History and Theory in Anthropology

Anthropology is a discipline very conscious of its history, and Alan Barnard has written a clear, balanced, and judicious textbook that surveys the historical contexts of the great debates in the discipline, tracing the genealogies of theories and schools of thought and considering the problems involved in assessing these theories. The book covers the precursors of anthropology; evolutionism in all its guises; diffusionism and culture area theories, functionalism and structural-functionalism; action-centred theories; processual and Marxist perspectives; the many faces of relativism, structuralism and post-structuralism; and recent interpretive and postmodernist viewpoints.

ALAN BARNARD is Reader in Social Anthropology at the University of Edinburgh. His previous books include *Research Practices in the Study of Kinship* (with Anthony Good, 1984), *Hunters and Herders of Southern Africa* (1992), and, edited with Jonathan Spencer, *Encyclopedia of Social and Cultural Anthropology* (1996).

History and Theory in Anthropology

Alan Barnard

University of Edinburgh

PUBLISHED BY THE PRESS SYNDICATE OF THE UNIVERSITY OF CAMBRIDGE
The Pitt Building, Trumpington Street, Cambridge, United Kingdom

CAMBRIDGE UNIVERSITY PRESS
The Edinburgh Building, Cambridge CB2 2RU, UK
40 West 20th Street, New York, NY 10011–421, USA
477 Williamstown Road, Port Melbourne VIC 3207, Australia
Ruiz de Alarcón 13, 28014 Madrid, Spain
Dock House, The Waterfront, Cape Town 8001, South Africa

http://www.cambridge.org

First published 2000
Reprinted 2001, 2002, 2003

Printed in the United Kingdom at the University Press, Cambridge

Typeset in Plantin 10/12pt [VN]

A catalogue record for this book is available from the British Library

Library of Congress cataloguing in publication data

Barnard, Alan (Alan J.)
History and theory in anthropology / Alan Barnard.
    p.   cm
Includes bibliographical references and index.
ISBN 0 521 77333 4 (hardback); 0 521 77432 2 (paperback)
1. Anthropology – Philosophy.   2. Anthropology – History.   I. Title
GN33.B34 2000
301'.01–dc21 00–045362

ISBN 0 521 77333 4 hardback
ISBN 0 521 77432 2 paperback

For Joy

Contents

Figures

Tables

Preface

This book began life as a set of lecture notes for a course in anthropological theory, but it has evolved into something very different. In struggling through several drafts, I have toyed with arguments for regarding anthropological theory in terms of the history of ideas, the development of national traditions and schools of thought, and the impact of individuals and the new perspectives they have introduced to the discipline. I have ended up with what I believe is a unique but eclectic approach, and the one which makes best sense of anthropological theory in all its variety.

My goal is to present the development of anthropological ideas against a background of the converging and diverging interests of its practitioners, each with their own assumptions and questions. For example, Boas' consideration of culture as a shared body of knowledge leads to quite different questions from those which engaged Radcliffe-Brown with his interest in society as an interlocking set of relationships. Today's anthropologists pay homage to both, though our questions and assumptions may be different again. The organization of this book has both thematic and chronological elements, and I have tried to emphasize both the continuity and transformation of anthropological ideas, on the one hand, and the impact of great figures of the past and present, on the other. Where relevant I stress disjunction too, as when anthropologists change their questions or reject their old assumptions or, as has often been the case, when they reject the premises of their immediate predecessors. The personal and social reasons behind these continuities, transformations and disjunctions are topics of great fascination.

For those who do not already have a knowledge of the history of the discipline, I have included suggested reading at the end of each chapter, a glossary, and an appendix of dates of birth and death covering nearly all the writers whose work is touched on in the text. The very few dates of birth which remain shrouded in mist are primarily those of youngish, living anthropologists. I have also taken care to cite the date of original publication in square brackets as well as the date of the edition to be found in the references. Wherever in the text I refer to an essay within a book, the date in square brackets is that of the original publication of the essay. In the references, a single date in square brackets is that of the first publication of a given volume in its original language; a range of dates in square brackets is that of the original dates of publication of all the essays in a collection.

A number of people have contributed to the improvement of my text. Joy Barnard, Iris Jean-Klein, Charles Jędrej, Adam Kuper, Jessica Kuper, Peter Skalník, Dimitri Tsintjilonis, and three anonymous readers have all made helpful suggestions. My students have helped too, in asking some of the best questions and directing my attention to the issues which matter.

1   Visions of anthropology

Anthropology is a subject in which theory is of great importance. It is also a subject in which theory is closely bound up with practice. In this chapter, we shall explore the general nature of anthropological enquiry. Of special concern are the way the discipline is defined in different national traditions, the relation between theory and ethnography, the distinction between synchronic and diachronic approaches, and how anthropologists and historians have seen the history of the discipline.

Although this book is not a history of anthropology as such, it is organized in part chronologically. In order to understand anthropological theory, it is important to know something of the history of the discipline, both its 'history of ideas' and its characters and events. Historical relations between facets of anthropological theory are complex and interesting. Whether anthropological theory is best understood as a sequence of events, a succession of time frames, a system of ideas, a set of parallel national traditions, or a process of 'agenda hopping' is the subject of the last section of this chapter. In a sense, this question guides my approach through the whole of the book. But first let us consider the nature of anthropology in general and the meaning of some of the terms which define it.

Anthropology and ethnology

The words 'anthropology' and 'ethnology' have had different meanings through the years. They have also had different meanings in different countries.

The word 'anthropology' is ultimately from the Greek (*anthropos*, 'human', plus *logos*, 'discourse' or 'science'). Its first usage to define a scientific discipline is probably around the early sixteenth century (in its Latin form *anthropologium*). Central European writers then employed it as a term to cover anatomy and physiology, part of what much later came to be called 'physical' or 'biological anthropology'. In the seventeenth and eighteenth centuries, European theologians also used the term, in this case to refer to the attribution of human-like features to their deity. The German word *Anthropologie*, which described cultural attributes of different ethnic groups, came to be used by a few writers in Russia and Austria in the late eighteenth century (see Vermeulen 1995). However, this usage did not become established among scholars elsewhere until much later.

Eighteenth- and early nineteenth-century scholars tended to use 'ethnology' for the study of both the cultural differences and the features which identify the common humanity of the world's peoples. This English term, or its equivalents like *ethnologie* (French) or *Ethnologie* (German), are still in use in continental Europe and the United States. In the United Kingdom and most other parts of the English-speaking world 'social anthropology' is the more usual designation. In continental Europe, the word 'anthropology' often still tends to carry the meaning 'physical anthropology', though there too 'social anthropology' is now rapidly gaining ground as a synonym for 'ethnology'. Indeed, the main professional organization in Europe is called the European Association of Social Anthropologists or l'Association Européenne des Anthropologues Sociaux. It was founded in 1989 amidst a rapid growth of the discipline across Europe, both Western and Eastern. In the United States, the word 'ethnology' co-exists with 'cultural anthropology'.

In Germany and parts of Central and Eastern Europe, there is a further distinction, namely between *Volkskunde* and *Völkerkunde*. These terms have no precise English equivalents, but the distinction is a very important one. *Volkskunde* usually refers to the study of folklore and local customs, including handicrafts, of one's own country. It is a particularly strong field in these parts of Europe and to some extent in Scandinavia. *Völkerkunde* is the wider, comparative social science also known in German as *Ethnologie*.

Thus, anthropology and ethnology are not really one field; nor are they simply two fields. Nor does either term have a single, agreed meaning. Today they are best seen as foci for the discussion of issues diverse in character, but whose subject matter is defined according to an opposition between the general (anthropology) and the culturally specific (ethnology).

The 'four fields' approach

In North America, things are much simpler than in Europe. In the United States and Canada, 'anthropology' is generally understood to include four fields or subdisciplines:

(1) biological anthropology,

(2) archaeology,
(3) anthropological linguistics,
(4) cultural anthropology.

The main concern of this book is with cultural anthropology, but let us take each of these branches of North American anthropology in turn.

(1) Biological anthropology is the study of human biology, especially as it relates to a broadly conceived 'anthropology' – the science of human-kind. Sometimes this subdiscipline is called by its older term, 'physical anthropology'. The latter tends to reflect interests in comparative anatomy. Such anatomical comparisons involve especially the relations between the human species and the higher primates (such as chimpanzees and gorillas) and the relation between modern humans and our ancestors (such as *Australopithecus africanus* and *Homo erectus*). The anatomical comparison of 'races' is now largely defunct, having been superseded by the rapidly advancing field of human genetics. Genetics, along with aspects of demography, forensic science, and palaeo-medicine, make up modern biological anthropology in its widest sense.

(2) Archaeology (or 'prehistoric archaeology', as it would be called in Europe) is a closely related subdiscipline. While the comparison of anatomical features of fossil finds is properly part of biological anthropology, the relation of such finds to their habitat and the search for clues to the structure of prehistoric societies belong more to archaeology. Archaeology also includes the search for relations between groups and the reconstruction of social life even in quite recent times. This is especially true with finds of Native North American material dating from before written records were available. Many American archaeologists consider their subdiscipline a mere extension, backwards in time, of cultural anthropology.

(3) Anthropological linguistics is the study of language, but especially with regard to its diversity. This field is small in comparison with linguistics as a whole, but anthropological linguists keep their ties to anthropology while most mainstream linguists today (and since the early 1960s) concentrate on the underlying principles of all languages. It might be said (somewhat simplistically) that whereas modern linguists study *language*, the more conservative anthropological linguists study *languages*. Anthropological linguistics is integrally bound to the 'relativist' perspective of cultural anthropology which was born with it, in the early twentieth-century anthropology of Franz Boas (see chapter 7).

(4) Cultural anthropology is the largest subdiscipline. In its widest sense, this field includes the study of cultural diversity, the search for cultural universals, the unlocking of social structure, the interpretation of

symbolism, and numerous related problems. It touches on all the other subdisciplines, and for this reason many North American anthropologists insist on keeping their vision of a unified science of anthropology in spite of the fact that the overwhelming majority of North American anthropologists practise this subdiscipline alone (at least if we include within it *applied* cultural anthropology). Rightly or wrongly, 'anthropology' in some circles, on several continents, has come to mean most specifically 'cultural anthropology', while its North American practitioners maintain approaches which take stock of developments in all of the classic 'four fields'.

Finally, in the opinion of many American anthropologists, *applied anthropology* should qualify as a field in its own right. Applied anthropology includes the application of ideas from cultural anthropology within medicine, in disaster relief, for community development, and in a host of other areas where a knowledge of culture and society is relevant. In a wider sense, applied anthropology can include aspects of biological and linguistic anthropology, or even archaeology. For example, biological anthropology may help to uncover the identity of murder victims. Anthropological linguistics has applications in teaching the deaf and in speech therapy. Archaeological findings on ancient irrigation systems may help in the construction of modern ones.

A survey for the American Anthropological Association (Givens, Evans, and Jablonski 1997: 308) found that applied anthropology, along with unspecified topics not covered within the traditional four fields, accounted for 7 per cent of American anthropology Ph.D.s between 1972 and 1997. Cultural anthropology Ph.D.s accounted for 50 per cent (and many of these also focused on applied issues); archaeology, 30 per cent; biological anthropology, 10 per cent; and linguistic anthropology, only 3 per cent. That said, some anthropologists reject the distinction between 'pure' and 'applied', on the grounds that all anthropology has aspects of both. In other words, applied anthropology may best be seen not as a separate subdiscipline, but rather as a part of each of the four fields.

Theory and ethnography

In social or cultural anthropology, a distinction is often made between 'ethnography' and 'theory'. Ethnography is literally the practice of writing about peoples. Often it is taken to mean our way of making sense of other peoples' modes of thought, since anthropologists usually study cultures other than their own. Theory is also, in part anyway, our way of making sense of our own, anthropological mode of thought.

However, theory and ethnography inevitably merge into one. It is

impossible to engage in ethnography without some idea of what is important and what is not. Students often ask what anthropological theory is for;
they could as easily ask what ethnography is for! Ideally, ethnography
serves to enhance our understanding of culture in the abstract and define
the essence of human nature (which is in fact predicated on the existence
of culture). On the other side of the coin, theory without ethnography is
pretty meaningless, since the understanding of cultural difference is at
least one of the most important goals of anthropological enquiry.

It is useful to think of theory as containing four basic elements:
(1) questions, (2) assumptions, (3) methods, and (4) evidence. The most
important *questions*, to my mind, are 'What are we trying to find out?', and
'Why is this knowledge useful?' Anthropological knowledge could be
useful, for example, either in trying to understand one's own society, or in
trying to understand the nature of the human species. Some anthropological questions are historical: 'How do societies change?', or 'What came
first, private property or social hierarchy?' Other anthropological questions are about contemporary issues: 'How do social institutions work?',
or 'How do humans envisage and classify what they see around them?'

Assumptions include notions of common humanity, of cultural difference, of value in all cultures, or of differences in cultural values. More
specifically, anthropologists may assume either human inventiveness or
human uninventiveness; or that society constrains the individual, or
individuals create society. Some assumptions are common to all anthropologists, others are not. Thus, while having some common ground,
anthropologists can have significant differences of opinion about the way
they see their subject.

Methods have developed through the years and are part of every fieldwork study. However, methods include not only fieldwork but, equally
importantly, comparison. *Evidence* is obviously a methodological component, but how it is treated, or even understood, will differ according to
theoretical perspective. Some anthropologists prefer to see comparison as
a method of building a picture of a particular culture area. Others see it as
a method for explaining their own discoveries in light of a more worldwide pattern. Still others regard comparison itself as an illusory objective,
except insofar as one always understands the exotic through its difference
from the familiar.

This last point begs the existential question as to what evidence might
actually be. In anthropology, as for many other disciplines, the only thing
that is agreed is that evidence must relate to the problem at hand. In other
words, not only do theories depend on evidence, evidence itself depends
on what questions one is trying to answer. To take archaeology as an
analogy, one cannot just dig any old place and expect to find something of

significance. An archaeologist who is interested in the development of urbanism will only dig where there is likely to be the remains of an ancient city. Likewise in social anthropology, we go to places where we expect to find things we are interested in; and once there we ask small questions designed to produce evidence for the larger questions posed by our respective theoretical orientations. For example, an interest in relations between gender and power might take us to a community in which gender differentiation is strong. In this case, we might focus our questions to elucidate how individual women and men pursue strategies for overcoming or maintaining their respective positions.

Beyond these four elements, there are two more specific aspects of enquiry in social anthropology. These are characteristic of anthropological method, no matter what theoretical persuasion an anthropologist may otherwise maintain. Thus they serve to define an anthropological approach, as against an approach which is characteristic of other social sciences, especially sociology. The two aspects are:

(1) observing a society as a whole, to see how each element of that society fits together with, or is meaningful in terms of, other such elements;
(2) examining each society in relation to others, to find similarities and differences and account for them.

Observing a society as a whole entails trying to understand how things are related, for example, how politics fits together with kinship or economics, or how specific economic institutions fit together with others. *Examining each society in relation to others* implies an attempt to find and account for their similarities and their differences. Here we need a broader framework than the one that a fieldworker might employ in his or her study of a single village or ethnic group, but still there are several possibilities. Such a framework can encompass: (1) the comparison of isolated cases (e.g., the Trobrianders of Melanesia compared to the Nuer of East Africa), (2) comparisons within a region (e.g., the Trobrianders within the context of Melanesian ethnography), or (3) a more universal sort of comparison (taking in societies across the globe). Most social anthropologists in fact engage in all three at one time or another, even though, as anthropological theorists, they may differ about which is the most useful form of comparison in general.

Thus it is possible to describe social or cultural anthropology as having a broadly agreed methodological programme, no matter what specific questions anthropologists are trying to answer. Theory and ethnography are the twin pillars of this programme, and virtually all anthropological enquiry includes either straightforward comparison or an explicit attempt to come to grips with the difficulties which comparisons entail. Arguably, the comparative nature of our discipline tends to make us more aware of our theoretical premises than tends to be the case in less comparative fields, such as sociology. For this reason, perhaps, a special concern with theory rather than methodology has come to dominate anthropology. Every anthropologist is a bit of a theorist, just as every anthropologist is a bit of a fieldworker. In the *other* social sciences, 'social theory' is sometimes considered a separate and quite abstract entity, often divorced from day-to-day concerns.

Anthropological paradigms

It is commonplace in many academic fields to distinguish between a 'theory' and a 'theoretical perspective'. By a theoretical perspective, we usually mean a grand theory, what is sometimes called a theoretical framework or a broad way of looking at the world. In anthropology we sometimes call such a thing a *cosmology* if it is attributed to a 'traditional' culture, or a *paradigm* if it is attributed to Western scientists.

The notion of a 'paradigm'

The theoretical perspective, cosmology, or paradigm defines the major issues with which a theorist is concerned. The principle is the same whether one is a member of a traditional culture, an anthropologist, or a natural scientist. In the philosophy of science itself there are differences of opinion as to the precise nature of scientific thinking, the process of gaining scientific knowledge, and the existential status of that knowledge. We shall leave the philosophers to their own debates (at least until chapter 7, where their debates impinge upon anthropology), but one philosopher deserves mention here. This is Thomas Kuhn, whose book *The Structure of Scientific Revolutions* (1970 [1962]) has been influential in helping social scientists to understand their own fields, even though its subject matter is confined to the physical and natural sciences. According to Kuhn, paradigms are large theories which contain within them smaller theories. When smaller theories no longer make sense of the world, then a crisis occurs. At least in the natural sciences (if not quite to the same extent in the social sciences), such a crisis eventually results in either the overthrow of a paradigm or incorporation of it, as a special case, into a newer and larger one.

Consider, as Kuhn does, the difference between Newtonian physics and Einsteinian physics. In Newtonian physics, one takes as the starting point the idea of a fixed point of reference for everything in the universe. In an Einsteinian framework, everything (time, space, etc.) is relative to everything else. In Newtonian physics magnetism and electricity are considered separate phenomena and can be explained separately, but in Einsteinian physics magnetism is explained as a necessary part of electricity. Neither Newton's explanation of magnetism nor Einstein's is necessarily either true or false in absolute terms. Rather, they derive their meanings within the larger theoretical frameworks. Einstein's paradigm is 'better' only because it explains some phenomena that Newtonian physics cannot.

There is some dispute about whether or not anthropology can really be considered a science in the sense that physics is, but most would agree that anthropology at least bears some relation to physics in having a single overarching framework (in this case, the understanding of humankind), and within this, more specific paradigms (such as functionalism and structuralism). Within our paradigms we have the particular facts and explanations which make up any given anthropological study. Anthropology goes through 'revolutions' or 'paradigm shifts' from time to time, although the nature of ours may be different from those in the natural sciences. For anthropology, fashion, as much as explanatory value, has its part to play.

Diachronic, synchronic, and interactive perspectives

Within anthropology, it is useful to think in terms of both a set of competing theoretical perspectives within any given framework, and a hierarchy of theoretical levels. Take evolutionism and diffusionism, for example. Evolutionism is an anthropological perspective which emphasizes the growing complexity of culture through time. Diffusionism is a perspective which emphasizes the transmission of ideas from one place to another. They compete because they offer different explanations of the same thing: how cultures change. Yet both are really part of the same grand theory: the theory of social change.

Sometimes the larger perspective which embraces both evolutionism and diffusionism is called the *diachronic* one (indicating the relation of things through time). Its opposite is the *synchronic* perspective (indicating the relation of things together in the same time). Synchronic approaches include functionalism, structuralism, interpretivism, and other ones which try to explain the workings of particular cultures without reference to time. A third large grouping of anthropological theories is what might be termed the *interactive* perspective. This perspective or, more accurately, set of perspectives, has both diachronic and synchronic aspects. Its adherents reject the static nature of most synchronic analysis, and reject also the simplistic historical assumptions of the classical evolutionist and

Table 1.1. *Diachronic, synchronic, and interactive perspectives*

DIACHRONIC PERSPECTIVES
  evolutionism
  diffusionism
  Marxism (in some respects)
  culture-area approaches (in some respects)

SYNCHRONIC PERSPECTIVES
  relativism (including 'culture and personality')
  structuralism
  structural-functionalism
  cognitive approaches
  culture-area approaches (in most respects)
  functionalism (in some respects)
  interpretivism (in some respects)

INTERACTIVE PERSPECTIVES
  transactionalism
  processualism
  feminism
  poststructuralism
  postmodernism
  functionalism (in some respects)
  interpretivism (in some respects)
  Marxism (in some respects)

diffusionist traditions. Proponents of interactive approaches include those who study cyclical social processes, or cause-and-effect relations between culture and environment.

Table 1.1 illustrates a classification of some of the main anthropological approaches according to their placing in these larger paradigmatic groupings. The details will have to wait until later chapters. The important point for now is that anthropology is constructed of a hierarchy of theoretical levels, though assignment of specific approaches to the larger levels is not always clear-cut. The various 'isms' which make these up form different ways of understanding our subject matter. Anthropologists debate both within their narrower perspectives (e.g., one evolutionist against another about either the cause or the chronology of evolution) and within larger perspectives (e.g., evolutionists versus diffusionists, or those favouring diachronic approaches against those favouring synchronic approaches).

Very broadly, the history of anthropology has involved transitions from diachronic perspectives to synchronic perspectives, and from synchronic perspectives to interactive perspectives. Early diachronic studies, especially in evolutionism, often concentrated on global but quite specific theoretical issues. For example, 'Which came first, patrilineal or matrilineal descent?' Behind this question was a set of notions about the relation between men and women, about the nature of marriage, about private property, and so on. Through such questions, quite grand theories were built up. These had great explanatory power, but they were vulnerable to refutation by careful counter-argument, often using contradicting ethnographic evidence.

For the synchronic approaches, which became prominent in the early twentieth century, it was often more difficult to find answers to that kind of theoretical question. 'Which is more culturally appropriate, patrilineal or matrilineal descent?' is rather less meaningful than 'Which came first?' The focus landed more on specific societies. Anthropologists began to study societies in great depth and to compare how each dealt with problems such as raising children, maintaining links between kinsfolk, and dealing with members of other kin groups. A debate did emerge on which was more important, descent (relations within a kin group) or alliance (relations between kin groups which intermarry). Yet overall, the emphasis in synchronic approaches has been on the understanding of societies one at a time, whether in respect of the function, the structure, or the meaning of specific customs.

Interactive approaches have concentrated on the mechanisms through which individuals seek to gain over other individuals, or simply the ways in which individuals define their social situation. For example, the question might arise: 'Are there any hidden features of matrilineal or patrilineal descent which might lead to the breakdown of groups based on such principles?' Or, 'What processes enable such groups to persist?' Or, 'How does an individual manoeuvre around the structural constraints imposed by descent groups?'

Thus anthropologists of diverse theoretical orientations try to tackle related, if not identical theoretical questions. The complex relation *between* such questions is one of the most interesting aspects of the discipline.

Society and culture

Another way to classify the paradigms of anthropology is according to their broad interest in either *society* (as a social unit) or *culture* (as a shared set of ideas, skills, and objects). The situation is slightly more complicated than the usual designations 'social anthropology' (the discipline as practised in the United Kingdom and some other countries) and 'cultural anthropology' (as practised in North America) imply. (See table 1.2.)

Table 1.2. *Perspectives on society and on culture*

PERSPECTIVES ON SOCIETY
  evolutionism
  functionalism
  structural-functionalism
  transactionalism
  processualism
  Marxism
  poststructuralism (in most respects)
  structuralism (in some respects)
  culture-area approaches (in some respects)
  feminism (in some respects)

PERSPECTIVES ON CULTURE
  diffusionism
  relativism
  cognitive approaches
  interpretivism
  postmodernism
  culture-area approaches (in most respects)
  structuralism (in most respects)
  poststructuralism (in some respects)
  feminism (in some respects)

Basically, the earliest anthropological concerns were with the nature of society: how humans came to associate with each other, and how and why societies changed through time. When diachronic interests were overthrown, the concern was with how society is organized or functions. Functionalists, structural-functionalists and structuralists debated with each other over whether to emphasize relations between individuals, relations between social institutions, or relations between social categories which individuals occupy. Nevertheless, they largely agreed on a fundamental interest in the social over the cultural. The same is true of transactionalists, processualists and Marxists.

Diffusionism contained the seeds of cultural determinism. This was elevated to an extreme with the relativism of Franz Boas. Later, interpretivists on both sides of the Atlantic and the postmodernists of recent times all reacted against previous emphases on social structure and monolithic visions of social process. Society-oriented anthropologists and culture-oriented anthropologists (again, not quite the same thing as 'social' and 'cultural' anthropologists) seemed to be speaking different languages, or practising entirely different disciplines.

A few perspectives incorporated studies of both culture and society (as conceived by extremists on either side). Structuralism, in particular, had

society-oriented concerns (such as marital alliance or the transition between statuses in ritual activities) and culture-oriented ones (such as
certain aspects of symbolism). Feminism also had society-oriented interests (relations between men and women within a social and symbolic
order) and cultural ones (the symbolic order itself). Culture-area or
regional approaches have come from both cultural and social traditions,
and likewise are not easy to classify as a whole.

In this book, chapters 2 (on precursors), 3 (evolutionism) and 4 (diffusionism and culture-area approaches) deal mainly with *diachronic perspectives*. Evolutionism has been largely concerned with society, and
diffusionism more with culture. Chapters 5 (functionalism and structural-functionalism) and 6 (action-centred, processual, and Marxist approaches) deal fundamentally with *society*, respectively from a relatively
static point of view and a relatively dynamic point of view. Chapters 7
(relativism, etc.), 8 (structuralism), 9 (poststructuralist and feminist
thought), and 10 (interpretivism and postmodernism) all deal mainly
with *culture* (though, e.g., poststructuralism also has strong societal elements). Thus the book is organized broadly around the historical transition from diachronic to synchronic to interactive approaches, and from
an emphasis on society to an emphasis on culture.

Visions of the history of anthropology

A. SEQUENCE OF EVENTS OR NEW IDEAS (e.g., Stocking 1987; 1996a; Kuklick 1991)
B. SUCCESSION OF TIME FRAMES, either stages of development or Kuhnian
   paradigms, each of which is best analysed internally (e.g., Hammond-
   Tooke 1997; and to some extent Stocking 1996a)
C. SYSTEM OF IDEAS, which changes through time and which should be
   analysed dynamically (e.g., Kuper 1988; and to some extent Harris
   1968; Malefijt 1976)
D. SET OF PARALLEL NATIONAL TRADITIONS (e.g., Lowie 1937; and to some
   extent Hammond-Tooke 1997)
E. PROCESS OF AGENDA HOPPING (perhaps implicit in Kuper 1996 [1973])

The form of anthropological theory really depends on how one sees the
history of the discipline. For example, is anthropology evolving through
stages, that is, developing through a sequence of events or new ideas? Or
does it consist of a succession of larger time frames, either stages of
development or Kuhnian paradigms? Is anthropology undergoing structural transformations? Is it developing through divergent and convergent

threads of influence between distinct national traditions? Or can the history of the discipline be seen essentially as 'agenda hopping'? As Roy D'Andrade explains:

What happens in agenda hopping is that a given agenda of research reaches a point at which nothing new or exciting is emerging from the work of even the best practitioners. It is not that the old agenda is completed, or that too many anomalies have accumulated to proceed with equanimity. Rather, what has happened is that as more and more has been learned the practitioners have come to understand that the phenomena being investigated are quite complex. Greater and greater effort is required to produce anything new, and whatever is found seems to be of less and less interest. When this happens, a number of practitioners may defect to another agenda – a new direction of work in which there is some hope of finding something really interesting. (D'Andrade 1995: 4–8)

Each of the five possibilities shown above is a legitimate view of the history of anthropology. Indeed, each is represented within this book at one point or another. An emphasis on events, as in A, represents the most objective view, but it fails to capture the complexity of relations between ideas. An emphasis on the internal workings of paradigms, as in B, is common among historians of science, but it does not allow the observer the dynamic perspective of C or the comparative perspective of D. In a sense, E is the inverse of B, as it amounts to the suggestion that anthropologists abandon their old questions rather than incorporate them into a new framework. C is tempting, but it is difficult to sustain the notion of anthropology as a single system when viewing its whole history, in all its diversity and complexity.

With some exceptions, A and B tend to be historians' views, and C, D, and E tend to be practising anthropologists' views. My own leanings are towards D and E, the former representing anthropology at its most conservative, and the latter representing it at its most anarchical.

Concluding summary

Theory in social and cultural anthropology is dependent on what questions anthropologists ask. The organizational structure of the discipline, and the relation of theory to ethnographic findings are integral to these questions. Broadly, theories may be classified as diachronic, synchronic, or interactive, in focus. Paradigms in the physical and natural sciences generally have clear-cut, agreed goals. Anthropological paradigms are not as easy to pin down. We may characterize much of the history of anthropology as a history of changing questions (agenda hopping), but it also has elements of paradigm shift and continuing, often nationally based, traditions.

The remainder of this book explores the development of anthropological ideas with these notions as guidelines. It is organized around historical transitions from diachronic to synchronic to interactive approaches, and from an emphasis on society (especially chapters 5 and 6) to an emphasis on culture (broadly chapters 7 to 10).

FURTHER READING

Ingold's *Companion Encyclopedia of Anthropology* (1994) presents a wide vision of anthropology, including biological, social, and cultural aspects of human existence. Other useful reference books include Adam Kuper and Jessica Kuper's *Social Science Encyclopedia* (1996 [1985]), Barnard and Spencer's *Encyclopedia of Social and Cultural Anthropology* (1996), Barfield's *Dictionary of Anthropology* (1997), and Bonte and Izard's *Dictionnaire de l'ethnologie et de l'anthropologie* (1991).

Chalmers' *What is This Thing Called Science?* (1982 [1976]) describes the major theories in the philosophy of science, including those of Kuhn and his critics.

Recent introductions to anthropological theory which take different approaches from mine include Barrett's *Anthropology* (1996), J. D. Moore's *Visions of Culture* (1997) and Layton's *Introduction to Theory in Anthropology* (1997). Barrett divides the history of anthropology into three broad phases: 'building the foundation', 'patching the cracks', and 'demolition and reconstruction'. He alternates discussion from theory to method in each. Moore summarizes the lives and works of twenty-one major contributors to the discipline, from Tylor to Fernandez. Layton concentrates on relatively recent and competing paradigms: functionalism, structuralism, interactionism, Marxism, socioecology, and postmodernism. See also the various histories of anthropology cited in table 1. 2.

2   Precursors of the anthropological tradition

Most anthropologists would agree that anthropology emerged as a distinct branch of scholarship around the middle of the nineteenth century, when public interest in human evolution took hold. Anthropology as an academic discipline began a bit later, with the first appointments of professional anthropologists in universities, museums, and government offices. However, there is no doubt that anthropological ideas came into being much earlier. *How much earlier* is a matter of disagreement, though not particularly much active debate. Rather, each anthropologist and each historian of the discipline has his or her own notion of the most relevant point at which to begin the story.

From a 'history of ideas' point of view, the writings of ancient Greek philosophers and travellers, medieval Arab historians, medieval and Renaissance European travellers, and later European philosophers, jurists, and scientists of various kinds, are all plausible precursors. My choice, though, would be with the concept of the 'social contract', and the perceptions of human nature, society, and cultural diversity which emerged from this concept. This is where I shall begin.

Another, essentially unrelated, beginning is the idea of the Great Chain of Being, which defined the place of the human species as between God and the animals. This idea was in some respects a forerunner of the theory of evolution, and later in this chapter we shall look at it in that context. Eighteenth-century debates on the origin of language and on the relation between humans and what we now call the higher primates are also relevant, as is the early nineteenth-century debate between the polygenists (who believed that each 'race' had a separate origin) and the monogenists (who emphasized humankind's common descent, whether from Adam or ape). Such ideas are important not only as 'facts' of history, but also because they form part of modern anthropology's perception of itself.

Natural law and the social contract

During the late Renaissance of Western culture and the Enlightenment which followed, there came to be a strong interest in the natural condition of humanity. This interest, however, was not always coupled with much knowledge of the variety of the world's cultures. Indeed, it was often tainted by a belief in creatures on the boundary between humanity and animality – monstrosities with eyes in their bellies or feet on their heads (see Mason 1990). In order for anthropology to come into being, it was necessary that travelogue fantasies of this kind be overcome. Ironically to modern eyes, what was needed was to set aside purported ethnographic 'fact' in favour of reason or theory.

The seventeenth century

The first writers whose vision went beyond the 'facts' were mainly jurists and philosophers of the seventeenth and eighteenth centuries. Their concerns were with abstract relations between individual and society, between societies and their rulers, and between peoples or nations. The times in which they wrote were often troubled, and their ideas on human nature reflected this. Politics, religion, and the philosophical discourse which later gave rise to anthropology, were intimately linked.

Let us start with Hugo Grotius. Grotius studied at Leiden and practised law in The Hague, before intense political conflicts in the United Provinces (The Netherlands) led to his imprisonment and subsequent escape to Paris. It was there he developed the ideas which gave rise to his monumental *De jure belli ac pacis* (1949 [1625]). Grotius believed that the nations of the world were part of a larger trans-national society which is subject to the Law of Nature. Although his predecessors had sought a theological basis for human society, Grotius found his basis for society in the sociable nature of the human species. He argued that the same natural laws which govern the behaviour of individuals in their respective societies should also govern relations between societies in peace and in war. His text remains a cornerstone of international law. Arguably, it also marks the dawn of truly anthropological speculation on the nature of human society.

Samuel Pufendorf (Puffendorf), working in Germany and Sweden, extended this concern. His works are surprisingly little known in modern anthropology, but intriguingly they long foreshadow debates of the 1980s and 1990s on human 'sociality'. 'Sociality' is a word of recent anthropological invention. Yet it much more literally translates Pufendorf's Latin *socialitas* than the more usual gloss of his anglophone interpreters, 'sociability'. Indeed, Pufendorf also used the adjective *sociabilis*, 'sociable' (or as one modern editor renders it, 'capable of society'). He believed that society and human nature are in some sense indivisible, because humans are, by nature, sociable beings.

Nevertheless, Pufendorf did at times speculate on what human nature might be like without society and on what people did at the dawn of civilization. His conclusions on the latter are striking. His notion of 'there' is where people lived in scattered households, while 'here' is where they have united under the rule of a state: 'There is the reign of the passions, there there is war, fear, poverty, nastiness, solitude, barbarity, ignorance, savagery; here is the reign of reason, here there is peace, security, wealth, splendour, society, taste, knowledge, benevolence' (1991 [1673]: 118).

Meanwhile in a politically troubled England, Thomas Hobbes (e.g. 1973 [1651]) had been reflecting on similar issues. He stressed not a natural proclivity on the part of humans to form societies, but rather a natural tendency towards self-interest. He believed that this tendency needed to be controlled, and that rational human beings recognized that they must submit to authority in order to achieve peace and security. Thus, societies formed by consent and common agreement (the 'social contract'). In the unstable time in which he wrote, his ideas were anathema to powerful sections of society: the clergy, legal scholars, and rulers alike; each opposed one or more elements of his complex argument. Nevertheless, Hobbes' pessimistic view of human nature inspired other thinkers to examine for themselves the origins of society, either rationally or empirically. His vision is still debated in anthropological circles, especially among specialists in hunter-gatherer studies.

John Locke's (1988 [1690]) view of human nature was more optimistic. Writing at the time of the establishment of constitutional monarchy in England, he saw government as ideally limited in power: consent to the social contract did not imply total submission. He believed that the 'state of nature' had been one of peace and tranquillity, but that a social contract became necessary in order to settle disputes. While human sinfulness might lead to theft and possibly to excessive punishment for theft in a state of nature, the development of society encouraged both the preservation of property and the protection of the natural freedoms which people in the state of nature had enjoyed.

The eighteenth century

Locke's liberal views inspired many in the next century, including Jean-Jacques Rousseau, though ironically Rousseau's essay *Of the Social Contract* fails to mention him at all. Rather, Rousseau begins with an attack on

Grotius' denial that human power is established for the benefit of the governed. Says Rousseau: 'On this showing [i.e. if we were to follow Grotius], the human species is divided into so many herds of cattle, each with its ruler, who keeps guard over them for the purpose of devouring them' (Rousseau 1973 [1762]: 183). For Rousseau, government and the social contract differed. Government originated from a desire by the rich to protect the property they had acquired. The social contract, in contrast, is based on democratic consent. It describes an idealized society in which people agree to form or retain a means of living together which is beneficial to all.

Social-contract theory assumed a logical division between a 'state of nature' and a 'state of society', and those who advocated it nearly always described it as originating with a people, living in a state of nature, and getting together and agreeing to form a society. The notion was ultimately hypothetical. The likes of Hobbes, Locke, and Rousseau, just as much as opponents of their view (such as David Hume and Jeremy Bentham), perceived the 'state of nature' essentially as a rhetorical device or a legal fiction. The degree to which they believed that early humans really did devise an *actual* social contract is difficult to assess.

Most anthropologists today would accept the view that we cannot separate the 'natural' (in its etymological sense, relating to birth) from the 'cultural' (relating to cultivation), because both are inherent in the very idea of humanity. We inherit this view from these early modern writers who sought to humanize our understandings of law and legal systems.

Definitions of humanity in eighteenth-century Europe

A number of important anthropological questions were first posed in modern form during the European Enlightenment: what defines the human species in the abstract, what distinguishes humans from animals, and what is the natural condition of humankind. Three life forms occupied attention on these questions: 'Wild Boys' and 'Wild Girls' (feral children), 'Orang Outangs' (apes), and 'Savages' (indigenous inhabitants of other continents).

Feral children

Feral children seemed to proliferate in the eighteenth century: 'Wild Peter of Hanover', Marie-Angélique Le Blanc the 'Wild Girl of Champagne' (actually an escaped captive, Native North American), Victor the 'Wild Boy of Aveyron', and so on. These were people found alone in the woods and subsequently taught 'civilized' ways. Peter was brought to

England in the reign of George I and lived to an old age on a pension provided by successive Hanoverian kings. He never did learn to say more than a few words in any language. Le Blanc, on the other hand, eventually learned French and wrote her memoirs, which were published in 1768. Victor, a celebrated case, was probably a deaf-mute; and efforts to teach him to communicate were to have lasting effects on the education of the deaf in general (see Lane 1977).

Anthropological interest in feral children has long since dwindled (see Lévi-Strauss 1969a [1949]: 4–5). This is largely because modern anthropologists are less interested in the abstract, primal 'human nature' which such children supposedly exhibited, and much more concerned with the relations between human beings as members of their respective societies.

The Orang Outang

The Orang Outang is a more complicated matter. In Enlightenment Europe this word, from Malay for 'person of the forest', meant very roughly what the word 'ape' means today (while 'ape' referred to baboons). 'Orang Outang' was a generic term for a creature believed to be almost human, and I retain the eighteenth-century-style initial capital letters and spelling to represent this eighteenth-century concept. More precisely, the Orang Outang was the 'species' that Carolus Linnaeus (1956 [1758]) and his contemporaries classified as *Homo nocturnus* ('night man'), *Homo troglodytes* ('cave man'), or *Homo sylvestris* ('forest man'). Travellers reported these nearly human, almost blind, creatures to be living in caves in Ethiopia and the East Indies. Apparently, neither travellers nor scientists could distinguish accurately between the true orang-utans (the species now called *Pongo pygmaeus*) and the chimpanzees (*Pan troglodytes* and *Pan paniscus*). Gorillas (the species *Gorilla gorilla*) were as yet unknown.

The importance of the Orang Outang is highlighted in the debate between two interesting characters, James Burnett (Lord Monboddo) and Henry Home (Lord Kames). Monboddo and Kames were judges of Scotland's Court of Session. Kames (1774) held a narrow definition of humanity. He argued that the differences between cultures were so great that population groups around the world could reasonably be regarded as separate species. He regarded Native Americans as biologically inferior to Europeans and incapable of ever attaining European culture.

Monboddo (1773–92; 1779–99) went to the other extreme. He maintained (incorrectly) that some of the aboriginal languages of North America were mutually intelligible with both Basque and Scots Gaelic. Not only did he regard Amerindians as fully human, he even thought they spoke much the same language as some of his countrymen! Furthermore, Monboddo extended the definition of humanity to include those who could not speak at all, namely the Orang Outangs of Africa and Asia. He believed that these 'Orang Outangs' were of the same *species* as 'Ourselves' (a category in which he included Europeans, Africans, Asians, and Amerindians alike).

Monboddo's views on the relation between apes and humans are rather more cogent than is generally credited. From the evidence he had, it appeared that his 'Orang Outangs', particularly the chimpanzees of Central Africa, might well be human. Travellers' reports claimed that they lived in 'societies', built huts, made weapons, and even mated with those he called 'Ourselves'. The reports said that they were gregarious, and Monboddo accepted this. Today, we know that orangs in Southeast Asia are relatively solitary, but chimps in Africa are indeed gregarious, make tools, and can certainly be said to possess both culture and society (McGrew 1991).

The essence of Monboddo's theory, however, is language. Just as intellectuals of his day accepted the relatively mute Peter the Wild Boy as human, they should, Monboddo argued, accept the speechless Orang Outang as human too (Monboddo 1779–99 [1784], III: 336–7, 367). In his view, natural humanity came first, then the 'social contract' through which society was formed, then speech and language. Kames, in contrast, did not even accept that Native North Americans had spoken the presumed common language of Eurasia before the biblical Tower of Babel. Thus Kames and Monboddo represent the two most extreme views on the definition of humanity.

Notions of the 'Savage'

'Savage' was not necessarily a term of abuse at that time. It simply connoted living wild and free. The prototypical savage was the Native North American who (although possessing 'culture' in the modern sense of the word) was, in the average European mind, closer to the ideal of 'natural man' than was the Frenchman or Englishman.

The idea of the 'noble savage' is commonly associated with Enlightenment images of alien peoples. This phrase originates from a line in John Dryden's play *The Conquest of Granada*, Part I, first produced in 1692:

> . . . as free as nature first made man,
> Ere the base laws of servitude began,
> When wild in woods the noble savage ran.

Dryden's words became a catch-phrase for the school of thought which argued that humanity's natural condition was superior to its cultured condition.

In the seventeenth and early eighteenth centuries the more typical view of human nature was that humans were but 'tamed brutes'. In the words of Hobbes (1973 [1651]: 65), savage life was 'solitary, poore, nasty, brutish, and short'. The relation between nature and society was a matter of much debate. Some conceived this in a Christian idiom. Nature was good, and society was a necessary evil, required in order to control inherited human sinfulness after the Fall of Adam and Eve. Others argued that society represented the true nature of human existence, since humans are pretty much found only in societies. As Pufendorf suggested, humankind's 'natural' existence is social and cultural, and nature and culture are impossible to separate.

Like Monboddo, Rousseau accepted Orang Outangs as essentially human, but unlike Monboddo he thought of them as solitary beings. This in turn was his view of the 'natural' human. He shared with Monboddo an idealization of savage life, but shared with Hobbes an emphasis on a solitary existence for 'natural man' (*l'homme naturel* or *l'homme sauvage*). Rousseau begins the main text of his *Discourse on the Origin of Inequality* (1973 [1755]: 49–51) with a distinction between two kinds of inequality. The first kind concerns 'natural inequality', differences between people in strength, intelligence, and so on. The second concerns 'artificial inequality', the disparities which emerge within society. It is artificial inequality that he tries to explain. Instead of being poor, nasty, or brutish, Rousseau's solitary 'natural man' was healthy, happy, and free. Human vices emerged only after people began to form societies and develop the artificial inequalities which society implies.

Rousseau's theory was that societies emerged when people began to settle and build huts. This led to the formation of families and associations between neighbours, and thus (simultaneously) to the development of language. Rousseau's 'nascent society' (*société naissante*) was a golden age, but for most of humankind it did not last. Jealousies emerged, and the invention of private property caused the accumulation of wealth and consequent disputes between people over that wealth. Civilization, or 'civil society' developed in such a way that inequalities increased. Yet there was no going back. For Rousseau, civil society could not abolish itself. It could only pass just laws and try to re-establish some of the natural equality which had disappeared. The re-establishment of natural equality was the prime purpose of government, a purpose which most European governments of his day were not fulfilling. Yet not all societies had advanced at the same rate. Savage societies, in his view, retained some of the attributes of the golden age, and Rousseau praised certain savage societies in Africa and the Americas for this.

Coupled with earlier doctrines about 'natural law', Rousseau's idealization of simple, egalitarian forms of society helped to mould both the American and the French republics. This idealization also influenced a generation of philosophers in Britain, especially in Scotland. Adam Smith tried to tackle two of Rousseau's key problems: the origin of language (Smith 1970 [1761]), and the development of the importance of private property (1981 [1776]). Adam Ferguson (1966 [1767]) praised Amerindian societies for their lack of corruption and held great sympathy with the 'savages' of all other continents. Indeed, it seems that the 'polished' residents of Lowland Edinburgh thought of him, a Gaelic-speaking Highlander, as a sort of local 'noble savage'.

I believe that we inherit much more than we might at first think from the eighteenth-century imagery of the 'noble savage'. In anthropological theories which emphasize the differences between 'primitive' and 'non-primitive' societies (such as evolutionist ones), the noble savage has survived as the representation of 'nature' in the primitive. In anthropological theories which do not make this distinction (such as relativist ones), the noble savage is retained as a reflection of the common humanity at the root of all cultures.

Sociological and anthropological thought

Standing somewhat apart from the romantic concerns with feral children, Orang Outangs, and noble savages was the sociological tradition embodied by Montesquieu, Saint-Simon, and Comte. Paralleling this, successors to the Scottish Enlightenment argued vehemently over the biological relationships between the 'races'. Both of these developments were to leave their mark in nineteenth- and twentieth-century anthropology.

The sociological tradition

The baron de Montesquieu's *Persian Letters* (1964 [1721]) chronicle the adventures of two fictional Persian travellers who make critical remarks on French society. That book foreshadows not only the genre of ethnography, but also reflexivity (see chapter 10). More importantly though, Montesquieu's *Spirit of the Laws* (1989 [1748]) explores the forms of government, the temperament of peoples, and the influence of climate on society, with true ethnographic examples from around the world. Central to his argument is the idea of the 'general spirit' (*esprit général*), which is the fundamental essence of a given culture: 'Nature and climate almost alone dominate savages; manners govern the Chinese; laws tyrannize Japan; in former times mores set the tone in Lacedaemonia; in Rome it was set by the maxims of government and the ancient mores' (1989 [1748]: 310). While Lévi-Strauss once argued that Rousseau was the founder of the social sciences, Radcliffe-Brown gave that honour to Montesquieu; and the styles of the later structuralist and structural-functionalist traditions do owe much to the respective rationalism of Rousseau and empiricism of Montesquieu.

At the dawn of the nineteenth century the comte de Saint-Simon and subsequently his pupil, Auguste Comte, put forward notions which combined Montesquieu's interest in a science of society with a desire to incorporate it within a framework embracing also physics, chemistry, and biology. Saint-Simon wrote little, and he wrote badly. However, in his writings and especially in Comte's famous lecture on social science (1869 [1839]: 166–208), we see the emergence of the discipline that Comte named *sociologie*. The proposed field of sociology comprised the ideas of Montesquieu, Saint-Simon, and other French writers, and also much of what we would later recognize as an evolutionist, anthropological thinking about society.

All the social sciences, sociology included, owe at least part of their origins to what in eighteenth-century English was known as Moral Philosophy. Modern biology grew from eighteenth-century interests in Natural History (as it was then called). Sociology in a sense originated from a deliberate naming of this new discipline by Comte, who clearly saw his sociology as similar in method to biology. Yet, while the linear development of sociology from pre-Comtean ideas, through Comte to his successors is clear, the development of anthropology or ethnology is not. Anthropological ideas preceded both the formation of the discipline and the name for it. As we saw in chapter 1, 'anthropology' and 'ethnology' as labels existed independently and with little association with what later came to be seen as mainstream social anthropology.

Polygenesis and monogenesis

It is often said that the early nineteenth century was an era of little interest to historians of anthropology. Those who might point to the eighteenth-century Enlightenment as the dawn of our science regard the early nineteenth century as a step backwards. Those who would begin in the late nineteenth century regard the earlier part of that century as an age before anthropology's basic principles came to be accepted. Certainly there is truth in both of these views. However, anthropology as we know it depends on the acceptance of the idea of monogenesis, and therefore the controversy between the monogenists and their opponents marks the first stirring of anthropology as a discipline.

Monogenesis means 'one origin', and polygenesis means 'more than one origin'. Monogenists such as James Cowles Prichard, Thomas Hodgkin, and Sir Thomas Fowell Buxton, believed that all humankind had a single origin, whereas their opponents, championed by Robert Knox and later by James Hunt, believed that humankind had many origins and that 'races' were akin to species.

Modern anthropology assumes all humankind to be fundamentally the same, biologically and psychologically. Such a view was inherent in Montesquieu's argument that it was climate, and not biology or mental ability, which made cultures different. In the early nineteenth century such monogenist or evolutionist thinking was regarded as politically liberal, and in some circles downright radical. Theories of cultural evolution, just as much as the later relativist theories of twentieth-century anti-racists (discussed in chapter 7), depend on the acceptance of the essential biological and intellectual similarity of all peoples. While nineteenth-century white European and American evolutionists did feel themselves superior to people of other 'races', they nevertheless believed that all societies had evolved through the same stages. Therefore, they reasoned, the study of 'lower' races could tell them something about the early phases of their own societies. However, polygenists of the early nineteenth century lacked this belief. Therefore, the polygenists did not invent, and could not have invented, anthropology as we understand it today.

Here is where we must part company with the history of ideas and turn instead to the politics of the emerging discipline. The monogenist camp was centred in two organizations: the Aborigines Protection Society or APS, founded 1837, and the Ethnological Society of London or ESL, founded 1843 (see Stocking 1971). The former was a human rights organization, and the latter grew from its scientific wing. Many of the leaders of both were Quakers. At that time, only members of the Church of England could attend English universities, so Quakers wishing to attend university were educated beyond its borders. Prichard (then a Quaker, though later an Anglican) and Hodgkin attended Edinburgh, and Buxton attended Trinity College Dublin. As it happened, Prichard and Hodgkin carried with them views picked up from the last remnant of the Scottish Enlightenment, Dugald Stewart – whose anthropological ideas stem ultimately from Montesquieu. They carried his small monogenist flame through the dark days of polygenist dominance. Prichard, Hodgkin, and Buxton were all medical doctors. They combined their vocation with the passionate furtherance of their beliefs in human dignity through the APS, and the natural, resulting scientific understanding of humankind through the ESL. Hodgkin helped establish ethnology in France, though he achieved greater fame from his important work in pathology. Buxton became an eminent, reforming Member of Parliament, and one of his particular interests was the improvement of living conditions for the indigenous inhabitants of Britain's African colonies.

The early leader of the polygenists was Robert Knox, the anatomist who dissected the bodies of the victims of Edinburgh's infamous grave-robbers turned murderers, William Burke and William Hare. In *Races of Men: A Fragment* (Knox 1850) he argued, as had Kames, that different human 'races' are virtually different species, and that they had originated separately. Prichard, in various editions of his *Researches into the Physical History of Man* (see, e.g 1973 [1813]), put the monogenist case. His book went into five editions and long stood as an early evolutionist tract. Prichard did not necessarily believe that members of the 'races' they defined were equal in intellectual ability, but he did believe that 'lower' races were capable of betterment. While such a view would be rightly regarded as reactionary today, it was a veritable beacon of liberalism then, in anthropology's darkest age.

With hindsight it is ironic that those who held to polygenesis did take an interest in the differences between human groups. They did call themselves 'anthropologists', whereas most in the monogenist camp preferred the less species-centred term 'ethnologists'. Their battles helped to form the discipline, and it would be denial of this fundamental fact if we were to ignore the battle and remember only our victorious intellectual ancestors, the monogenists, in isolation. We should recall too that the discipline encompasses the study of both the human nature common to all 'races' and the cultural differences between peoples.

Concluding summary

It is impossible to define an exact moment when anthropology begins, but anthropological ideas emerged long before the establishment of the discipline. Crucial to the understanding of what was to come were notions of natural law and the social contract, as formulated in the seventeenth and eighteenth centuries. Though these ideas have long since been jettisoned by most social scientists, they mark a baseline for debate about the nature of society.

Eighteenth-century anthropological concerns included feral children, the 'Orang Outang', and notions of 'savage life'. Ethnography as we know it did not then exist. Montesquieu and Rousseau are both today claimed as founders of social science, and the sociological tradition descended from the former has parallels with the anthropological one. One view of the founding of anthropology is that it stems from the debate between the polygenists and the monogenists of the early nineteenth century. All anthropology today inherits the monogenist premise that humankind is one species.

FURTHER READING

Slotkin's *Readings in Early Anthropology* (1965) presents an excellent selection of short pieces from original sources, while Adams' *Philosophical Roots of Anthropology* (1998) covers in more depth some of the issues touched on here. The classic work on natural law is Gierke's *Natural Law and the Theory of Society* (1934).

My essay '*Orang Outang* and the definition of *Man*' (Barnard 1995) gives further details of the debate between Kames and Monboddo. See also Berry's *Social Theory of the Scottish Enlightenment* (1997) and Corbey and Theunissen's *Ape, Man, Apeman* (1995). A useful reference book on the period is Yolton's *Blackwell Companion to the Enlightenment* (1991). See also Daiches, Jones, and Jones' *A Hotbed of Genius* (1986).

Levine's *Visions of the Sociological Tradition* (1995) presents an excellent overview of sociology and general social theory. His approach is similar to the one given in this book for anthropology, though with a greater emphasis on national traditions. Stocking's essay 'What's in a name?' (1991) describes the founding of the Royal Anthropological Institute against a background of dispute between monogenists and polygenists. See also Stocking's introductory essay in the 1973 reprint of Prichard's *Researches into the Physical History of Man*.

3   Changing perspectives on evolution

By the 1860s the stage was set for evolutionist anthropology to come into its own within what was then, in Britain as on the Continent, usually called ethnology. It had already done so in archaeology, especially in Denmark. There the three-age theory (Stone Age, Bronze Age, and Iron Age) had been systematically propagated from around 1836 by Christian Jürgensen Thomsen, Sven Nilsson, and others (see, e.g., Trigger 1989: 73–86). Yet what became British anthropology grew not so much from this source, nor from evolutionary ideas in biology, but from questions of the relation between contemporary 'savage' or 'primitive' societies and Victorian England.

This chapter examines some parallels and disjunctions between the biological and anthropological traditions. It chronicles the rise of evolutionist anthropology, mainly in Britain in the middle of the nineteenth century, and its rapid development as the major paradigm for understanding human society prior to functionalism and relativism. It also covers the return to evolutionist thought in the middle of the twentieth century, mainly in America, and the growth of evolutionist ideas towards the end of the twentieth century.

Essentially, there are just four broad strands of evolutionist thinking in anthropology: unilinear, universal, and multilinear evolutionism, plus neo-Darwinism. The first three have been gradualist approaches, and their labels come from Julian Steward (1955 [1953]: 11–29), a practitioner of multilinear evolutionism. Neo-Darwinism comes in different guises, from 1970s sociobiology and its aftermath to more recent approaches to the origin of symbolic culture.

Biological and anthropological traditions

Encyclopedists of the Middle Ages classified the universe from high to low – God to angels to man; man to apes, and apes to worms; animals to plants. They believed the world was ordered, and they thought they could deduce its order according to principles embodied in the 'Great Chain of

Being' which united all living things. The term was in use well into the eighteenth century, and arguably the modern theory of evolution is an elaboration of this notion (see Lovejoy 1936).

However, there are two important differences between the Great Chain of Being and the theory of evolution. First, the concept 'evolution' has a temporal as well as a spatial aspect: things change or evolve through time. Secondly, whereas the classic notion of the Great Chain of Being was based on the idea of the fixity of species, the theory of evolution, in its biological form, depends on the contrary notion of the mutability of species. Lower forms evolve into higher forms.

Social evolution has parallels with biological evolution. This is obvious today, in a world where most book-educated people learn biological evolution before they learn of other cultures. It was also obvious in the late nineteenth century, when social advancement was often seen as analogous to biological evolution. However, to view social evolution *merely* in this way would be to invert historical precedent. The widespread acceptance in intellectual circles of the notion of 'progress' predates the theory of evolution as we know it. Eighteenth-century thinkers accepted the idea of the progress of humankind within the framework of biological immutability; it was only in the late nineteenth century that modern notions of social evolution became associated with ideas like 'mutual struggle' or 'survival of the fittest'.

The boundary between the Great Chain of Being and evolutionism is hardly a precise one, and beliefs concerning the mechanisms of biological change were varied. Linnaeus, essentially an anti-evolutionist, believed in a system of hybridization, whereby hybrids constantly form and produce new genera. The comte de Buffon seems to have changed his mind in the course of completing his forty-four-volume *Histoire naturelle* (1749–1804), at first rejecting any ancestral connection between different species, and later moving towards a degenerativist, or anti-evolutionist view. He argued that a small number of pure, ancestral animal forms developed into a multiplicity of less-pure, modern forms.

In *Philosophie zoologique*, Jean-Baptiste de Lamarck (1914 [1809]) suggested that each line of descent evolves to produce more-and-more-sophisticated life forms, but that the earliest forms continue to be reproduced by spontaneous generation. The earliest amoebas, he claimed, evolved into jellyfish. These evolved eventually into fishes, and later to reptiles, then later to mammals. Meanwhile, more recently generated amoebas evolved into jellyfish and fishes, but they will not yet have become reptiles or mammals. More recently still, other amoebas will have reproduced to form jellyfish, but not yet fishes. Lamarck believed that organs improve or decay according to whether they are used to their potential or not. He also held that individuals acquired characteristics which could be passed on to their descendants. For example, if a girl learned to paint at an early age, later she could pass on such talents to her children in the womb. Plainly, Lamarck had the idea of evolution, but he misunderstood its mechanism.

Charles Darwin (1859) rejected the Lamarckian view. He argued instead that evolution proceeds only through the passing down of what we now call genetic traits. Accidental mutation produced greater variety, and the forms which were most successful in their respective environments would reproduce more efficiently. Darwin, along with Alfred Russel Wallace (who came to similar conclusions), described the mechanism of evolution as 'sexual selection'. Since only those individuals that survive to reproduce will pass on their genes, mutations which enable this survival will be favoured. Isolation encourages greater change, and ultimately the formation of new species. As Darwin's ideas became well known, they came to have wide implications in Western societies, where they were seen as a threat to Christian orthodoxy. Their impact in the social sciences has, of course, been profound too (see Kuper 1994).

However, it would be wrong to see all developments in evolutionist anthropology simply as an extension of Darwinian theory. Evolutionist thinking in anthropology predates Darwin. Darwin published his most 'anthropological' work (he preferred the word 'ethnological'), *The Descent of Man*, in 1871 – the same year as important works by Lewis Henry Morgan and Edward Burnett Tylor. Arguably, Lamarck's theory, though flawed in biology, makes better sense than Darwin's as an analogy to explain gradual, unilinear, or universal, cultural evolution. Although biological traits may not be passed on in the womb as Lamarck thought, nevertheless newly invented cultural traits may be passed rapidly from individual to individual. New culture traits have the capacity to transform existing social relations. Societies become more complex as this process continues.

Unilinear evolutionism

Unilinear evolutionism is the notion that there exists one dominant line of evolution. In other words, all societies pass through the same stages. Since societies will progress at different rates, those societies which have been slower will remain at a 'lower' level than those which progress more rapidly. Of course, all this begs the question of what exactly it means for social institutions to be 'progressing' or 'evolving'. Different unilinear evolutionists have emphasized different things: material culture, means of subsistence, kinship organization, religious beliefs. But unilinear evolutionists, in general, believed that these phenomena are interrelated, and that therefore changes, say in means of subsistence, create evolutionary changes in kinship organization, religious belief and practice, and so on.

Maine, Lubbock, and Morgan

The idea of unilinear evolution grew from the early nineteenth-century monogenist theorists, but its high point was in the late nineteenth century, when it stood as the central idea of anthropological thought. The first major issue was that of the *family* versus the *social contract*: the outcome would lead directly to kinship theory, a central stage of anthropological debate ever since.

The social contract had stood for nearly two hundred years as a cornerstone of legal thought. Then, in 1861, Scots-born jurist Sir Henry Maine turned against the idea. He objected to it because of its artificial nature and its use in what he regarded as faulty legal fictions. Recalling his specialized knowledge of Roman law (and assuming its great antiquity), Maine argued that society originates instead in the family and in kinship groups built upon the family. In the absence of much opposition from inside the anthropological fraternity, family and kinship easily emerged victorious. However, this led ultimately to a host of vehement debates about the prehistory of the family and descent systems, and the relation of those systems to 'primitive promiscuity', the idea of 'private property', totemism, and the incest taboo (see Kuper 1988).

About a decade after Maine's book, two sometime politicians from opposite sides of the Atlantic came to prominence as anthropologists. Sir John Lubbock sat in the House of Commons as the Liberal Member of Parliament for London University, and was later elevated to the Peerage as Lord Avebury. He was a banker by profession, and is remembered today for his bill which established 'bank holidays' (so-called because he knew he could get more support among the Conservative opposition by calling them that than by calling them 'workers' holidays'). He also wrote prolifically on anthropology, archaeology, and the natural sciences.

Lewis Henry Morgan's career had certain similarities: success in business coupled with politics, and indeed amateur authorship of books on natural history. He was a part-time railroad tycoon and an upstate New York Republican state senator. His political renown was far less great than Lubbock's. Nevertheless his influence was profoundly ironic – because his key anthropological ideas were taken up by Karl Marx and especially by Friedrich Engels (1972 [1884]). The Republican state senator's emphasis on private property as the driving force of evolution struck a chord with his Communist admirers. In 1871, Lubbock and

Morgan met and discussed such matters, when the latter visited England.

Morgan is remembered primarily for two things. First, he was one of very few theorists of the nineteenth century to conduct serious field research. After a chance encounter with a Western-educated Iroquois named Ely Parker, Morgan was to spend many years working with Iroquois and other Native American peoples. He studied especially their kinship systems and their traditional political institutions, and he was active on their behalf as a campaigner for land rights. Secondly, after his discovery of 'the classificatory system of relationship' (essentially, the classifying of parallel cousins by the same terms as brothers and sisters), he developed a comparative model for the understanding of kinship systems worldwide. This was, in his view, the key to unlocking the prehistory of human society.

Matrilineality versus patrilineality

Most nineteenth-century scholars believed that matrilineality came before patrilineality, but they had different views about the evidence for this and the reasons why one system of unilineal descent might emerge first and the other evolve from it. Lubbock (1874 [1870]) maintained some scepticism about the significance of primitive matrilineality, but he accepted that existing matrilineal societies had evolved along similar lines. He believed that matrilineality had once been more common, when marriage was not fully developed. With fully developed marriage, he believed, property would go from a man to his own children (patrilineally) rather than to his sisters' children (matrilineally). Yet Lubbock also pointed out that in the most 'savage' of societies, marriage is unknown, 'female virtue' is not highly regarded, and women are treated as inferior to men. Thus he could not support the more radical matriarchal theories which were emerging. On the more clearly patrilineal side, Maine (1913 [1861]) had thought the Romans were quite ancient, and they, along with the Hebrews, Greeks, and Teutonic nations, all had patrilineal descent: he saw no reason to look to distant ethnography or to further speculation beyond the works of his predecessors in jurisprudence.

Those who favoured the primacy of matrilineality debated both with the patrilineal theorists and with other matrilineal theorists. Morgan and his arch-enemy John Ferguson McLennan (also a lawyer, and parliamentary draftsman for Scotland) left the patrilineal theorists behind and reserved their most vehement criticisms for each other. The debate centred on the reasons *why* matrilineality might have preceded patrilineality. McLennan (1970 [1865]) thought that a struggle for food in early times led to female infanticide. The resulting shortage of women led to polyandry (i.e., one woman with several husbands). Members of these ancient societies could not determine the father of any given child, so they came to reckon descent matrilineally. Patrilineality developed later, as men began first to capture, and subsequently to exchange women with men from other bands.

Morgan (1871; 1877) rested his case on kinship terminology – something which McLennan regarded as of little or no significance. Part of Morgan's argument was diffusionist. The Iroquois of New York State and Ontario (with whom Morgan worked in the 1840s and 1850s) had matrilineal descent and inheritance and a relationship terminology similar in some ways to South Asian ones. He noted too that the neighbouring Ojibwa had a terminology of similar structure even though they spoke a very different language. He reasoned that the First Peoples of North America must have migrated from Asia, a fact today firmly established though in his time still one of speculation. He argued, further, that Asian peoples must once have been matrilineal. Their common classification of the father and the father's brother by one relationship term, and their classification of parallel cousins as 'brothers and sisters', implied to Morgan a system of marriage of several brothers to the same woman. From such a system, he reasoned, matrilineal descent emerged.

Morgan believed that relationship terminologies are conservative, and as such reflect ancient social facts. In other words, they preserve hints of past forms of social organization because other aspects of society change faster than the terminology its members use. In his scheme, patrilineality came rather late, with the rise in private property and its associated laws of inheritance, from father to son. The matrilineal Iroquois represented an in-between stage in evolution, before patrilineal descent but long after what he called the stage of 'promiscuous intercourse'. The early phase of promiscuity evolved into a system of cohabitation or intermarriage between brothers and sisters, which gave rise to a 'communal family' and a custom, reported in Hawaii, whereby a group of brothers and their wives, or sisters and their husbands, once held common 'possession' over one another. This was reflected in his own time by the Hawaiian custom of such a kinship grouping still describing their relationship as *pinalua*, or one of intimacy, though no longer maintaining the practice of common sexual possession (if it ever really existed). The relationship terminology system of Hawaiian and other Polynesian languages, in turn, classifies only by generation, with parents and their siblings all called 'father' and 'mother', and both siblings and cousins called 'brother' and 'sister'.

Swiss jurist J. J. Bachofen, in *Das Mutterrecht* (1967 [1861]: 67–210), presented yet another notion of matrilineal pre-eminence. His theory rested on a supposed early feminist movement which overthrew primeval male dominance. This, he said, was followed by a subsequent resurgence of male authority. Bachofen's evidence involved mainly survivals of notions about female deities (from the matriarchal phase) and the ethnographic discovery of South American *couvade* (from the male overthrow of female authority). This French word designates the custom in which husbands of pregnant wives act as if they are pregnant themselves. Native South Americans reportedly did this in order to deflect malevolent spirits and keep them away from the unborn baby. Bachofen, in fact, here confused matrilineality (descent through the mother) with matriarchy (rule by mothers), but his theory had some following in his own time. It also anticipated more recent revolutionist, and indeed feminist, perspectives on 'primitive society'.

It is important to remember that all these arguments were made *within* the framework of unilinear evolution. There was little concern with cultural diversity for its own sake. To the unilinear evolutionists, cultural diversity was only important as an indicator of different stages within a grand evolutionary scheme. Perhaps the fact that most of the key protagonists were lawyers is significant too. As a pastime they debated over descent as in work they might have argued over competing inheritance claims. The logic and nuance of argument was important to them. There is a real sense in which anthropology as we know it began with law – whether with the notion of natural law (and the social contract) or with the squabbles over family and kinship which, from Maine onwards, became a central focus of the anthropological discourse.

Theories of 'totemism'

In the last quarter of the nineteenth century, though interest in kinship remained strong, other aspects of culture became focal points. Among these was religion, especially *totemism*. A short ethnographic excursion into 'totemism' may help to clarify the points of debate.

'Totemism' is today often written in quotation marks because there is a real question as to whether the category itself represents a single, specific phenomenon. Many have argued that when we talk about totemism, we are actually talking about quite different things in different cultures. However, nineteenth-century writers generally perceived totemism as a worldwide phenomenon, found in Native North and South America, Australia, Asia, Africa, and the Pacific. Arguably, elements of 'totemism' – the symbolic representation of the social by the natural – are found in European thought too, but not to the same degree, and certainly not with the same coherence as in, say, Australian Aboriginal thought. Military symbolism is one obvious example – calling units or operations by the names of animal species.

The word *totem* is from the Ojibwa. The word was introduced into the English language in 1791 by a British merchant, but the first good description of Ojibwa totemic ideas was in 1856, by one Peter Jones, who was both a Methodist missionary and an Ojibwa chief. The next ethnographer, in 1885, was also an Ojibwa, and all subsequent cross-cultural notions of totemism emanate, at least in part, from these two indigenous accounts (see, e.g., Lévi-Strauss 1969b [1962]). In Ojibwa thought, the *totem* is contrasted to the *manitoo*. The totem is represented by an animal species, and it symbolizes a patrilineal clan. It appears in mythology, and there is a rule that a person cannot marry one who shares his or her totem. The manitoo is also represented by an animal species, but it is the guardian spirit of an individual rather than a group. It comes in dreams, and a person cannot kill or eat his or her manitoo.

Similar notions are found in other cultures, but there are differences. For example, ethnographers of Australia have recorded some six forms of 'totemism', with each Aboriginal society possessing some two or three. There are (1) 'individual totems' which resemble the manitoos of the Ojibwa, though they often belong specifically to medicine men rather than to ordinary individuals. There are (2) 'clan totems', like the totems of the Ojibwa. These can be emblems of patrilineal clans, or of matrilineal ones. There are also (3) phratry totems, a phratry being simply a group of clans; and (4) moiety totems, where society is divided in 'half' (French *moitié*), on either patrilineal or matrilineal principles. There are (5) section and subsection totems, these divisions being marriageable categories defined by a combination of descent and generational principles. Finally, there are (6) land-based totems, for example, belonging to spirits of sacred sites. Usually in Australia, all these kinds of totem represent beings whose flesh cannot be eaten *and* whose fellow members cannot be taken as lovers or spouses. So they tend to incorporate the abstract principles of both the Ojibwa manitoos and the Ojibwa totems.

As ethnographic literature on 'totemism' grew, especially of the Australian varieties, armchair theorists in Europe used that literature to speculate on the origin and psychological nature of totems. French sociologist Emile Durkheim (1963 [1898]) argued that the most 'primitive' of men were in awe of blood and refused to cohabit with females of their respective clans, since they believed that their totemic gods inhabit this clan blood. Scottish folklorists Andrew Lang and Sir James Frazer emphasized the consubstantial relation between a man and his totem. Sir Edward Burnett Tylor saw totemism simply as a special case of ancestor worship. Yet whatever their considerable disagreements, almost all theorists of the day saw a relation between totemism and exogamy, and most held that totemism had evolved first. Furthermore, by implication at least, almost all of them saw this as an answer to the problem of primal human society, because these evolutionists believed that Australian Aboriginal culture represented a survival of early culture (for further details, see Kuper 1988: 76–122; Barnard 1999). The prime example of 'primal culture' had moved from Sir Henry Maine's Romans to the Aborigines.

Interesting among theories of totemism is that of Sigmund Freud (1960 [1913]: 140–55 *passim*). Though essentially a Lamarckian, he built his theory on the ideas of Darwin and also of theologian William Robertson Smith. What he sought to explain was no less than the origin of totemism, sacrifice, and the incest taboo all at once. Freud imagined a primal horde of males and females in which one male eventually became dominant. This male alone controlled the females, and he alone had sexual access to them. Members of the horde ultimately came to revere him as a god, but the young males resented his authority. They killed him and had sex with their sisters and their mothers. Then they felt guilty for doing such a horrible thing, so, it seems, they invented totemism! More precisely, the alpha-male primate, patriarch of the horde came to be remembered as a totemic being. His descendants invented sacrifices to appease his spirit. They instituted rules forbidding incest to stop the 'natural' proclivity of males to mate with their mothers. Thus, according to the Freudian view, the horrible deeds of murder and incest came to be forgotten, though vestiges of it remained deep in the totemic systems of Australian Aborigines, and very deep in the subconscious of all humanity. Freud saw both the Greek myth of Oedipus and the 'Oedipus complex' as 'memories' of these distant events.

Tylor and Frazer on 'early' religion

Religion attracted the attention of several scholars. Two are worthy of special note because of their position in the discipline, their great influence, and indeed for the high quality of their work: Tylor and Frazer. Both had the advantage of great longevity (Tylor lived from 1832 to 1917, and Frazer 1854 to 1941). Thus, for decades, their successive publications and public pronouncements represented the established, unilinear evolutionist view. Especially in Frazer's case, this view competed with emerging diffusionist, functionalist, and relativist ideas as later generations rebelled against evolutionism.

Sir Edward Tylor's introduction to anthropology came during a trip to North America. In Havana he met Henry Christie, a gentleman adventurer and like himself an English Quaker, who was about to set off for

Mexico. Tylor went with him and later published his first book on what he found (Tylor 1861). There and in subsequent works, especially *Primitive Culture* (Tylor 1871), Tylor explored the evolution of culture through the doctrine of 'survivals'. The idea is that present-day culture retains elements which have now lost their function, but whose present existence is a testimony to their past importance. Morgan's kinship terminologies are an example. Others, which Tylor was fond of, include items of clothing which formerly were functional but which in his time were only decorative: unused buttons behind the waist of a jacket, or cut-away collars always kept turned down. One of the most curious aspects of Tylor's method was his study of school children in London, for he believed that they, being less mature and less educated, might hold clues to primitive thought. In the realm of religion, he argued that survivals of ancient rituals and beliefs continue long after the original meaning has been forgotten, while the more instinctual and primitive thoughts of civilized humanity may still hold hints of the earlier development of religious ideas.

Tylor's theory of religion consisted of a scheme of evolution from 'animism', the all-embracing doctrine that souls (Latin *animi* or *animae*) exist independently of the material world. He noted that in virtually every human society, there is a common belief in a spiritual essence which survives death. People the world over make offerings to the dead, or to revere things such as trees or streams in which souls are believed to dwell. Tylor postulated that the earliest peoples held this notion through dreams in which souls appeared to them; and that societies eventually developed the practices of making offerings, and later, sacrifices, to such souls, fairies, and deities. He believed that fetishism (when humans control their deities through material objects) and totemism (in which animal or plant species are vested with souls) developed from animism.

In a number of respects, Tylor agreed with Lubbock, though it was in fact the latter who more simply stated the unilinear scheme many nineteenth-century anthropologists seem to have accepted: *atheism* (the absence of definite ideas on a deity), to *fetishism*, to *nature-worship* or *totemism*, to *shamanism* (where deities are believed to be remote and powerful, accessible only through shamans), to *idolatry* (when gods become like men), to *theism* (Lubbock 1874 [1870]: 119). Tylor avoided making such an explicit sequence as this, perhaps because he viewed the evolution of religion as a complex matter, with survivals of earlier stages overlapping with newer ideas and different kinds of animism emerging simultaneously. Tylor's contribution therefore was less substantive and more theoretical and methodological, and as such it still stands as an achievement of evolutionist thought – however flawed the paradigm of unilinear evolutionism may be.

Sir James Frazer was, for most of his career, a classics scholar and Fellow of Trinity College, Cambridge. The University of Liverpool granted him the title of Professor of Social Anthropology in 1907, but he held this as an honorary position. A shy man, he is said to have disliked teaching, but earned sizeable royalties from his voluminous, influential, and widely read books. His *Golden Bough* is one of the great books of anthropology, and it was widely read by generations of intellectuals of all kinds (the young Bronislaw Malinowski, then still a mathematician, read it in order to improve his English). On the surface, *The Golden Bough* represents an attempt to explain the origin and meaning of the slaughter of ancient Italian priest-kings, each by his successor. On a deeper level, it merges myth and history, ethnography and reason, to build a fanciful, poetic overview of the human psyche and social order. *The Golden Bough* was first published in 1890, and expanded to twelve volumes in 1900. Let me quote the final words of the 1922 abridged edition:

Without dipping so far deep into the future we may illustrate the course which thought has hitherto run by likening it to a web woven of three different threads – the black thread of magic, the red thread of religion, and the white thread of science . . . Could we then survey the web of thought from the beginning, we should probably perceive it to be at first a chequer of black and white, a patchwork of true and false notions, hardly tinged as yet by the red thread of religion. But carry your eye farther along the fabric and you will remark that, while the black and white chequer still runs through it, there rests on the middle portion of the web . . . a dark crimson stain, which shades off insensibly into a lighter tint as the white thread of science is woven more and more into the tissue. (Frazer 1922: 713)

What is intriguing here is that while Frazer privileges one realm of culture (namely science) over the others, he nevertheless attributes it to the most primitive as well as the most civilized cultures. From a relativist point of view (see chapter 7), magic in so-called primitive societies may be thought of as nothing more than applied science, or technology. Frazer here sees religion as evolving after primitive science, and modern culture as containing both these threads. This is interesting in light of more recent debates between fundamentalist Christians, who call themselves 'creation scientists', and American anthropologists who in their view have blind faith in the 'false doctrine' of Darwinism (see, e.g., Williams 1983; Stipe 1985). Both sides claim for themselves the status of 'scientist' and claim for science the truth which Frazer also believed it represented.

All the unilinear evolutionists, whether they specialized in kinship or in religion, held a vision of anthropology as a science which tied the present and the past. They sought origins, and they found them among their 'primitive' contemporaries. Their methodological flair, however, was dampened as succeeding generations turned away from the question of origins. Anti-evolutionists turned to diffusion, social function, and cultural diversity. We shall take up those stories later. Yet it is important to see the next phase in evolutionist thought, universal evolutionism, as an attempt to return to grand questions, if not of origins then of universal history.

Universal evolutionism

Universal evolutionism emerged in the early twentieth century as a softening of the tenets of unilinear evolutionism. In light of new ethnographic and archaeological evidence, precise unilinear phases, consistent cross-culturally and throughout the world, could no longer be sustained. So instead, broad, 'universal' phases of evolution were postulated, such as the classical division between 'savagery', 'barbarism', and 'civilization' (championed by Morgan, among others). Debates on matters like matrilineality versus patrilineality were jettisoned as too speculative to merit further consideration. Also thrown aside were the *details* of, for example, Frazer's many analyses of totemism (see especially Frazer 1910: vol. IV), in favour of generalities similar to those of Frazer's passage above, which foreshadowed universal evolutionist thinking. Yet it is of the greatest importance that the universal evolutionism which emerged in the 1930s owed more to Morgan's materialism than to Frazer's quest for the aesthetic and esoteric in the human spirit. The new generation of evolutionists reacted against the functionalist, and especially the relativist bent of most anthropologists of their day (see chapters 5 and 7).

The main proponents of universal evolutionism were Australian archaeologist V. Gordon Childe and American cultural anthropologist Leslie White. Their left-wing political concerns led them to review the theories of Marx and Engels, and those anthropologists, notably Morgan, who had influenced Marx and Engels.

V. Gordon Childe

Childe was prominent as a leftist member of the Australian Labour Party, and his views found no favour in the conservative Australian universities in which he sought employment. He emigrated to Britain in 1921 and travelled widely in Europe before accepting a chair in archaeology, in 1927, at Edinburgh. He later moved to the Institute of Archaeology in London, before returning to Australia to end his days. In Britain Childe achieved fame, both as a field archaeologist and as a theoretician. His ideas became widely accepted within archaeology, where universal evolutionism is perhaps a more natural theory than it is in cultural anthropology. The ages of humankind, seen through their technology, are readily apparent in the archaeological record; and Childe's belief that prehistory and history ought to be the same subject, but with different methodologies, was attractive to archaeologists of his time.

Childe wrote many books, but among them two short popular texts stand out as his most influential. *Man Makes Himself* (Childe 1936) examined human history as a whole, and branched out across the continents, whereas his previous work had largely been confined to Europe. It traced evolution from hunting and gathering, to the dawn of agriculture, to the formation of states, the urban revolution and the 'revolution in human knowledge'. *What Happened in History* (Childe 1942), intended as a sequel, turned out to be much more pessimistic. Written during the early part of the Second World War, it suggested that Europe was heading for a new 'dark age' (albeit only a temporary one). At his death in 1957, Childe's desire to see archaeology and universal history established as social sciences was a long way off.

Leslie A. White

White's place as an isleted evolutionist in a sea of relativism (which American anthropology then was) must have been even more problematic than Childe's. For forty years (1930 to 1970) he taught at the University of Michigan, where he gradually built up a following of 'neo-evolutionist' students and colleagues. Although he did publish five ethnographies on Pueblo peoples, White is far better known for his theoretical works. In a series of essays collected as *The Science of Culture* (White 1949), he put forward the notion of culture as an integrated, dynamic, and symbolic system whose most important component is technology. His proposed science, 'culturology', would be the study of that phenomenon. It would steal subject matter from psychology, but it would oppose conventional psychological theory in seeing history as comprised of cultural forces driven by technology. Its relation to sociology would be similar, in that it would explain what sociology, focused as it is on social interaction, could not.

In *The Evolution of Culture* (White 1959), White turned his attention to the course of evolution from the 'Primate Revolution' to the fall of Rome. He argued that 'energy' is the key mechanism of cultural evolution. In the earliest phase, energy existed in the form of the human body alone. Later, men and women harnessed other sources: fire, water, wind, and so on. Advances in the manufacture of tools, in the domestication of animals and plants, and in the intensification of agriculture all increased efficiency and spurred on cultural evolution.

White's style of evolutionism continued after his death through the work of his students. Marshall Sahlins (especially in his early work), Elman Service, and Marvin Harris, among many others, owe an intellectual debt to Leslie White. However, with the dawn of cultural ecology, their vision became more particularistic than White's, and their approaches decidedly more multilinear. It is ironic too that all these later scholars have acknowledged debts to Marx and Engels, whereas White himself remained largely silent on this in his major texts.

Multilinear evolutionism and cultural ecology

Unilinear evolutionism's assertions were problematic, because they were either untestable or (when falsified by ethnographic cases) clearly non-universal. Unilinear evolutionism rested on an assumption that things occur and change everywhere in the world in the same way, if not at the same time. According to a strictly unilinear approach, specific culture changes have but one explanation, though theorists might disagree as to what explanation this might be.

Universal evolutionism was a much less powerful theory precisely because it was harder to debate. Many would agree that technology advances and societies become more complex with time, but what would they do with this information? What was needed was a more sophisticated and more controversial approach.

Julian H. Steward

Multilinear evolutionism was devised by Julian Steward, of the University of Illinois, as an explicit attempt to get away from both the vague generalities of universal evolutionism and the problematic assertions of unilinear evolutionism. It gets around such difficulties by positing diverse trajectories of technological and social evolution in different regions of the world. These trajectories were essentially limited by ecological circumstances, that is, by historical determinations of technology and the very important further limiting factor of the natural environment. Thus multilinear evolutionism became closely bound with the idea of cultural ecology. It also shares a certain similarity with Darwinian thought in biology, by its analogy with the biological theory of speciation.

The main breakthrough came in 1955, when Steward's major essays to that date were published in book form. Although he went on later to look at technologically advanced societies, his ethnographic work on the Shoshone of California and his comparative essays on hunter-gatherers (which formed the major portion of *Theory of Culture Change*) set the scene. Steward, and later Service (e.g., 1962), propounded the notion that hunter-gatherers developed characteristic ways of exploiting resources to their best advantage not only through technology but also through seasonal migrations, territorial arrangements, and group structures suited to the purpose (see Barnard 1983).

George Peter Murdock

Meanwhile, a quite different but equally multilinear and ecological approach was being developed by George Peter Murdock, first at Yale and later at Pittsburgh. Murdock founded the Cross-Cultural Survey, later the Human Relations Area Files, through which he tried to assemble cultural facts from all the cultures of the world. His purpose was to enable scholars to correlate the distribution of culture traits and work out historical trajectories both in general and for particular culture areas or similar culture types. His best known work was the somewhat mis-titled monograph *Social Structure* (1949), which employed a sample of 250 representative societies for such a purpose. A handful of other scholars followed, notably Melvin Ember and Carol Ember at the Human Relations Area Files (New Haven Connecticut), and in some of his work, Jack Goody at Cambridge.

Let me illustrate the method and theory Murdock espoused with an example. It had been known before Murdock's work that certain rules of descent are more commonly found with certain patterns of postmarital residence, for example, patrilineal descent with virilocal residence (with the husband), or matrilineal descent with either uxorilocal (with the wife) or viri-avunculocal residence (with the husband's mother's brother). Murdock established more precisely statistical correlations between such patterns, and then sought to explain the reasons behind them, and relate them statistically to other patterns, such as means of subsistence and kinship terminologies.

Supposing, let us say, hoe agriculture is commonly practised by women. Women in such a society might tend to pass on both their skills and their fields to their daughters, who would bring in their husbands upon marriage. *De facto* matrilineal groups would be established, and an ideology of matrilineal descent might be expected to emerge. Matrilineal descent is further correlated either with what Murdock called 'Iroquois-type terminology', in which cross-cousins are distinguished from parallel cousins, or with 'Crow-type terminology', in which, in addition, father's sister and father's sister's daughter are called by the same term. The apparent reason for this peculiarity is that a person's father's sisters and father's sisters' daughters would reside in the same locale. If matrilineal descent is recognized, they would also belong to the same matrilineal kin group. Actually, 'Crow-type terminology' makes sense in a strongly matrilineal society, and it would make little sense in most other kinds of society. Murdock reasoned that when modes of descent change, so too should kinship terminologies. Therefore, we can posit a causal, and evolutionary, relationship between these elements of culture.

Neo-Darwinism

Neo-Darwinism is a broad set of perspectives comprising two basic and very different schools of thought: sociobiology and what might be called 'revolutionist' (as opposed to narrowly evolutionist) thinking. The former tradition is in continuity with biology. The latter takes up the nineteenth-century quest for origins and even returns to nineteenth-century interests in totemism and primitive promiscuity.

Sociobiology

By the late 1970s a new grand evolutionist tradition was encroaching on the social sciences, especially in the United States. This was 'sociobiology', sparked off by E. O. Wilson's (1975) book by that title – a book which treated human culture and society as simply adjuncts of humankind's animal nature. Wilson pulled together a variety of strands of biological thinking, and like Darwin considered the implications for the understanding of humanity. Yet unlike Darwin, he took on the whole of human culture. Wilson argued that the application of Darwinian principles makes it possible to explain culture in much the same way as one explains the social life of termites, frogs, or wolves. Analysing anthropological data, he considered the effects of group selection on human warfare, sexual selection on the development of political organization, art as a special manifestation of tool use, ritual music as derivatives of communication, and even ethics as an extension of the desire to pass on one's genes. Altruism within family or community, he suggested, fulfils the function of enabling those who share one's genes to do better than those who do not.

One anthropologist who was influenced by the sociobiology movement was Robin Fox. His approach is interesting because it illustrates clearly the view that human society has its basis in animal sociality. Fox (1975) argued that aspects of human kinship systems are found also among non-human primates. Some primate species have the makings of 'descent' (which he defines as pan-generational relations within a group) while others have only 'alliance' (defined as mating relations between groups). This argument contradicts the mainstream theory of structural-ist anthropology, following Claude Lévi-Strauss (1969a [1949]), that the incest taboo marks the boundary between animals and humans. Only humans have the capability of instituting a taboo. For Lévi-Strauss, the incest taboo is part of (human) nature because it is present in all societies, but it is the essence of culture because it is defined differently from culture to culture. Some cultures, Lévi-Strauss points out, prohibit sex between cross-cousins, while other cultures recognize the category of cross-cousins as precisely the one within which sex is allowed.

However, few anthropologists apart from Fox were taken in, and some reacted strongly against the perceived threat. Among the latter were two influential American scholars of broadly evolutionist persuasion: Marvin Harris and Marshall Sahlins. Harris (1979: 119–40) attacked sociobiology as biological reductionism. Taking on the biologists in their own terms, he pointed out that 'genotypes never account for all the variations in behavioural phenotype' (1979: 121): even in simple organisms, learned behaviour is a factor. Culture, as he says, is 'gene free'. Sahlins, in his devastating little book, *The Use and Abuse of Biology*, pointed out that there was a vast gulf between aggression and war, between sexuality and cross-cousin marriage, and between socially functional 'reciprocal altru-ism' and formalized gift exchange. 'Within the void left by biology', as he put it, 'lies the whole of anthropology' (Sahlins 1977 [1976]: 16).

Thus sociobiology turned out not to be the 'new synthesis' its adher-ents hailed it as. Its impact may have been great among biologists, but it never succeeded in overtaking anthropology. There was simply too much it left unexplained.

The symbolic revolution?

Revolutionist thinking was, in retrospect, characteristic of many thinkers in the eighteenth century. We also see it in the work of Morgan, Marx, and Engels, and more especially in Freud's theory of the origin of to-temism and Lévi-Strauss' theory of the incest taboo as the origin of culture. White's notion of a 'Primate Revolution' is also a clear example. Yet it emerged as a paradigm in its own right – at once evolutionist and anti-evolutionist (in the sense that it puts instantaneous change over slow evolution) – only in the 1980s (e.g., Cucchiari 1981). Its central feature today is the search for the origin of symbolic culture, or *culturo-genesis*. It turns Freud on his androcentric head by giving the instigating force of that first human revolution to the females of the species.

One eccentric version of this approach is that of Chris Knight, a British anthropologist who argues that symbolic culture began with a sex strike

Table 3.1. *Evolution (Maine, Morgan, and others) versus revolution (Rousseau, Freud, Knight, and others)*

	Human/animal 'kinship'	Basis of society	Development of ritual
Evolution	continuity	family	gradual, increasing complexity
Revolution	discontinuity	social contract	catastrophic event leading to the invention of ritual, taboo, totemism, and so on.

on the part of anatomically modern women demanding food for sex (see, e.g., Knight 1991; Knight, Power, and Watts 1995). In the 'primal horde' (to use Freud's term) males impregnated females indiscriminately, and the females were left to care for their young themselves. At some point within the last 70,000 years, females – or rather, the women of some specific horde or band – took charge of the situation and collectively demanded that their menfolk hunt for them before sex was allowed. The women symbolized their refusal of sex by menstruating or pretending to menstruate, and they did this together, in synchrony. The period of hunting and sexual taboo was from new moon to full moon, and the period of feasting and sex was between full moon and new moon.

Knight's theory is evolutionist in that it emphasizes the trajectory from pre-symbolic to symbolic-cultural humankind, but the focal point is on instantaneous revolution. Knight's approach to ritual and symbolic activity generally resembles Lévi-Strauss on kinship, and Rousseau on his vision of the social contract as the basis of society. It directly opposes most other theories of evolution on ritual, and implicitly opposes Fox's gradualist view of the relation between human and animal 'kinship', as well as Maine's and Morgan's idea of the family as the basis of society. The problem is that while it is ingenious, it is untestable.

The relation between the most significant of these ideas is illustrated in table 3.1.

Current trends

The debate between gradualists and those who see the origin of symbolic culture as revolutionary is very much the way anthropological evolutionism, in the broad sense, is moving. In Britain, new links are being forged between social anthropology and linguistics, archaeology, and human biology, as all these bear on the issue. This may seem strange in North

America, where these fields have long been seen as anthropological subdisciplines which are moving away from each other.

While some evolutionists today, such as Tim Ingold (e.g., 1986: 16–129) in Britain, and a number of ecological anthropologists in Japan and the United States, are pursuing the boundary between animals and humans, Knight is perusing the boundary between pre-symbolic humanity and humankind as we know it. The former boundary rests on factors such as the social relations of technology use, while the latter rests on affective aspects of culture and society. Clearly, the former is easier to define. While the latter has an intrinsic fascination, its specific theories are essentially untestable and unlikely to survive if presented (as they tend to be) as part of what Leslie White liked to call 'a scientific theory of culture'.

Concluding summary

Evolutionism in anthropology has parallels with evolutionism in other fields, including archaeology and biology. However, it is also unique in having three classic and easily definable forms: unilinear, universal, and multilinear (though the attribution of these Stewardian ideal types to individual theorists is not always as easy as Steward made out). Unilinear evolutionism took monogenesis for granted and treated cultures as so similar that they would all invent things in the same order and pass through the same stages of development. Universal evolutionism, still characteristic of much thinking in archaeology, recognizes greater complexity than this but seeks to simplify by focusing on the broad, general stages rather than the specifics. Multilinear evolutionism has focused on the specifics of historical development, especially those related to ecological factors. Of the three approaches, it bears the closest relation to the Darwinian notion of evolution.

Bachofen once wrote: 'Generally speaking, the development of the human race knows no leaps, no sudden progressions, but only gradual transitions; it passes through many stages, each of which may be said to bear within it the preceding and the following stage' (1967 [1861]: 98). This gradualist statement characterizes much in evolutionist anthropology from the unilinear, to the universal, to the multilinear approaches. Yet it is contradictory to the ideas of both Darwin and Marx (see chapter 6). The debate today between gradualists and revolutionists seems set to continue, whether today's specific theories of culturo-genesis survive or not.

FURTHER READING

Stocking's *Victorian Anthropology* (1987) and *After Tylor* (1996a) present fine overviews of relevant eras in the history of anthropology in Britain. For more of a social history approach, see Bowler's *The Invention of Progress* (1989). His book on Darwin (Bowler 1990) is also of interest, while Kuper's *The Chosen Primate* (1994) is both lighter in tone and wider in scope.

The classic statement on the three evolutionist approaches in social anthropology is in Steward's *Theory of Culture Change* (1955: 11–29). Harris' critical overview, *The Rise of Anthropological Theory* (1968), has a good deal of relevance; though his negative attitude to those he discusses is not to everyone's liking.

In general, the primary sources cited in this chapter are readable, particularly those by Tylor (1871), Childe (1936; 1942), White (1949; 1959), Steward (1955), and E. O. Wilson (1975). There is also an abridged edition of Wilson's *Sociobiology* (1980).

4   Diffusionist and culture-area theories

Diffusionism stresses the transmission of things (material or otherwise) from one culture to another, one people to another, or one place to another. An implicit presupposition of extreme diffusionism is that humankind is uninventive: things are invented only once, and then are transmitted from people to people, sometimes across the globe. This can be effected either by direct transmission between stable populations or through migrations by culture-rich peoples. In contrast, classical evolutionism assumes that humankind is inventive: each population has the propensity to invent the same things as the next, though they will do so at different rates.

By the time diffusionism was dwindling in importance, around the 1930s, it had left behind ideas which were picked up within other traditions: the idea of 'culture areas' is the most prominent example. This had already become an important facet of the ethnographic tradition of Franz Boas and his followers (see chapter 7). It also appeared within the evolutionism of Julian Steward (chapter 3) and within the functionalist and structuralist traditions which emerged in the first half of the twentieth century (chapters 5 and 8). Culture-area and regional approaches are a logical outgrowth of an emphasis on diffusion, and this chapter will cover these approaches with this point in the background.

Antecedents of diffusionism: philology, Müller, and Bastian

Diffusionism originated in the eighteenth-century philological tradition which posited historical connections between all the languages of the Indo-European language family.

The philological tradition: diffusionism before the diffusionists?

The breakthrough came in 1787, when Sir William Jones, an English Orientalist and barrister serving as a judge in India, discovered similarities between Sanskrit, Greek, and Latin. In the early nineteenth century, Wilhelm von Humboldt, Prussian diplomat and brother of the explorer Alexander, Baron von Humboldt, concentrated his interest on Basque – a European but non-Indo-European language. Echoing earlier ideas of Johann Gottfried von Herder, Wilhelm von Humboldt put the case for a close interrelation between language and culture. About the same time, Jacob Grimm, famous along with his brother Wilhelm for collecting European fairy tales (the 'brothers Grimm'), established the sound shifts which distinguish Germanic from other Indo-European languages, and Franz Bopp took up the comparative study of Indo-European grammar. All these writers touched on ideas which later came into anthropology as diffusionism.

The development of theoretical ideas in linguistics has throughout the history of that discipline foreshadowed the development of related ideas in social and cultural anthropology, though in this case their ideas were very slow to catch on. The thread that links early philological or historical linguistic theories to anthropology was of greater influence in evolutionist Britain than in Germany, where diffusionism was to take hold late in the nineteenth century.

The connection to British evolutionism runs through the work of several scholars, but none as obviously as that of the German-British orientalist, Friedrich Max Müller. Dissuaded by his godfather Felix Mendelssohn from studying music, the young Max Müller turned to Sanskrit, first at Leipzig and then, under Bopp, at Berlin. In 1846 further studies took him to Oxford, where he settled and eventually took up chairs in modern languages and comparative philology. Like Lubbock, Müller was active in Liberal politics and knew many in positions of power. Apparently through his friendship with the Royal Family, he was granted the very rare honour of being made a Privy Councillor.

Müller spent much of his life editing a fifty-one-volume series of sacred texts of the East. He also helped to propagate both the essentially evolutionist idea of psychic unity or psychical identity (i.e., that all humankind shares the same mentality) and the diffusionist idea that the religions as well as the languages of ancient Greece and Rome were related to those of India. He explored the latter through both anthropological comparisons of funeral customs and philological comparisons of the names of Greek and Hindu deities (see, e.g., Müller 1977 [1892]: 235–80). It is noteworthy that Müller (1977: 403–10) argued against the notion that there is one kind of 'totemism', and strongly criticized those who believed that all societies pass through the same stages of religious belief. Through both positive contributions in diffusionist thinking and negative comments on the extremes of unilinear evolutionism, Müller helped temper the tendencies of his British evolutionist contemporaries.

Like Müller, Adolph Bastian was an ambiguous figure. His broad approach was evolutionist rather than diffusionist, but he was a staunch opponent of Darwinism. In the late 1860s he helped establish both museum ethnography and theoretical ethnology in Germany. Thus he influenced the rise of diffusionism by providing the institutional base for it to develop from, even though his immediate successors became critical of his own theoretical contributions.

Bastian spent much of his working life as a ship's surgeon, travelling the world and writing on the exotic cultures he encountered. Unfortunately, his writings were absurdly metaphorical and virtually untranslatable, and have hardly ever been rendered into English. Let me quote one sentence, as translated by Robert Lowie, to give the flavour. The topic under discussion is the avoidance of premature generalization:

Thereby would be tailored for us a beggar's cloak of mottled shreds and patches, whereas if we wait calmly for the facts to be gleaned for a definite survey, a magnificent peplos will be woven, as though spread by Zeus over a sacred oak, as a radiantly reflected image of reality. (Bastian [1881], quoted in Lowie 1937: 33)

But for all that, Bastian did give the world a theoretical contrast which was well ahead of its time: his distinction between *Elementargedanken* ('elementary thoughts') and *Völkergedanken* ('folk thoughts', or more literally 'folks' thoughts'). The former consist of what were later called 'cultural universals' and which, taken together, formed the psychic unity of humankind. Bastian noted the many similarities between cultures in different parts of the world, and he attributed such similarities to evolutionary convergence along lines pre-determined by these 'elementary thoughts'. His notion of 'folk thoughts', in contrast, represents the aspects of culture which differ from place to place. He attributed such differences to the influence of the physical environment and the chance events of history. The eventual focus of German-Austrian anthropology on 'folk thoughts', in turn, paved the way for diffusionism.

Diffusionism proper

Diffusionism came to prominence in the work of German and Austrian geographer-anthropologists in the late nineteenth century. As we shall see, it then fell into obscurity and absurdity (albeit interesting absurdity) in Britain, in the hands of two early twentieth-century Egyptologists.

German-Austrian diffusionism

The first great diffusionist was Friedrich Ratzel. He trained as a zoologist, but soon turned to geography and saw his theory in terms of a discipline which came to be called 'anthropogeography' (*Anthropogeographie*). Ratzel advocated the mapping of regions and the search for routes of migration and diffusion across the globe. He argued against Bastian's assumption of psychic unity and, wherever possible, sought evidence of culture contact as the cause of cultural similarity. This, together with the fact that he regarded humankind as uninventive, made him a true 'diffusionist' though he did not use the label himself.

Ratzel argued that single items of culture tended to diffuse, whereas whole 'culture complexes' (clusters of related cultural features) were spread by migration. His most famous example was the similarity between hunting bows found in Africa and New Guinea (Ratzel 1891). He postulated a historical connection between them and related this to what he regarded as the similar psychological makeup of peoples in the two areas. He argued further that culture *developed* mainly through massive migrations and conquests of weaker peoples by stronger, and more culturally advanced, ones. Thus, just as evolutionists like Morgan and Tylor (without necessarily knowing it) incorporated elements of diffusionism in their theories, Ratzel, the first great diffusionist, retained a strong element of evolution in his theoretical stance. Where they differed was in the mechanism they chose to emphasize: progress itself or the transmission of culture.

From his base at Leipzig, Ratzel taught a great number of scholars. He influenced not only immediate followers in Germany and later proponents of culture-area theory in North America, but also Tylor in England. Specifically, Tylor praised Ratzel's important three-volume masterpiece *Völkerkunde* – which appeared in English translation as *The History of Mankind* (1896–8 [1885–8]). From this time, evolutionism and diffusionism came to be recognized as two logically opposed but nevertheless complementary perspectives, which depended on each other for a full explanation of human culture history.

Ratzel was probably the first to divide the world into what we now call 'culture areas', but Leo Frobenius greatly extended his method and theory. Frobenius, a self-trained African explorer and museum ethnologist, enjoyed looking for parallels in cultural development worldwide. He came up with the idea of 'culture circles' (*Kulturkreise*), conceived as great culture areas which in some cases spread across the globe and overlapped those which had existed before: for example, bow-and-arrow culture over spear culture. The definition of these culture circles was to dominate German and Austrian anthropology from the 1890s to the 1930s.

However, in his later work Frobenius turned his attention to what he called the *Paideuma*. The term is Greek for 'education' (roughly translated), but in Frobenius' usage it took on a meaning akin to the classic

romantic idea of the *Volksgeist*. This is the 'soul' of a culture, a basic psychic principle which determined any given configuration of culture traits. Furthermore, through his search for African culture configurations, he helped develop the notion of 'worldview' (German, *Weltanschauung*) which was to dominate American anthropology in its relativist period. For Africa, Frobenius (e.g., 1933) postulated two basic worldviews: 'Ethiopian' (characterized by cattle and cultivation, patrilineality, ancestor cults, cults of the earth, etc.) and 'Hamitic' (characterized by cattle and hunting, matrilineality, avoidance of the dead, sorcery, etc.). The former he located in Egypt and most of East, West, and Central Africa. The latter was supposedly the worldview of the Horn of Africa, much of North Africa and South Africa.

Playing upon these basic worldviews were a set of more specific culture configurations which, Frobenius believed, had spread either within Africa, or in other cases, from Asia or Europe to Africa. These overlay earlier cultural elements, such as hunting and gathering, which either were subsumed under, or remained encapsulated within, the culture areas which formed through successive waves of cultural diffusion. Thus Frobenius' vision of African culture was of a complex of layers whose historical relations could be determined by comparative study. Ethnology in his eyes was akin to archaeology, but with contemporary ethnographic work as its methodological basis.

After Ratzel and Frobenius, Fritz Graebner and Wilhelm Schmidt took the lead in *Kulturkreis* studies. Graebner, a museologist, concentrated on similarities in material culture, first across Oceania and later throughout the world. Ratzel had emphasized the qualities of cultures, and Frobenius had favoured a quantitative dimension. Graebner put these together in stressing both form and quantity as separate criteria for gauging the likelihood of any two cultures being historically related. By this method he defined culture circles such as the 'Tasmanian' (reputedly the earliest and most primitive), 'Australian boomerang', 'Melanesian bow', and 'Polynesian patrilineal', which he believed represented increasingly advanced cultural waves, surging across the Pacific. Graebner's career was hampered by internment in Australia during the First World War (allegedly for smuggling documents), and by mental illness which afflicted him from around 1926 until his death in 1934. Nevertheless, his attempts to place on a scientific basis the search for geographical culture circles and overlapping culture strata marked a high point in diffusionist thinking. His book *Die Methode der Ethnologie* (Graebner 1911) became a classic.

Schmidt, a Catholic priest with a special interest in African religions, argued that 'African Pygmy culture' was more 'primitive' than Graebner's 'Tasmanian culture'. He distinguished four basic culture circles

(Schmidt 1939 [1937]). After the Primitive Culture Circle of hunters and gatherers came the Primary Circle of horticulturists. At this stage, patrilineal and matrilineal descent first appeared. Schmidt argued that the greater confidence people felt in their own technological abilities led to a reduction in the importance of worship and to a dependence on magic. The Secondary Circle consisted in the mixing of Primitive and Primary traits. These led to intensive agriculture, sacred kingship, and ultimately polytheism. His Tertiary Circle consisted of a complex blending of traits from different cultures of the Secondary Circle, creating the ancient civilizations of Asia, Europe, and the Americas.

One of Schmidt's goals was establishing the history of world religion, a subject on which he wrote more than a dozen volumes. He hypothesized that religion began with a primitive monotheism, derived from early humanity's knowledge of his own, one true God. He believed that each succeeding culture circle developed better technology and more complex social organization, while at the same time it moved away from the primal monotheistic religion. Thus Schmidt's stance had elements of both primitivism and evolutionism, a fact which highlights the contradictions of diffusionism as a unitary perspective.

British diffusionism

While diffusionism reigned in Germany and Austria, elsewhere it infiltrated anthropological thinking mainly as a restraint on the simplicity of unilinear evolutionism. In archaeology, Swedish writer Oscar Montelius, in the 1880s and 1890s, refined the typology of the European Neolithic and Bronze Ages. He argued that regional variations and specific small developments across Europe could be accounted for by diffusion, rather than by evolution (see Trigger 1989: 155–61). In ethnology, things were more subtle, but it is important to recall that Morgan's thinking about kinship terminologies depended heavily on both migration and diffusion, and Tylor often spoke of diffusion and described cultures as having 'adhesions', or elements of culture usually found together. German and American anthropologists called these 'culture complexes'.

However, the co-existence of evolutionism and diffusionism was soon to be challenged in Britain, perhaps spurred on by a growing pessimism after Queen Victoria's death in 1901 and the political manoeuvring of European states which foreshadowed the First World War. Nineteenth-century Britons had firmly believed that Victorian values and the scientific inventions and discoveries personified by Prince Albert's sponsorship were pinnacles of human endeavour. In the pessimism of the first decades of the twentieth century, though, these achievements came to be deni-

grated. The new symbol of human cultural achievement was ancient Egypt, and degeneration rather than evolution marked the British diffusionists' trajectory from Egyptian to Victorian society.

Sir Grafton Elliot Smith (an eminent Australian-born anatomist) and his disciple William James Perry (a geographer) devised the fanciful theory that all great things had come from the Egypt of pharaohs, mummies, pyramids, and sun worship, and that all the cultures of their own times were but pale remnants of that once grand place. Based at Manchester and later at University College London, they propagated their theory both in academic journals and in public discussions. Elliot Smith's inspiration was his studies of Egyptian mummies (he had worked in Egypt between 1900 and 1909), but the stance of both men is perhaps best exemplified by Perry's *The Children of the Sun* (1923). In this widely read book, Perry argues that Egypt, and only Egypt, was the source of agriculture, the domestication of animals, the calendar, pottery, basketry, permanent dwellings, and towns. The extremist position of Elliot Smith and Perry became known as 'heliocentrist' diffusionism, that is, centred on the sun (with reference to sun worship among Egyptian and other ancient cultures). It met with few adherents among professional anthropologists, though it did prove popular among the Edwardian public.

Together with the great pre-Malinowskian fieldworker W. H. R. Rivers (who had been with Elliot Smith in Egypt and announced his own conversion from evolutionism to diffusionism in 1911), Elliot Smith and Perry fought a rearguard action, first against evolutionism. After Rivers' death in 1922 they continued their battle, but now against the growing tide of functionalism, institutionally established in that year through the appointment of both Malinowski and Radcliffe-Brown to chairs of social anthropology.

The heliocentrists had neither the base of a university anthropology department nor the methodological skills to sustain interest among the new breed of functionalist scholars, whose influence rose rapidly in the 1920s and 1930s (see chapter 5). The functionalist concerns were with modern Asia, the Americas, or sub-Saharan Africa, rather than Ancient Egypt; and with fieldwork and comparison, rather than speculation. Ultimately, the scientific advances in archaeology in the 1940s proved beyond doubt that the Egypt of 4000 BC could not have been the source of all human culture, and gave the *coup de grâce* to British diffusionism: Elliot Smith in 1937, and Perry in 1949. Of anthropological writers in the late twentieth century, only Thor Heyerdahl, an eccentric Norwegian adventurer with a penchant for testing diffusionist theories, maintained a belief in historical connections between Egypt and the Americas. British anthropology went in other directions entirely, whereas American

anthropology developed from the foundations of German-Austrian rather than British diffusionist methods.

Diffusionism today?

Of all theories, diffusionism is probably the least popular in present-day social anthropology. However, it is not dead. There is today a great debate in archaeology and biological anthropology between those who favour the 'Out of Africa' or 'Replacement Model' and those who favour the 'Regional-Continuity Model' of human expansion (see, e.g., Gamble 1993). This debate bears close relation to an age-old problem within diffusionism: whether similarities stem more from the transmission of genes or culture between stable populations or more from migration of peoples from one place to another. A number of 'diffusionists', including Ratzel, actually favoured the latter, and the nuances of debate within the diffusionist school foreshadow those of modern studies of world prehistory.

In yet another sense, diffusionism lives on through ideas such as that of the 'culture area', now a part of standard anthropological thinking within all schools of thought. World-systems or globalization theory is another indicator that diffusionism lives (see chapters 6 and 10), though practitioners of it would no doubt repudiate a connection between their school of thought and that of Ratzel and his followers, much less Elliot Smith and his. The irony is that if a connection exists between classic diffusionism and such recent trends, it is precisely at a level of high theory or analogy. It is not one of the diffusion of the idea of diffusion itself.

Culture-area and regional approaches

Each and every anthropologist specializes in the study of some culture area – that where he or she does fieldwork. Yet the importance of the culture area varies according to the theoretical interest of the ethnographer. Broadly, it is useful to distinguish two kinds of culture-area approach. The first is that of American anthropology as it developed from German-Austrian diffusionism. The other, a much more diffuse approach, and in no sense a single school of thought or national tradition, is that of 'regional comparison'. This perspective characterizes quests for cause and regularity. Adherents have variously espoused multilinear evolutionism, functionalism, and structuralism, while maintaining an implicit belief in the historical relation between cultures of their respective regions.

The culture-area approach in American anthropology

Anthropology in Germany and Austria was largely destroyed in the 1930s and 1940s. Those who had opposed the Nazis were persecuted during the Third Reich, and those who sympathized with the Nazis found their theories discredited after the Second World War, when new German traditions (Marxism in the East; and an eclectic, foreign-influenced anthropology in the West) emerged. However, already in the 1920s an interest in historical relations between cultures and notions of 'culture area' and 'culture complex' had become commonplace in American anthropology. It is worth remembering that, although North America may have been colonized by the English in the seventeenth century, American anthropology began with the migration of Franz Boas, a German, and became established across the North American continent through the work of people like Robert Lowie, Edward Sapir, A. L. Kroeber, Clyde Kluckhohn, and Abram Kardiner – all of whom either spoke German in the home or studied in Germany or Austria.

Of these, Boas, Lowie, Sapir, and especially Kroeber (e.g., 1939) helped to develop the notion of the culture area. They directed their efforts towards the definition of specific areas and the recording of 'culture traits', the minimal units of culture, within each. From Boas onwards, American anthropologists of the early twentieth century tended to emphasize the particular over the general (see, e.g., Stocking 1974). In the 1930s and 1940s, more-and-more-detailed studies of cultural comparison within culture areas generated longer lists of culture traits to search for. These ran to the many thousands, with any given activity, for example, hunting or fishing, accounting for several dozen. Boas' rejection of evolutionism, his downplaying of diffusion, and above all his insistence on the meticulous gathering of ethnographic data, all contributed towards changing the agenda of anthropology as a whole, from historical questions to other ones (see chapter 7). Yet, as we shall see, some in his school did turn to history and to conjecture, and with some success.

The best-known example of a 'culture complex' or 'trait complex' was one proposed by the famous American anthropologist of Africa and African-America, Melville Herskovits (1926). He called it the 'cattle complex of East Africa'. Where cattle are found, so too are nomadism, patrilineal descent, age sets, bridewealth, the association of livestock with the ancestors, and a host of other interrelated culture traits. Both Herskovits and the German writers spoke of distributions of traits existing in relation to each other, that is, not distributed randomly. The difference is that Herskovits resisted attempts to put their ideas into either diffusionist or evolutionist schemes (see also Herskovits 1930).

In retrospect, the leading theorist of the school and one who did tackle historical questions, was a museum curator called Clark Wissler. However, Wissler was underrated in his own time. His lack of a university job meant that he trained no students to propagate his theories. His originality lay not so much in his specific new ideas (though he did have many), but in his ability to synthesize the mood of his time and present clear and coherent theoretical statements about what others were thinking. While others were content to record the distribution of prehistoric stone ornaments in eastern North America or of decorative pots in the Rio Grande Valley, Wissler (e.g., 1923: 58–61; 1927) explained such distributions in relation to the development, expansion, and contact of culture areas.

Wissler's greatest contribution was the age-area hypothesis, which both developed from and contributed to the interplay between archaeological and ethnological research (see Kroeber 1931). In the days before radiocarbon dating, archaeologists lacked a means to tell the real age of material they dug up. Relative age could be inferred from stratigraphy within a site, but not easily between sites. Moreover, ethnologists were collecting data on living cultures, but cultures known to have changed through the centuries. Wissler's hypothesis was that culture traits tended to spread from the centre to the periphery of any culture area. Therefore those traits found at the periphery were older, and those found at the centre were newer. When put to the test, the hypothesis seemed to work, and it gave a dynamic aspect to culture-area research which had been lacking. Implicitly, it also brought together diffusion and evolution within a framework of culture-area studies: evolution took place at the centre of a given culture area, and diffusion was from centre to periphery.

The interplay between evolution and diffusion became yet more apparent when American anthropology left behind the extreme relativism of Boas to take up evolutionism again. Thus it took on special meaning in Steward's work. We met him in chapter 3 as the architect of multilinear evolutionism, but his theories also had a diffusionist basis. Crucial here is his distinction between the 'cultural core' (which is determined by environment and evolution) and the 'total culture' (which contains elements of culture susceptible to diffusion). Steward developed the culture-area idea within a framework which emphasized natural environment as the limiting factor for culture, and technology as its enabling component (see, e.g., 1955: 78–97).

Wissler had defined fifteen culture areas for all the Americas (including the Caribbean): Plains, Plateau, California, North Pacific Coast, and so on. Kroeber first altered the names and boundaries of the culture areas, but not their number. Later, in his most important culture-area work, Kroeber (1939) mapped eighty-four 'areas' and 'sub-areas' which he grouped into seven 'grand areas' of North America only. He left South America to Steward, who edited a six-volume study of the culture areas of that continent (Steward 1946–50). Frequently culture areas turned out to be correlated with ecological zones: in North America, the Arctic, the Great Plains, the Eastern Woodlands, and others; and in South America, the Andes, Amazonia, and so on. If the environment is a limiting or determining force upon culture, then its influence should be apparent regionally. Steward and his followers both demonstrated this general principle and tested the limits of environmental determinism by comparative studies both within and between culture areas. All this left the problem of what constitutes 'a culture', but it did help both to fill in the ethnographic map and to increase interest in cross-cultural comparison as a goal of anthropological research.

Regional comparison, national traditions, and regional traditions

It is useful to distinguish three types of comparison in anthropology (see Sarana 1975): illustrative, global, and controlled (which includes regional comparison).

Illustrative comparison involves choosing examples to make some point about cultural difference or similarity. This is the basis of much introductory teaching in anthropology. We might choose Nuer as an example of a patrilineal society, and compare Nuer to Trobrianders, as an example of a matrilineal society. We might choose an element of one society which is unfamiliar to our audience, say gift-giving in Bushman society, and compare it to a similar practice in a more familiar case, say gift-giving in American society. Such comparisons may show similarities (e.g., the practice of gift-giving itself), but usually the illustrations are designed to show differences which reveal aspects of the less-familiar society.

Global comparison, or more accurately, *global-sample comparison*, involves comparing a sample of the world's societies to find statistical correlations among cultural features, or (in ecological anthropology) between environmental and cultural features. George Peter Murdock's approach, discussed in chapter 3, is the best-known example.

Controlled comparison lies in-between in scope. It involves limiting the range of variables, usually (though not always) by confining comparisons to those within a region. Regional comparison has been prevalent in the work of a number of anthropologists of a variety of schools. Among the diffusionists, Frobenius (in his studies of African culture areas) followed a mainly regional approach. Among the evolutionists, Steward employed a form of regional comparison. Among the functionalists, A. R. Radcliffe-Brown (writing on Australia) and Fred Eggan (writing on Native North

America) sought an understanding of specific cultures through a wider understanding of their place within regional structures. At a deeper level, structuralist anthropologists have sought to comprehend such regional structures and define generative principles peculiar to a given region, common structures which set the limits of variation, or culture traits which stand in relation to one another in interesting ways – often capable of transformations when they move between cultures.

The Dutch scholars who studied the Dutch East Indies (now Indonesia) in the 1920s and 1930s originated a structuralist form of regional comparison. Their regions are known within Dutch anthropology as 'fields of ethnological study' (*ethnologisch studievelden*), each defined by a set of features known as its 'structural core' (*structurele kern*). In the case of the former Dutch East Indies, the structural core includes, for example, a system of marriage in which a wife's lineage is of higher status than her husband's. Within a given society, each lineage is linked to every other by a circle of intermarrying units. The most articulate statement of the theory of this school is J. P. B. de Josselin de Jong's (1977 [1935]) inaugural lecture at the University of Leiden. Although in recent decades anthropology in The Netherlands has moved on towards Marxist theory, the understanding of indigenous knowledge, and the anthropology of Third World development, nevertheless 'regional structural comparison' (as it is now called) remains strong in the folk perception of the Dutch tradition.

One of the best-known proponents of regional structural comparison is Adam Kuper, a South African-British anthropologist who once taught at the University of Leiden. Indeed, his 1977 inaugural lecture at Leiden echoed that of J. P. B. de Josselin de Jong more than forty years before (Kuper 1979a [1977]), but with Africa as his area of concern. In a number of articles and books, most notably *Wives for Cattle* (1982), Kuper has sought to explain the regional-structural basis of Southern Bantu kinship, traditional politics, household economics, and symbolism. Any given culture trait can best be interpreted, he argues, in relation to corresponding traits in related cultures. What at first may appear to be random traits are intelligible within a framework which takes account of the Southern Bantu region as a whole. Take three examples where close kin marriage is common: Tswana men tend to marry women of lower status, and bridewealth in Tswana society is relatively low; Southern Sotho men tend to marry higher status women, and bridewealth in their society is relatively high; Swazi men may marry either way, but those who marry 'down' (like the Tswana) pay less bridewealth than those who marry 'up' (like the Southern Sotho). By comparing these societies, each set-up can be seen as a transformation of another, and the entire regional system can be analysed in terms of the ability of powerful individuals to perpetuate their power through bridewealth transactions. Interestingly, where close kin marriage is forbidden (e.g., among Tsonga and Chopi), marriage between commoners lends itself much less to such manipulation, and egalitarian marriage structures occur.

Kuper's method shows promise in other ethnographic areas too, both in Africa and elsewhere. As anthropologists become more regionally focused, both because of the plethora of recent ethnographic data and because of the ease of comparison between closely related and well-studied societies, the trend towards regional studies is likely to continue (see Barnard 1996).

Furthermore, as Richard Fardon and his colleagues have pointed out (Fardon 1990), there is an additional twist: 'regional traditions' in ethnographic writing. These work to ensure that regional understanding is a strong determinant of anthropological theory in general. If one does fieldwork in India, for example, one cannot help but develop theoretical insights specifically relevant to the Indianist literature. A Melanesianist cannot help but comment on Melanesianist debates, an Amazonianist on Amazonianist debates. Thus both the cultural characteristics of regions themselves and the interests of those anthropologists who have worked in them, help determine the agenda of new scholars setting off for fieldwork. Theoretical emphases differ accordingly.

Concluding summary

Diffusionism at the end of the nineteenth century, and well into the twentieth, offered anthropologists one of many points of departure from the pervasive dominance of evolutionism. The extreme ideas of the British school, with its emphasis on Ancient Egypt as the source of high culture the world over, proved of little merit. The more moderate notions of the German-Austrian school filtered into American anthropology and emerged transformed as 'the culture-area approach'. Ultimately, a number of culture-area approaches came into being, including evolutionist, functionalist, and structuralist varieties.

Diffusionist and culture-area approaches constitute one of the most interesting sets of ideas anthropology has produced. Yet unlike evolutionist ideas, diffusionist ones today (e.g., globalization theory) have lost continuity with the past. The primary legacy of diffusionism in its classic form is in the study of culture areas – both historical relations between such areas and, more importantly, the intensive study of regions.

FURTHER READING

Zwernemann's *Culture History and African Anthropology* (1983) gives a good overview of German-Austrian diffusionism. Classic studies of that school and of the American culture-area approach include respectively the essays by Kluckhohn (1936) and Wissler (1927). The relations between them are touched on in some of the essays in Stocking's *Volksgeist as Method and Ethic* (1996b). For a contemporary overview of German-Austrian, American, and British traditions, see Lowie's *History of Ethnological Theory* (1937: 128–95, 279–91). For an anti-culture-area approach, see Herzfeld's essay on the Mediterranean (1984).

On British diffusionism, see Langham's *The Building of British Social Anthropology* (1981: 118–99). For an overview of comparative methods, see Sarana's *The Methodology of Anthropological Comparisons* (1975).

Dutch anthropology is well documented as a national tradition. For further discussion of Dutch structuralism, see chapter 8. See also P. E. de Josselin de Jong's *Structural Anthropology in the Netherlands* (1977). Kloos and Claessen have edited three collections on contemporary Dutch anthropology, most recently *Contemporary Anthropology in the Netherlands* (Kloos and Claessen 1991).

5 Functionalism and structural-functionalism

The terms 'functionalist' and 'structural-functionalist' and their corresponding 'isms' are now quite stable in their meanings. However, this was not always the case. Before looking at the theories, a brief tour of the changing nuances of the terms is in order.

'Functionalism' is a broad term. In its widest sense, it includes both functionalism (narrowly defined) and structural-functionalism. I use it mainly in the narrower sense, that is, to refer to ideas associated with Bronislaw Malinowski and his followers, notably Sir Raymond Firth. It is the perspective concerned with actions among individuals, the constraints imposed by social institutions on individuals, and relations between the needs of an individual and the satisfaction of those needs through cultural and social frameworks. 'Structural-functionalism' tends to be concerned less with individual action or needs, and more with the place of individuals in the social order, or indeed with the construction of the social order itself. Typically, the latter term identifies the work of A. R. Radcliffe-Brown and his followers. In Britain these included E. E. Evans-Pritchard (in his early work), Isaac Schapera, Meyer Fortes, and Jack Goody, among many others.

Yet the boundary between structural-functionalism and functionalism was never rigid. Some of Radcliffe-Brown's followers did not mind the term 'functionalist'; others took to the labels 'structural-functionalist' or 'structuralist' (to distinguish their work from that of Malinowski). Furthermore, the term 'British structuralist' was heard in the 1950s to distinguish Radcliffe-Brownianism from Lévi-Straussianism or 'French structuralism' (described in chapter 8). Confusingly, when in the early 1960s a new generation of British anthropologists turned to Lévi-Strauss, they assumed the label 'British structuralist' for themselves. In broader terms, the latter 'British structuralism' was actually a British version of 'French structuralism'!

As if all that is not bad enough, both Radcliffe-Brown and Lévi-Strauss drew inspiration from the sociology of Emile Durkheim. And although he did not like being called a 'functionalist', Radcliffe-Brown was happy to call his discipline 'comparative sociology'.

Evolutionist precursors and the organic analogy

Radcliffe-Brown recalled more than once that anthropology has two points of origin. He dated one to 'around 1870', the heyday of evolutionist thinking. The other he dated to Montesquieu's *Spirit of the Laws* (published in French in 1748). This sociological tradition respected the idea that society is systematically structured, and that its structures are the proper study of the disciplines we now call the social sciences. It also, at least from Comte onwards, held to the view that its object of study may be likened to a biological organism, made up of functioning systems. Evolutionists, especially Herbert Spencer (an English member of this otherwise mainly French tradition) saw the transformation of societal types as the focal point for research. He also made the most explicit statements on the organic analogy (see, e.g., Andreski 1971 [Spencer 1876]: 108–20). Spencer argued the case for a science of society based on the science of life (biology), then decidedly evolutionist and Darwinian in outlook. Spencer saw societies as passing through stages analogous to infancy, childhood, adolescence, adulthood, middle life, and old age. He, and Durkheim as well, saw them as made up of parts, each with its own function. And they saw the parts as increasing in heterogeneity with evolution. Even the diffusionist Leo Frobenius joined the organic-analogy bandwagon. The idea was amenable to synchronic and diachronic, evolutionist and diffusionist approaches alike.

This early functionalist perspective was itself transformed in the early twentieth century, partly by Durkheim in his more synchronic work, but decidedly by Radcliffe-Brown. While neither Durkheim nor Radcliffe-Brown denied the importance of evolution, they became known for their emphasis on contemporaneous societies. We can imagine a society functioning smoothly like a healthy organism, made of many parts put together in larger systems; and these systems, each with its own special purpose of function, working together with the others. Societies have structures similar to those of organisms. Social institutions, like the parts of the body, function together within larger systems. The social systems, such as kinship, religion, politics, and economics, together make up society, just as the various biological systems together form the organism. A simple representation of this, essentially Radcliffe-Brownian, analogy is shown in figure 5.1.

To take the analogy further, look at, say French or British society. The systems which make up each society are composed of parts which Rad-

Reproductive system	Circulatory system
Digestive system	Nervous system

Systems of an organism

Kinship	Religion
Economics	Politics

Systems of a society

Figure 5.1 The organic analogy: society is like an organism

cliffe-Brown called 'social institutions'. How do we understand the relation between these and the systems they form? 'Marriage' in France or Britain might be designated an institution within the kinship system, but it can also have religious, political, and economic aspects. Therefore 'marriage' is not just part of kinship, because it functions within other systems too. This does not make the analogy useless or wrong, but it does make it problematic. It also shows that it is simplistic. Any institution can have a function in fitting together with some other institution. Everything is, therefore, in some sense 'functional'.

To my mind, the reason the organic analogy succeeded is that it was such a simple model, and one capable of being put to use in either diachronic or synchronic analyses. Yet this was also to be its failing, as successive post-functionalist generations have all clamoured for something more sophisticated.

Durkheimian sociology

Perhaps the most important source for structural-functionalist ideas is the sociology of Emile Durkheim. After an undistinguished student career and a spell of philosophy teaching, Durkheim gained a university post (the first in the social sciences in France) at Bordeaux in 1887. He moved to the Sorbonne in 1902 and taught there until his death in 1917. He gathered around him a devoted group of philosophers, economists, historians, and jurists, who shared his vision of an integrated science of society. In 1898, Durkheim and his band of young scholars founded the *Année sociologique*, an interdisciplinary journal which quickly achieved great influence. Several of this band contributed to anthropological ideas, and especially to the anthropology of religion. Marcel Mauss, Lucien Lévy-Bruhl, Robert Hertz, Marcel Granet, and Henri Hubert, in particular, influenced our discipline, though in some cases their influence was slow, only culminating years after death when later generations read their works in posthumous translations.

It has been said that anthropologists and sociologists agree that Durkheim wrote one great book, but that they disagree about which book this might be. The empirical tradition alive today in sociology is derived from Durkheim's early works. In *Suicide* (1966 [1897]), Durkheim reports from archival sources that statistics differ for suicide rates among Catholics and Protestants, rural people and city dwellers, married and unmarried, young adults and older people, and so on. There are also differences for different countries, and these remain constant through time. Thus even that apparently most individual of acts, the taking of one's own life, has at its heart a social basis.

As *their* choice of Durkheim's one great book, most anthropologists would cite *The Elementary Forms of the Religious Life* (Durkheim 1915 [1912]), or perhaps *Primitive Classification* (Durkheim and Mauss 1963 [1903]), which foreshadows it. *The Elementary Forms* deals with religion in 'early' societies. Durkheim first defines 'religion' and asserts its social basis: religions distinguish the 'sacred' from the 'profane' and take the sacred as their special concern. He traces theories of the origin of religion, notably Tylor's animism, Müller's naturism, and McLennan's totemism. Durkheim himself favours totemism, and he puts forward his ideas on the specifics of its evolution. He makes good use of the growing ethnographic literature on Aboriginal Australia, as well as Native North America. Although still couched in evolutionist terms, towards the end of the book, Durkheim's explanations take on a more strongly functionalist flavour as he moves from belief to ritual. In ritual, he argues, people venerate society itself, as the cosmological order is constructed upon the social order. Ritual helps to validate that order in the minds of its participants.

Durkheim co-authored *Primitive Classification* with his nephew and student, Marcel Mauss. In this short work (first published as an article in the *Année sociologique*), they tackle the question of how the human mind classifies. The authors review ethnographic evidence from Aboriginal Australia, from the Zuñi and Sioux of North America, and from Taoist China, and they conclude that there exists a close relation between society and the classification of nature. Furthermore, they see a continuity between primitive and scientific thinking. The advanced culture of

China possesses elements of classification which reflect those of 'primitive' Aboriginal Australian cosmology, and in turn the structural divisions
of Australian Aboriginal society. There are cross-cultural similarities in
the classification of time, place, animals, and things – all built up from
divisions into twos, fours, sixes, eights, and so on. Australia, North
America, China, and ancient Greece provide Durkheim and Mauss'
examples. The theory they put forward has elements not only of structural-functionalism, but also of evolutionism and structuralism – all
theories which rest on an explicit recognition of the psychic unity of
humankind.

Mauss' work proved seminal in several areas of anthropology. His
writings, mainly in the *Année sociologique*, include essays on aspects of
cultural ecology, sacrifice, magic, the concept of the person, and the
exchange of gifts (see Lévi-Strauss 1988 [1950]). Probably the most
important of these, and certainly the most functionalist, was his 'essay on
the gift' (Mauss 1990 [1923]). He argues that though gifts are in theory
voluntary, they nevertheless stem from expectation on the part of the
recipient. Moreover, though they may be free from expectation of direct
return, there is always an element of repayment, either in the form of a
later gift or in the form of deference or some other recognition of social
status between giver and recipient. The gift, in other words, is not free;
and it is embedded in a system of rights and obligations which in any
society make up part of the social structure, and in some societies form a
system of 'total services'. Mauss' examples include ceremonial exchanges
among Polynesians and Melanesians (including Malinowski's Trobrianders) and among North West Coast peoples (including Boas' Kwakiutl).
He also records survivals of 'archaic' exchange in Roman, Hindu, Germanic, and Chinese law, thereby enabling his conclusion that the spirit of
the gift is a widespread if not universal institution.

Durkheim and especially Mauss remain inspirational for anthropologists of various theoretical perspectives. Sociology has since gone its own
way, though with cross-influences and parallel developments (see
Swingewood 1984: 227–329). This is not the place to recount that story,
though it is perhaps worth keeping in mind the fact that sociology and
anthropology once had the potential to become one discipline.

The functionalism of Malinowski

Malinowski's position in British anthropology is analogous to that of Boas
in American anthropology (see chapter 7). Like Boas, Malinowski was a
Central European natural scientist brought by peculiar circumstances to
anthropology and to the English-speaking world. Like Boas, he objected
to armchair evolutionism and invented a fieldwork tradition based on the

use of the native language in 'participant observation'. Furthermore, both Boas and Malinowski were pompous but liberal intellectuals who built up very strong followings through their postgraduate teaching.

Malinowski was born in Cracow in 1884, the son of a professor of Slavic philology. He graduated from the Jagiellonian University in Cracow in 1908, in mathematics, physics, and philosophy, and with the highest honours in the Austrian Empire. He studied anthropology at the London School of Economics (LSE), under C. G. Seligman and Edward Wester-marck, then set off for Australia in 1914. Although technically an enemy alien, Malinowski (unlike Graebner) was treated well in Australia during the First World War; he was permitted to carry out fieldwork in areas of New Guinea which were administered by Australia. Between September 1914 and October 1918 Malinowski spent some thirty months, in three separate trips from Australia, conducting his work in New Guinea. All except the first six-month stint was spent in the Trobriand Islands. After the War Malinowski turned down a chair at the Jagiellonian University and returned to the LSE, where he taught from 1922 to 1938. It was in this period that his influence was greatest. At the outbreak of the Second World War he was in the United States. He chose to remain there for the duration, but died in 1942, shortly after accepting a permanent post at Yale.

Functionalism and fieldwork

The phrase 'Malinowskian anthropology' evokes two rather different images today. One is an image of the fieldwork method and its implicit theoretical assumptions and ethnographic style reminiscent of Malinowski's monographs on the Trobriand Islanders. The other is a more explicit theory of culture and cultural universals based on assumptions in Malinowski's late writings, especially his posthumous collection, *A Scientific Theory of Culture* (1944).

The functionalism of Malinowski's fieldwork style was not dissimilar to that of Radcliffe-Brown, but Malinowski was the better researcher. Many of Malinowski's students picked up theoretical ideas from Radcliffe-Brown, especially the emphasis on social institutions functioning within larger social systems. Yet the methods of Malinowski's well-known students, such as Raymond Firth, Phyllis Kaberry, Isaac Schapera, Eileen Krige, Monica Wilson, and Hilda Kuper, are best characterized as 'Malinowskian'. Malinowski encouraged long stints of fieldwork, with close contact with informants over a long period of time.

The most famous of Malinowski's works is *Argonauts of the Western Pacific* (1922). *Argonauts* begins with a statement on subject, method, and scope, then describes the geography of the Trobriands and his arrival in the islands. He moves on to the rules of *kula* exchange, facts about canoes, sailing, and canoe magic and ceremony. He then gives more detailed and specific accounts of aspects touched on earlier, including canoe journeys, the *kula* and magic. He ends with a 'reflective' (we would now say 'reflexive') chapter on 'the meaning of the *kula*'. Here he explicitly declines to venture into theoretical speculations, but rather comments on the importance of ethnology for encouraging tolerance of alien customs and enlightening readers on the purpose of customs very different from their own. This is the Malinowski most passionately admired by his students.

For me, the most striking case of Malinowski's insights came a few years after *Argonauts*. This is in his work on parent–child relations, which tested the central tenets of Freudian psychology (Malinowski 1927a; 1927b). For the Trobrianders, the father is a figure of supreme indulgence, not the authority figure postulated as a cultural universal by Freud. Rather, a boy's mother's brother is in the position of authority. This is because the mother's brother's power is derived from his place as a senior member of the boy's matrilineal kin group. According to Malinowski, the Trobrianders were ignorant of physiological paternity; thus the role of the father would be quite different from that in patrilineal societies, where the biological relationship between father and son is considered the basis of their social relationship. Much later, Radcliffe-Brown (1952 [1924]: 15–31) and Lévi-Strauss (1963 [1945]: 31–54) were to debate this classic set of relations between a boy and his father and a boy and his mother's brother. What makes Malinowski's contribution to the 'avunculate' problem of special interest is that his argument is from deep ethnographic insight and not simply from cross-cultural comparison. This is perhaps what gave him the edge, at least against Freud.

In more general terms, Kaberry (1957: 81–2) describes three levels of abstraction in Malinowski's theory of function. At the first, 'function' denotes the effects of an institution on other institutions, that is, the relation between social institutions. This level is similar to that in Radcliffe-Brown's work. The second involves the understanding of an institution in terms defined by members of the community. The third defines the way in which the institution promotes social cohesion in general. Malinowski himself was not very explicit in print about these levels, and it is likely that Kaberry has inferred them from isolated comments in Malinowski's ethnographic writings. However, in a rare venture into theoretical comment cited by Kaberry as an example of the first level, Malinowski argued that custom is 'organically connected' with the rest of culture and that the fieldworker needs to search for the 'invisible facts'

which govern the interconnection of the different facets of social organization. These, he said (Malinowski 1935: I, 317), are discovered by 'inductive computation'.

A scientific theory of culture?

When, late in his life, Malinowski sat down to summarize his perspective
he explained things in a rather different, and indeed quite peculiar way.
This marks the second of the perspectives Malinowski is known for.

Malinowski claimed that the basis of his approach was a set of seven
biological needs and their respective cultural responses (table 5.1). After
defining 'culture', Malinowski (1944: 75–84) proposes a theory of 'vital
sequences', which he says are biological foundations incorporated into all
cultures. There are eleven of these sequences, each composed of an
'impulse', an associated physiological 'act', and a 'satisfaction' which
results from that act. For example, the impulse of somnolence is associated with the act of sleep, resulting in satisfaction by 'awakening with
restored energy' (1944: 77). He follows this eleven-fold paradigm with a
slightly simpler one. This is the one built on the relationship between
seven 'basic needs' and their respective 'cultural responses' (1944: 91–
119). He then goes on to a four-fold one, relating what he sees as four,
rather complex, 'instrumental imperatives' with their respective 'cultural
responses'. The latter comprise economics, social control, education, and
political organization (1944: 120–31). Finally, he tackles 'integrative imperatives' and the 'instrumentally implemented vital sequence' (1944:
132–44).

None of the ideas of Malinowski's *Scientific Theory of Culture* found
favour with his contemporaries, though in a collection of commemorative
essays published fifteen years after his death (Firth 1957) some of his
students tried to find worth in them. As Malinowski's final statement, and
as the most theoretical of all his writings, it does deserve study. However,
the fact is that his students were embarrassed by it. The biological
assertions seem to have little to do with culture, and much of what he said
is either self-evident (e.g., sleep relieves tiredness) or impenetrable (e.g.,
integrative imperatives and the instrumentally implemented vital sequence). Phyllis Kaberry (1957: 83), a favourite among Malinowski's
students, points out that Malinowski's late concerns with biological needs
were of little interest to any, whereas his earlier work on social institutions
was of great interest. The problem was that Malinowski's work on social
institutions remained submerged within his erudite and ethnographic
prose and, unlike his statement on biological needs, was never the subject
of theoretical generalization.

Table 5.1. *Malinowski's seven basic needs and their cultural responses*

Basic needs	Cultural responses
1. metabolism	1. commissariat
2. reproduction	2. kinship
3. bodily comforts	3. shelter
4. safety	4. protection
5. movement	5. activities
6. growth	6. training
7. health	7. hygiene

Sadly, in a way, the relation between the two Malinowskian perspectives is hinted at in Malinowski's introduction to a volume by one of his other students: 'The most important thing for the student, in my opinion, is never to forget the living, palpitating flesh and blood organism of man which remains somewhere in the heart of every institution' (Malinowski 1934: xxxi). S. F. Nadel commented:

Putting it somewhat crudely, Malinowski's thought moved on two levels only – on the level of the particular society, the Trobriands, where he did his fundamental and exemplary field research; and on the level of primitive man and society at large, and indeed Man and Society at large. In his more general writings Malinowski did refer also to other primitive societies; but he did so in the main only for the sake of supporting evidence, of secondary importance. He never thought strictly in comparative terms. His generalizations jump straight from the Trobrianders to Humanity, as undoubtedly he saw the Trobrianders as a particularly instructive species of Humanity. (Nadel 1957: 190)

What comes out in the final assessment of Malinowski by virtually all his students (i.e., in Firth 1957) is Malinowski's failure to grasp the significance of kinship terminology, the intricacies of economic exchange, the precision required for writing on law, or the meaning of anthropological comparison. Yet we still remember him as the founder of the greatest fieldwork tradition of anthropology. If his own analysis did not live up to expectation, his exemplary fieldwork methods and his inspiring teaching at the LSE seminars in the 1920s and 1930s have left a legacy that is the essence of the British tradition.

Malinowski and Boas both died, not far from each other, in 1942. Yet the year of their passing somehow holds less symbolic significance than that of Rivers, twenty years before, which marked the end of a pre-Malinowskian fieldwork tradition as well as that of diffusionism's most respected British proponent. Perhaps in 1942 the anthropological world was too preoccupied with the horrors of war, but the Boasian spirit stayed with American anthropology, while Malinowskian methodology and (for a time) Radcliffe-Brownian theory remained the backbone of the British tradition.

The structural-functionalism of Radcliffe-Brown

Alfred Reginald Brown was born in Birmingham in 1881. Following his older brother's lead, he adopted the style A. Radcliffe Brown (adding their mother's maiden name) around 1920, and became A. R. Radcliffe-Brown by deed poll in 1926. He was known to his friends as Rex, R-B, or in his university days, Anarchy Brown, because of his political inclinations. In fact, he knew the anarchist writer Peter Kropotkin, whose vision of society as a self-regulating system, functioning by mutual aid in the absence of the state, anticipated Radcliffe-Brown's interest in the functions of social institutions (see, e.g., Kropotkin 1987 [1902]: 74–128).

After completing his bachelor's degree at Cambridge in 1904, Radcliffe-Brown did postgraduate work there and subsequently conducted fieldwork in the Andaman Islands (1906–8) and Western Australia (1910–11). During the First World War he served as Director of Education in the Kingdom of Tonga. Then he travelled around the world, establishing chairs of anthropology as he went, at Cape Town (1920–5), Sydney (1926–31), Chicago (1931–7), and Oxford (1937–46). He also taught for shorter periods at other universities in England, South Africa, China, Brazil, and Egypt.

A natural science of society?

In his Australian ethnography, Radcliffe-Brown (e.g., 1931) advocated a comparative perspective and explained the diversity in Aboriginal kinship systems in terms of the full complex of Aboriginal social structure found at the time. An inductivist, he believed that anthropology would one day discover through comparison the 'natural laws of society' (though he himself did not get very far in the effort). As an empiricist, he opposed speculation about the origins of the systems or institutions which make up society and argued that anthropologists should study just what they find. He wanted facts, and the simplest facts to come by were facts about the present, not the past; and the simplest way to connect them was through the study of society as a unit composed of living, interacting parts (see, e.g., Radcliffe-Brown 1952 [1935]: 178–87).

My favourite among Radcliffe-Brown's works is *A Natural Science of Society*, originally presented as a series of lectures at the University of Chicago in 1937 and transcribed for eventual, posthumous publication by his students (as Radcliffe-Brown 1957). These lectures were designed to propose the idea of a single, unified social science. He explicitly rejected the claims of the dominant social sciences at Chicago at that time – psychology, economics, and so on – that *they* might be that unified social science (1957: 45–50, 112–17). He also rejected the idea of a 'science of culture' (1957: 106–9; cf. 1957: 117–23) and implicitly attacked the Boasian emphasis on this. What really mattered to him was that in Boasian anthropology, the dominant version in America at the time, 'society' (as relations between people) was lost to the vagaries of 'culture', which could not be analysed scientifically. In fairness to Boas and his followers though, Radcliffe-Brown's notion of 'culture' was essentially synonymous with *enculturation* or (more accurately) *socialization*: a way of learning to live in a society. Radcliffe-Brown simply could not comprehend Boas' desires to extol differences between peoples and place the highest value on the richness of the human experience.

Radcliffe-Brown summarized his 'natural science of society' lectures as follows:

I HAVE ADVANCED several theses. The first of these was that a theoretical natural science of human society is possible. My second thesis was that there can only be one such science; the third, that such a science does not yet exist except in its most elementary beginnings. The fourth thesis, which seems to me important, was that a solution of any of the fundamental problems of such a science must depend on the systematic comparison of a sufficient number of societies of sufficiently diverse types. The last was that the development of the science therefore depends at this time on the gradual improvement of the comparative method and its refinement as an instrument of analysis . . . (Radcliffe-Brown 1957: 141)

The emphasis on comparison as an objective was crucial. Indeed, he praised his evolutionist predecessors for their comparative objectives, though he rejected their conjectural methods. He rejected the relativist objectives of his American contemporaries, though he found nothing wrong in their methods of observation and description. This contradiction was at the crux of his vision of the discipline (see Leach 1976a; Barnard 1992).

Function, structure, and structural form

In his work on the Andaman Islanders, Radcliffe-Brown (1922) explained rituals in terms of their social functions – their value for the society as a whole, rather than their value for any particular individual member of society. This emphasis on society over the individual was to remain strong in his own work and to influence both the theoretical interests and the ethnographic approaches of the next generation. His clearest statement on *function* is in a paper in which he takes up both diachronic and synchronic implications of the 'organic analogy' he inherited from Spencer and Durkheim (Radcliffe-Brown 1952 [1935]: 178–87). More specifically, he attacks an American critic's assertion that there is a conflict between 'historical' and 'functional' interests. For Radcliffe-Brown, the opposition is rather between the historical and the sociological, and to him they are not in conflict, but rather, represent different kinds of study. He places the emphasis on synchronic (sociological) aspects: the way given institutions 'function' within a social system, rather than how they change through time.

In another famous analogy, Radcliffe-Brown likened the study of society to the study of sea shells (Kuper 1977 [Radcliffe-Brown 1953]: 42). Each sea shell has its own 'structure', but the structure of one may resemble the structure of another. In this case, the two are said, in Radcliffe-Brown's terms, to share a common 'structural form'. The analogy is that *social structure* is about actual observations, that is, what the anthropologist actually sees and hears about individual people, whereas *structural form* is about generalization, that is, what an anthropologist infers about a particular society on the basis of his or her observations of individuals. Suppose Edward is a chief. Suppose George is another chief among the same people. Perhaps George has succeeded Edward after Edward's death. The anthropologist observes the two chiefs in action, and the relation between each chief and his people constitutes an example of social structure. When the anthropologist generalizes about the role of 'the chief' (rather than the role of Edward or George), he or she is now describing the structural form. To Radcliffe-Brown, the concern of an anthropologist should be not with describing individual chiefs and individual subjects (as Boas might have done), but with understanding among a particular people the relationship between the typical chief and his typical subjects, between the typical father and his typical children, a typical lecturer and her typical students, and so on. Then, at a later stage of analysis, an anthropologist can compare the structural form of one society to that of another, and might even (Radcliffe-Brown hoped) come up with general laws about the way in which societies work.

There are two common criticisms of this line in Radcliffe-Brown's thinking. First, confusingly, Radcliffe-Brown used the phrase 'structural form' to mean what others have usually called 'social structure', and the phrase 'social structure' to mean what others call just 'data'. Secondly, and more seriously, he appeared to be going about things backwards. One cannot get at universal, general laws by counting up instances of anything. One can only get there by reasoning from logical premises, a point made repeatedly through structuralist studies such as those of Claude Lévi-Strauss.

Hardly anyone in social anthropology today claims to be a follower of Radcliffe-Brown. Nevertheless, he was right about the basis of the subject. Virtually all anthropological enquiry is in some sense about relationships between things. Evolutionists, structuralists, interpretivists, and even anti-theorists at their best (when relations of interconnectedness lie implicitly in their descriptions) have this in common. Where they differ is in the ways in which they seek such connections, in the kinds of connections they regard as significant, and in the analogies they use in order to explain them.

Let us turn now to a couple of examples from Radcliffe-Brown's work: kinship terminology and totemism. I choose these because they show, in the case of kinship terminology, a facet of structural-functionalism which has won the argument against earlier approaches; and, in the case of totemism, the transformation from structural-functionalist to structuralist thinking.

Semantic structure or social structure?

What are kinship terms for? Are they simply aspects of language, independent of social implications, or are they more closely tied to the society which possesses them? The answer has wide implications, not just for kinship, but for any domain of classification. Essentially there are three viewpoints: the classical formulations of these are attributed respectively to A. L. Kroeber, W. H. R. Rivers, and A. R. Radcliffe-Brown (figure 5.2).

Kroeber's (1909) view was that kinship terminology reflects *not* society, as Morgan and other nineteenth-century theorists had supposed, but what he called 'psychology'. His notion of 'psychology' was not the university subject which is today called by that term. Rather, Kroeber's 'psychology' concerned specifically the formal properties of human thought, and he anticipated Lévi-Strauss in seeing these mainly in terms of binary oppositions. Kroeber suggested that these formal properties, or principles of classification, may have social implications, but he explicitly denied that there is any direct connection between the terminology itself (also ultimately derived from these principles) and the social implications of the underlying 'psychological' principles. 'Psychology' determines kinship terminology through language, of which the terminology is a part; it determines social behaviour independently and only indirectly. The formal properties he defined were: generation, lineal versus collateral, relative age within a generation, sex of the relative, sex of the speaker, sex of the person through whom the relationship is traced, blood relative versus relative by marriage, and 'condition of life' of the person through whom

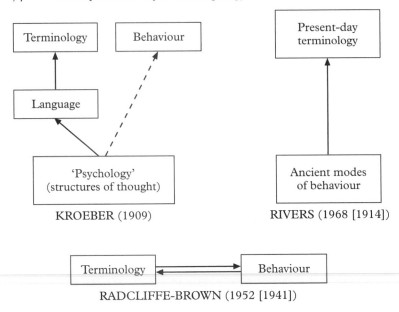

Figure 5.2 Relations between kinship terminology and social facts

the relationship is traced (e.g., living or dead, married or unmarried).

Rivers (1968 [1914]: 37–96) reacted against Kroeber's paper by re-articulating the earlier view which Kroeber was attacking. Rivers' formulation became the best representation of the traditional view that kinship terminology did directly stem from social facts, which was the prevailing theory in the late nineteenth century. Being conservative, he argued, terminology tends to reflect ancient, and often extinct, social facts. Thus it could be used as a kind of linguistic archaeology in order to understand historical changes in social organization. This is precisely what Morgan (1877) had done. Rivers here represented the last of the classic evolutionists, though he had in fact already announced his conversion to diffusionism; and his student, Radcliffe-Brown, was on the verge of a new approach based on a denial of the importance of conjectural history.

Radcliffe-Brown (1952 [1941]: 49–89) rejected Kroeber's claim that terminology was divorced from social behaviour and reflected merely language or 'psychology'. He also rejected Rivers' claim that it reflected only ancient social facts. For Radcliffe-Brown, its importance was its relation to existing social facts: the terminology, no matter what its history, would bear a connection to contemporary society. If one called one's father and father's brother by the same term, then one must treat them in a similar way. The origin of the custom is, in his view, lost in prehistory and can never be recovered. The meaning of the custom, however, is embedded in contemporary society. With few exceptions, Radcliffe-Brown's emphasis on contemporary classification over historical speculation remains with anthropology to this day.

Two theories of totemism

Radcliffe-Brown held not just one, but two theories of totemism. The contrast between them is of significance for understanding the relation between his structural-functionalism and the incipient structuralism which pervades his second theory, devised very late in his life.

Radcliffe-Brown's first paper on the subject is called 'The sociological theory of totemism'. It was delivered at a conference on the island of Java in 1929 and is reprinted in *Structure and Function in Primitive Society* (Radcliffe-Brown 1952: 117–32). There Radcliffe-Brown tries to explain how Australian Aborigines classify the world, and especially how Aborigines classify people as members of social groups. He builds on Durkheim's ideas of totemism, as he agrees with Durkheim that totems have the function of expressing clan solidarity.

However, he disagrees with Durkheim about the relationship between species and ritual. Durkheim argues that because given species represent social groups, these species are made the objects of ritual activity. Radcliffe-Brown argues the opposite. A species is chosen to represent a group because that species is already of ritual importance. But once a species is selected, the interrelationship between ritual, the symbolism of the species, and the solidarity of the group is what is important. For Radcliffe-Brown, totemism is a special development of the symbolism of nature. Totemistic ideas are found in many societies, though only some come to identify local groups specifically with truly totemic species.

Australian totemism, as Radcliffe-Brown points out, is characterized by the relations between four things: (1) the patrilineal local group (or 'horde' as Radcliffe-Brown called it); (2) the totems (certain animals, plants, the rain, the sun, hot and cold weather, and so on); (3) certain sacred spots within the local territories; and (4) certain mythical beings who, in the Dreamtime, made the sacred sites sacred. What Radcliffe-Brown does not quite do is put these relations together into a single framework. He concentrates instead on his disagreement with Durkheim, the relations between one group and another, and the relation between a group and its totemic species.

In his second essay on totemism, 'The comparative method in social anthropology', Radcliffe-Brown goes further. This theory was first presented as a public lecture in 1951 and published in 1952, and is reprinted in the compilations of Radcliffe-Brown's writings by Srinivas (Radcliffe-Brown 1958: 108–29) and Kuper (1988: 53–69). The second theory is not just about how the Aborigines classify people as members of social groups, but also about how they classify animals as members of species. And it concerns the relation between these systems of classification. Radcliffe-Brown anticipates Lévi-Strauss in comparing diverse societies (Australian Aborigines and the Indians of the North West Coast of North America) and expressing a 'general law' based on the notion of structural opposition.

This scheme also goes beyond the social structure into the cosmological structure. Radcliffe-Brown, and following him Lévi-Strauss, have come to ask: Why this particular species? For example, the eaglehawk and the crow represent moieties in parts of Western Australia; and similar birds, the eagle and the raven, represent moieties among the Haida of the North West Coast of North America. The question is not just 'Why have moieties and associate them with species?' It is also 'Why the eagle? Why the crow?' and further, 'What is the symbolic relation between the eagle and the crow?' The last question is answered by appeal to the respective myths of the peoples who revere such species, because myths explain (among other things) the 'kin' relations which connect the species. For example, in Western Australia the mythical Eaglehawk is the mythical Crow's mother's brother.

But for Lévi-Strauss, and I think also Radcliffe-Brown, the question is even deeper. Why do such birds represent exogamous moieties in both Australia and North America? Is it because there is something alike about the indigenous inhabitants of these two continents? Or is there some general principle, or pattern, imprinted on the human mind which is found everywhere, and of which this particular configuration of species and moiety is a trace? Is this, perhaps, a conscious example of an unconscious universal? If this is what Radcliffe-Brown was thinking in 1951, then he had indeed gone beyond his own structural-functionalist paradigm into the realms of Lévi-Straussian structuralism.

The influence of Malinowski and Radcliffe-Brown

Both Malinowski and Radcliffe-Brown demanded loyalty from their students. Between them they persuaded virtually every anthropologist in the British Commonwealth that the old interests of anthropology – in evolution and diffusion – were no longer appropriate areas for major research. Most anthropologists in Britain and many in America followed Radcliffe-Brown's line. They conceived of anthropology as being about filling in the details of ethnography: generalizing about particular societies and comparing them to other societies, working out how the social system functions without conjecturing about the past, de-emphasizing individual action and seeking the broader pattern, and above all, fitting the pieces together to see how elements of the social structure functioned in relation to each other.

Malinowski's greatest influence was in Britain, especially in the establishment of his tradition of 'participant observation'. Radcliffe-Brown's influence was predominant in South Africa and Australia (several famous 'British' anthropologists were in fact South Africans by birth and education). In the United States he left his mark through the work of Sol Tax, Fred Eggan, and others, especially at Chicago. A. P. Elkin and his students at Sydney continued the tradition there, while 'English' South African anthropology through Isaac Schapera (who later emigrated to Britain and worked with Malinowski), Monica Wilson (another student of Malinowski), and others grew to be a major intellectual force, and ultimately a political force against apartheid (see Hammond-Tooke 1997). Radcliffe-Brown's spell also reached India. Indian anthropologist M. N. Srinivas did postgraduate work with Radcliffe-Brown and Evans-Pritchard, then taught for three years at Oxford. In 1951 Srinivas returned to his own country and helped establish there an empirical but essentially structural-functionalist social science tradition.

It has often been said that Radcliffe-Brown's primary influence was as a teacher rather than a writer. He possessed a charismatic personality and was a brilliant lecturer, generally performing without any notes whatsoever. He published relatively little. What he did publish had a conversational style and very little jargon, as more often than not his writings were versions of his public lectures. His writings also exhibit a consistency in theoretical viewpoint through some four decades (see Radcliffe-Brown 1952; 1958; Kuper 1977).

Ironically, the substantive contribution most strongly associated with structural-functionalism is one he wrote little about (but see Radcliffe-Brown 1952 [1935]: 32–48). This is 'descent theory'. Evans-Pritchard (1940: 139–248), Fortes (1945), and others among his followers argued that localized patrilineal or matrilineal descent groups formed the basis of many societies, especially in Africa. Yet the idea was strongly contested, both through confrontation by its opposite, Lévi-Strauss' 'alliance theory' (discussed in chapter 8), and through empirical tests of its validity by close readings of the paradigm cases (see, e.g., Kuper 1988: 190–209).

Radcliffe-Brown intensely disliked being labelled with any 'ism'. The reason he would give (e.g., 1949, included in Kuper 1977: 49–52) is that 'sciences' do not have isms; only political philosophies (Communism,

Liberalism, Conservatism, etc.) have isms. One does not call a botanist interested in the structures and functions of plants a 'structural-function-alist', so why should one call an anthropologist with like interests by this label? He objected most strongly to being put in the 'functionalist' box with Malinowski, whose theory of biological needs and cultural responses he explicitly opposed. Yet outsiders, and some inside, gave the label 'functionalist' to Radcliffe-Brown's work too. And so for a time, this 'functionalist anthropology' did become a 'school' in spite of both its scientific trappings and the ambivalent relationship between its founders. While no one today claims to be a 'functionalist', there remains some-thing 'functionalist' about both anthropological fieldwork and anthropo-logical comparison – in spite of the challenges from processualist, Marx-ist, and more recent approaches.

Concluding summary

Functionalism had its beginnings in evolutionist thought. It came into its own as an anthropological perspective, partly through the influence of Durkheim (on the cusp of evolutionist-functionalist thinking), but more definitively through the writings of Malinowski and Radcliffe-Brown. Also crucial was the institutional base these latter two and their immedi-ate successors created for the discipline worldwide.

Although Malinowski succeeded in building up a great following, his major venture into grand theory failed. His theory of 'seven basic needs and their cultural responses' never caught on. Radcliffe-Brown's theoreti-cal ventures fared better: especially his emphasis on social structure and his encouragement of comparison. However, his brave vision of 'a natural science of society', analogous to the biological sciences, never bore fruit.

FURTHER READING

Good histories of the sociological tradition are Swingewood's *Short History of Sociological Thought* (1984) and Levine's *Visions of the Sociological Tradition* (1995). The best treatment of functionalism and structural-functionalism (and the after-math) in anthropology is Kuper's *Anthropologists and Anthropology* (1996 [1973]).

For an evaluation of Malinowski's work by his own students, see Firth's *Man and Culture* (1957). On the fieldwork methods of Malinowski and others, see Stock-ing's *Observers Observed* (1983). A useful evaluation of the work of Radcliffe-Brown is Firth's (1956) obituary of him.

There are three collections of Radcliffe-Brown's essays: *Structure and Function in Primitive Society* (Radcliffe-Brown 1952), *Method in Social Anthropology* (Rad-cliffe-Brown 1958), and *The Social Anthropology of Radcliffe-Brown* (Kuper 1977). Some of the best examples of structural-functionalist ethnography are in the edited volumes, *African Political Systems* (Fortes and Evans-Pritchard 1940) and *African Systems of Kinship and Marriage* (Radcliffe-Brown and Forde 1950). A useful reader on kinship, which includes relevant selections from the Kroeber–Rivers debate, is Graburn's *Readings in Kinship and Social Structure* (1971).

Classic functionalist ethnographies include Evans-Pritchard's *Kinship and Marriage among the Nuer* (1951a), Firth's *We the Tikopia* (1936), and Fortes' *Dynamics of Clanship* (1945) and *Web of Kinship* (1949). Two with an ecological twist are Evans-Pritchard's *The Nuer* (1940) and Richards' *Land, Labour and Diet* (1939). One dealing with social change is Schapera's *Migrant Labour and Tribal Life* (1947). A regional-comparative ethnography in the functionalist tradition is Eggan's *Social Organization of the Western Pueblos* (1950).

6 Action-centred, processual, and Marxist perspectives

From the 1950s onwards there were a number of attempts to move anthropology away from the formal, society-centred paradigms, especially structural-functionalism, towards more individual and action-centred ones. Among these are the transactionalism of Fredrik Barth, various interrelated approaches of the 'Manchester School', and 'processual' offshoots of structuralism, including much of the work of Edmund Leach (see chapters 8 and 9).

Earlier ideas on social and cultural processes include the sociological theories of Georg Simmel and Max Weber, some of A. L. Kroeber's perceptive comments on 'culture patterns and processes' (1963 [1948]) and Arnold van Gennep's (1960 [1909]) seminal study of 'rites of passage'. The last was picked up especially by structural processualists such as Edmund Leach and Victor Turner. Relations between structures, processes, and historical events returned with a vengeance in the 1980s in debates such as that between Marshall Sahlins and Gananath Obeyesekere on the death of Captain Cook, and between Richard Lee and Edwin Wilmsen on the political economy of the Kalahari. Meanwhile, a Marxist revolution had succeeded in turning many away from functionalist and structuralist interests towards Marxism, a processual theory based on the social relations of production.

However, Marxism's status in anthropology is ambiguous: it contains aspects of several other theoretical positions. As a trajectory, evolutionist history was firmly in Karl Marx's own mind and in the minds of Marxists of later times. Diffusionism is there too, exemplified by the spread of the revolutions of past and future which so concerned Marx and Engels. Marxism is even more firmly grounded in functionalism, with the idea of societies as self-regulatory systems, but systems which are transformable by revolutionary change. It is also loosely relativist in the sense that different modes of production are said to entail ideologies which need to be understood in their own terms – albeit their own terms of 'false consciousness'. Marxist anthropology has structuralist elements too: a number of its proponents, particularly in France from the 1960s to the

1980s, aligned themselves with structuralist positions in traditional areas such as kinship studies. Marxist-feminists have been prominent in equating class consciousness with gender consciousness (see chapter 9), and Marxism has links with poststructuralism and postmodernism in its concern with power relations.

I group Marxism with processual approaches, as in anthropology (if less so in other disciplines) that is its closest association in both historical time and field of debate. Both processual approaches and Marxism reached prominence in Western anthropology in the 1970s. And while the placement of Marxism with functionalism would have been rejected by mainstream functionalists and Marxists alike, both Marxists and processualists in their heyday saw themselves as at least arguing from common ground. Over the last decade or more Marxism has declined as a predominant paradigm in anthropology. In the West, this has little to do with the revolutionary changes in Eastern Europe and elsewhere. It has more to do with the prior movement of former Marxist scholars away from explicitly Marxist endeavours towards concerns which align them with their former enemies, the (postmodern) relativists, who have in the past couple of decades taken an interest in things like power, oppression, and global politico-economic relations.

Action-centred and processual approaches

Roots in sociology

Two figures stand out among sociological thinkers whose classic understandings of social process and individual action have influenced anthropological ideas: Weber and Simmel.

Georg Simmel was a German philosopher active at the turn of the nineteenth to the twentieth century and author of treatises on social differentiation, the philosophy of history, the philosophy of money, fashion, literature, music, and aesthetics generally (see, e.g., Wolff 1950; 1965). Simmel's approach was formalistic and highly theoretical, but it gave prominence to the individual. He introduced the idea of the *Wechselwirkung* (reciprocal effect), which anticipated Mauss' theory (1990 [1923]) of 'the gift', developed not long after. The idea is that the social exists when two or more people engage in interaction with each other, and when the behaviour of one is seen as a response to the behaviour of the other. These dyadic relations provided Simmel with a notion of structural opposition which was dynamic rather than static, and one focused as much on the individual as on society in the abstract.

Max Weber was a German economist and founder of one of the three great traditions of sociology (the others being Marx and Durkheim). Weber wrote on economics, economic history, social science methodology, charisma, bureaucracy, social stratification, differences between Eastern and Western societies, ancient Judaism, and religion in China and India. His fame, though, rests especially on *The Protestant Ethic and the Spirit of Capitalism* (1930 [1922]), which he composed between 1904 and 1905. He died in 1920; most of his works were published after his death, and a collection of his key essays appeared in 1946 (Gerth and Mills 1946).

Weber borrowed from Simmel and, at first glance, he was the more formalist of the two. He developed the anti-empiricist notion of 'ideal types' – our imagined understandings of how things work. He argued that these are necessary in order to comprehend individual events in a social system. In his eyes, social action should be the central concern of sociology, but he also emphasized the notion of 'spirit' (*Geist*) within society. For example, in his study of relations between the feudal economy of rural Germany and the emergent market economy, he argued that not only were these in interaction, but that each was driven by a different 'spirit'. In his work on the Protestant Ethic, he argued that Calvinism and modern capitalism have the same 'spirit', and thus that Calvinist countries are conducive to the development of capitalist economies. Weber made contributions to early debates on the nature of 'interpretation' (*Verstehen*), and his writings consider values, objectivity, and causal explanation. His ideas were picked up by anthropologists, including those of the Manchester School in the 1950s, and they still influence anthropology today. Both transactionalists and interpretivists derive important elements of their thinking from their roots in Weberian sociology.

Roots in anthropology

Within the Boasian tradition, social and cultural change also received some comment, and sometimes even functional analysis. For example, Kroeber (1963 [1948]: 142–4) pointed out that European women's fashion goes through periods of stability and instability. Using statistics on skirt length and width, and waist height and width, for eight selected years between 1789 and 1935, he noted that fashion stability is correlated with times of socio-political stability, and fashion instability with times of strife and restlessness such as those occasioned by revolution and world war.

Transactionalism, the perspective which emphasizes the relations between individuals and the decisions these individuals make in social behaviour, has roots in Malinowski's functionalism, especially as championed by his successor at the London School of Economics, Sir

Raymond Firth (e.g., 1961 [1951]). Firth's approach stresses the importance of 'social organization' (which in sociological terms is made of the roles people play) rather than 'social structure' (the statuses people occupy).

Another precursor was Oscar Lewis, an American anthropologist who conducted a restudy of Robert Redfield's fieldwork site, the village of Tepoztlan in Mexico. Redfield (1930), in an apparent mixing of Boasian, functionalist, evolutionist, and German sociological traditions, had concentrated on the normative rules which are supposed to govern social behaviour. Lewis (1951) concentrated on behaviour itself, which turned out not to conform to Redfield's rules at all. Redfield's idealist representation of Tepoztlan portrays a quiet place in which the inhabitants live in peaceful harmony. Lewis describes it as full of factionalism, with personal antagonism, drunkenness, and fighting as the prevalent characteristics. The village described had not so much undergone social change as a change of paradigm in the hands of these two very different ethnographers.

It was characteristic of the classic functionalist monographs that they should end with a section, a chapter, or even a collection of chapters on 'culture contact' or 'social change' – apparently often perceived as the same thing (e.g., Ottenberg and Ottenberg 1960: 475–564). However, as social change gradually came to be regarded as the norm and social dynamics recognized as a subject worthy of study in its own right, new perspectives appeared which focused directly on change, both linear and oscillating. At first drawing heavily on both functionalism and structuralism, anthropologists from the 1950s began to examine deficiencies in their own received paradigms and adapt them to suit their ethnographic and their archival findings. From the Manchester School to the debates between Leach and Friedman and between Sahlins and Obeyesekere (both discussed later in this chapter), the roots of anthropological discourse in functionalist and structuralist understandings are clearly present.

Transactionalism

The main proponent of transactionalism has always been Fredrik Barth – a Cambridge-trained Norwegian, who has taught both in Norway (at Oslo and later Bergen) and in the United States (at Emory University, and at Boston). Barth was no doubt influenced by the functionalist tradition and especially by his teacher Meyer Fortes, but from his earliest writings he reacted against what he saw as excessive equilibrium in models of social organization current in 1950s British anthropology. Working in field areas as diverse as Pakistan, Norway, Sudan, Bali, and

Papua New Guinea, Barth devised an approach which gave prominence to social action, the negotiation of identity, and the production of social values through reciprocity and decision-making.

Barth's (1959) study of politics among Swat Pathan showed that the position of leaders is dependent on maintaining the allegiance of followers through transaction, and a constant 'game' oscillating between conflict and coalition. He developed these ideas further in his short monograph *Models of Social Organization* (1966), as well as in the introduction to his famous edited volume, *Ethnic Groups and Boundaries* (1969). Barth has shown himself to be a consistent thinker, as his recent work, and indeed that of his students and students' students, still echoes his early studies. Barthian models have proved especially valuable in the study of ethnicity and nationalism, where negotiation of identity is readily apparent. Although the specifics of his Swat ethnography were questioned by later writers (e.g., Ahmed 1976), Barth's analytical insights have withstood the challenge.

Transactionalism proceeded through work by, among others, Czech-British Africanist Ladislav Holy, British-American Melanesianist Andrew Strathern, Dutch Mediterraneanist Jeremy Boissevain, American South Asianist F. G. Bailey, and Australian South Asianist Bruce Kapferer. Each has brought his own theoretical twist into the paradigm. For example, Holy was interested in the relation between folk models, normative rules, and the creation of representations (e.g., Holy and Stuchlik 1983). In his last book (Holy 1996), he turned his attention to the understanding of national identity in his native Bohemia as it underwent the transition from Communist Czechoslovakia to the creation of a new Czech Republic. Holy also borrowed from the poststructuralist tradition of Bourdieu, which has parallels with both transactionalist and processualist approaches (see chapter 9). Indeed, there is a sense in which all these perspectives merge into one, though adherents to each school would, for reasons of their own historical, scholastic, national, and literary identities, probably prefer to see them as unique.

Thus transactionalism never fully became a 'school of thought', but remains a powerful analytical tool amenable to use in combination with others. It has both ardent adherents and quiet users among young anthropologists today.

The Manchester School

The Manchester School consisted of a close-knit group of scholars, mainly Oxford educated at first, then transplanted to Manchester and the Rhodes-Livingstone Institute (RLI) in Livingstone, Northern Rhodesia (now Zambia). It was at its height in Manchester between the 1950s and early 1970s, though arguably one could trace its origins to Max Gluckman's arrival at the RLI in 1939. Anthropology at Manchester today is far more eclectic, as testified by the annual debates in anthropological theory held under the auspices of the department there since 1988 (see, e.g., Ingold 1996). However, the term 'Manchester anthropology' once implied an allegiance both to group and to the agreed line, and for a time even to Gluckman's favourite soccer team, Manchester United.

Those associated either with the Institute in colonial times or with Manchester in its heyday include J. A. Barnes, A. L. Epstein, Scarlett Epstein, Elizabeth Colson, Clyde Mitchell, Godfrey Wilson, and Monica Wilson; and those of more recent times include Richard Werbner, John Comaroff, and Jean Comaroff. Each made distinctive and original contributions, and there were variations in approach. For example, Mitchell and (in some of his work) A. L. Epstein favoured 'network analysis', showing the ways in which individuals interacted socially and economically and the lines of connection built up from such interactions. This approach had much in common with Barth's.

However, two names stand out above all the others as providing the distinctive characteristics of the Manchester School: Max Gluckman and Victor Turner. Gluckman was a South African, trained in anthropology and law. He conducted fieldwork with several Central and Southern African groups, including Barotse, Tonga, Lamba, and Zulu, and maintained a strong interest in social change and the relation between 'tribal' and 'town' life. Yet he reacted against the Malinowskian notion that social change was all about culture contact, and sought instead the complex dynamics of African society. He also reacted against functionalist assumptions that African societies were essentially stable, and he set about the study of social action, differences between rules and behaviour, contradictions in social norms, the anatomy of conflict, and the means of dispute settlement. In general works such as *Custom and Conflict in Africa* (1955) and *Politics, Law and Ritual in Tribal Society* (1965), as well as in a number of specific ethnographies, Gluckman examined the relations between stability and change, the ways in which order is maintained in stateless societies, and the role of conflict in creating order. This last issue was one on which he expressed somewhat different views in different publications, but his classic statements in *Custom and Conflict* assert that cross-cutting ties of loyalty strengthen the social order, that social cohesion results from conflict itself, and even that 'the whole system depends on the existence of conflicts in smaller sub-systems' (Gluckman 1955: 21). Gluckman's interest in indigenous African law, including the ways in which disputes are handled, also brought into social anthropology new methodological tools, notably the 'extended case study'.

Perhaps contrary to his own theory of conflict, Gluckman's charismatic leadership fostered a climate of intellectual engagement and general agreement on the central aims of anthropology at Manchester. It also engendered a dread on the part of outsiders when they went to present seminar papers there, that they would be savaged by Gluckman and a room full of his followers. This sense even continued after Gluckman's death in 1975, when his successors were known, on occasion, to kick the wastepaper basket in disapproval of the ideas of visiting speakers.

Turner was a Scotsman transplanted to England, Central Africa, and, from 1964, the United States. In later life he studied pilgrimage in Mexico, Brazil, and Ireland, but he is best known for his research on the symbolism and rituals of the Ndembu people of what is now Zambia. Turner's *Schism and Continuity in an African Society* (1957) has been called 'a centerpiece for understanding the Manchester School's principal currents of ideas, orientations, and empirical concerns' (Werbner 1984: 176). It is built around the idea of 'social drama', with pre-crisis and post-crisis phases. This notion, borrowed in part from the famous study of rites of passage by Arnold van Gennep (1960 [1909]), became a recurrent theme in Turner's rich corpus on Ndembu ritual (cf., e.g., Turner 1967) and his later work on pilgrimage (e.g., Turner and Turner 1978). Others (e.g., Myerhoff 1978) have developed the idea of social dramas further, though Turner's work remains the classic foundation of the 'social drama' approach.

In the ritual process, participants pass through a *liminal phase* (as van Gennep termed it, after the Latin for 'threshold'), which is characterized by what Turner called *communitas*. Communitas is an 'unstructured' realm of 'social structure', where often the normal ranking of individuals is reversed or the symbols of rank inverted. In structural terms (and there is a clear sense in which Turner was *the* structuralist of the Manchester School), one might envisage it as a realm which is simultaneously one thing and not that thing (as in the Venn diagram, figure 6.1)

The diverse interests of Turner and Gluckman provided the Manchester School with a range of pursuits. United by their focus on Central Africa, by their basic theoretical assumptions and, at least at first, by their institutional affiliations, the school they led presented British anthropology with a challenge when perhaps it most needed it. While Gluckman leaned towards the functionalism of the past (even in his concern with rejecting functionalist dogma), Turner turned to structuralist interests in the systematic relations between symbolic aspects of culture. Even Marxism was present in the school – quite apart from the alleged Communist sympathies of Gluckman and others. Specifically, Peter Worsley's (1956) re-analysis of Fortes' (1945) study of lineage organization among

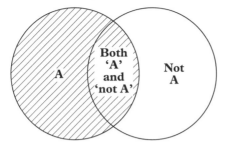

Figure 6.1 The liminal phase as both 'A' and 'not A'

the Tallensi of Ghana emphasized control by elders over the productive power of the land. In contrast, Fortes' functionalist ethnography had stressed merely the continuity of the lineage through association with ancestors buried in the land.

Marxist approaches

In the 1960s a new school was emerging: Marxism. It had a profound influence over the next two decades, especially in France, and also in Britain, South Africa, India, The Netherlands, Scandinavia, Canada, and Latin America. For obvious political reasons, it had less impact in the United States. Even evolutionist Leslie White, though influenced by Marxist thought, remained largely silent on explicitly Marxist issues and debates.

While Marxist ideas had been the established anthropological ortho-doxy in the Soviet Union from the 1920s, the more liberal French version offered something different. French Marxists, like Russian ones, were often politically Communist; but they were decidedly more open to theoretical ideas from French structuralism, British functionalism, and non-Marxist materialist approaches such as Steward's cultural ecology. Some writers stuck close to Marx (see especially Marx 1965 [1857–58]), with interests in land, labour, capital, and the like. Others sought to apply the spirit of Marx to questions he had never looked at. For example, one subject of debate in the 1960s and 1970s was whether in West Africa gender and age hierarchy could be analysed in the same manner that classical Marxism analysed class hierarchy (see, e.g., Terray 1972 [1969]; Kahn 1981). Marxists seemed to argue with each other on such matters as much as they argued with non-Marxists, who opposed them at a much deeper level. Nevertheless, a number of widely agreed ideas emerged, and some remain prominent even in our post-Marxist age, both among anthropologists who follow non-Marxist materialist approaches and among those interested in the anthropology of colonialism and imperialism.

Key concepts in Marxist anthropology

The most important of all concepts in Marxist anthropology is *mode of production*, based on Karl Marx's ideas in *Capital*, Vol. 1 (see especially Marx 1974 [1867]: 667–724). The classic commentary on its usage is that by Barry Hindess and Paul Hirst (1975: 9). They define a mode of production as 'an articulated combination of relations and forces of production structured by the dominance of the relations of production'. The notion of 'articulation' here refers to the interaction between these elements, although in Marxist theory more generally it usually refers to an interaction between different modes of production. Hindess and Hirst (1975: 9–10) go on to say that the relations of production 'define a specific mode of appropriation of surplus-labour and the specific form of social distribution of the means of production corresponding to that mode of appropriation of surplus-labour'. Surplus-labour, in their view, is found in all societies, but different societies 'appropriate' it differently. For example, primitive communist and advanced socialist societies appropriate it collectively, whereas in feudal and capitalist societies it is appropriated by classes of non-labourers (i.e., by feudal lords and modern capitalists respectively). Forces of production involve 'the mode of appropriation of nature' (1975: 10). Means of production are simply those economic activities such as food-gathering, horticulture, or pastoralism which individuals practise. Hindess and Hirst (1975: 11) sum up their definitions with the comment that 'there can be no definition of the relations or of the forces of production independently of the mode of production in which they are combined'.

Marxist anthropologists have debated, for example, whether there is a distinctive 'foraging' mode of production, or whether foraging as a means of production is included within a larger mode of production involving other means of production which have similar effects (see, e.g., Lee 1981 [1980]). Those who hold the latter view might argue that what they call the 'domestic' mode, that is, where the household is the unit of producing and distributing goods, characterizes not only foraging societies but also small-scale horticultural ones. Beyond this on a scale of evolving complexity, there are 'lineage', 'feudal', and 'capitalist' modes of production.

On another front, Marx made a distinction between the *base* or *infrastructure* and its *superstructure* (e.g., Godelier 1975). The base consists of elements of a social formation (the Marxist term for 'society') which are closely related to production, such as subsistence technology, settlement patterns, and exchange relations. The superstructure consists of things which are more distant from production, such as ritual and religious belief. Of course, there may be a connection between production and religion, but it is not usually as direct as that between, say, production and politics. In fact by the 1970s, if not earlier, Marxists and cultural ecologists were coming to similar conclusions on a number of issues. Steward (1955) called the Marxist base the 'cultural core' (that related to exploitation of the environment and upon which, he argued, cultural evolution operated). Likewise, the Marxist idea of superstructure resembled Steward's idea of the 'total culture' (upon which cultural diffusion operated).

Yet another distinction common in Marxist anthropology is that between *centre* and *periphery*. The centre, in this sense, is the place where power is exercised, such as the colonial or national capital. The periphery is one of the places affected by decisions made at the centre, such as a rural area where peasants produce for redistribution or trade from the centre. According to Immanuel Wallerstein (1974–89), a centre–periphery relation has characterized economic relations on a global scale since the end of the fifteenth century.

In the 1970s and 1980s, interest grew in the *reproduction* of society through processes involving technology and labour (see, e.g., Meillassoux 1972), and in the articulation of (or interaction between) different modes of production (e.g., Friedman 1975). Interest turned equally towards arguing the rightful place of Marxist theory in anthropology generally (e.g., Kahn and Llobera 1981; Bloch 1983).

The structural Marxism of Godelier

While non-Marxist political anthropologists have sometimes argued an evolutionary trajectory, from band societies to clan-based societies, to chiefdoms, to states, Marxists have always emphasized the significance of economic relations in determining political structures. Still, Marxists differed from each other in how they incorporated non-economic issues, in other words, how important they saw the superstructure.

Structural Marxists regarded superstructure as fundamental. Some even reinterpreted superstructural elements (such as religion or kinship) as being infrastructural, in that they were seen as embedded in a socio-economic framework rather than constructed on top of it. The most prominent member of this school, Maurice Godelier carried out ethnographic research in Melanesia and has long actively undertaken and encouraged research in traditional realms of anthropology. His approach drew on conventional structuralism as well as on Marxism, though his overriding concern in the 1970s was with the description and analysis of modes of production (see, e.g., Godelier 1975; 1977 [1973]). As hinted above, Godelier's structural Marxism also built on cultural ecology and paralleled it in seeking an understanding of relations between environment, technology, and society. The difference was that structural Marxism emphasized relations of production (i.e., social relations) over either technologies or individual activities. Societies as bounded universes remained the units of analysis, though they were called by their Marxian term, 'social formations'. Likewise, culture became 'ideology', and the economy was the 'mode of production'. Structural Marxism had much in common with functionalism too, as both emphasized the synchronic and the functional qualities of ritual, lineage organization, and so on.

Even mainstream economic anthropologists were influenced by the trend. Marshall Sahlins' *Stone Age Economics* (1974 [1972]) is an example. An American anthropologist much taken with Marxism during a year in France, Sahlins eventually repudiated the structural Marxist tradition on the grounds that it gave too little emphasis to culture and therefore had little analytical power to explain the workings of pre-capitalist societies (see Sahlins 1976). Yet it was through *Stone Age Economics* that the notion of the 'domestic mode of production' (where the household is the dominant unit of production and exchange) became popularized.

Another American influenced by but opposed to new directions in Marxist anthropology, Marvin Harris (e.g., 1979: 216–57), built his attack on the notion that the structural Marxists were too structuralist and not materialist enough. Harris' 'cultural materialism' – labelled 'vulgar materialism' in an important Marxist attack by Jonathan Friedman (1974) – sought to reduce culture to virtually pure material forces. Harris argued that even religious taboos, such as that against eating cattle in Hindu India, have a material basis. In this case, it is the preservation of such animals for use in ploughing. Thus, Harris argued, ecological constraints prevail over all others; and culture is essentially a product of material forces (see chapter 3; see also Harris 1977).

The 'land and labour' Marxism of Meillassoux

Claude Meillassoux was critical of Lévi-Straussian structuralism (and perhaps implicitly structural Marxism) for leaving aside the question of exploitation and the material causes of transformation in kinship systems. He distinguishes societies in which land is the subject of labour from those in which it is the instrument of labour. In his view, the domestic economy ensures the reproduction of labour and therefore contributes to the existing power structures. For him, it is control over the means of reproduction (that is, over women) which is most important, not control over the means of production *per se* (see, e.g., Meillassoux 1972; 1981 [1975]). For this reason, Meillassoux's work is often used in feminist anthropology as a starting point for debate.

However, feminists have levelled a number of critiques (see, e.g., H. L. Moore 1988: 49–54). Women are largely invisible in his discussion, though they are central to it. Where they are visible, they form a homogeneous category and are taken out of the essential kinship context in which they belong ('woman' as wife is not the same as 'woman' as mother-in-law). Also, he seems to conflate the notion of biological reproduction with that of social reproduction; and ironically, he seems to see women mainly as reproducers of the labour force rather than as labourers or producers (see, e.g., Edholm, Harris, and Young 1977; Harris and Young 1981).

In fact Meillassoux's Marxism has strong functionalist elements, as well as relying to a great extent on technology as a determinant of mode of production. His arguments reflect his own ethnography, on the Guro of the Ivory Coast (see Meillassoux 1964), perhaps more than is generally the case among Marxists. He argues that capitalism does not destroy pre-capitalist modes of production but rather, maintains them 'in articulation' with a capitalist mode.

Political economy and globalization theory

A third school, still influential, is that of political economy, derived in part from the 'world systems' approach of Immanuel Wallerstein (1974–89) and the 'underdevelopment' ideas of Andre Gunder Frank (e.g., 1967). Whereas structural Marxism and interests in land, labour, and capital within small-scale societies were predominantly European interests, political economy as a school of thought took hold more in North America and the Third World. The influence of this school in Britain is also apparent in the shift in focus, during the late 1970s and 1980s, to large 'regional systems' (e.g., Hart 1982). Unlike other Marxist schools within anthropology, the political economy school stresses history. It also opposes the notion, implied in Meillassoux's work, that capitalist and pre-capitalist modes of production can simply co-exist in a state of 'articulation'.

Wallerstein's idea of a 'world system' which links the economies of the smallest societies to the powerful capitalist economies of the West and the Far East has proved a powerful one. Relations between these economies are unequal, in that developed capitalist ones benefit at the expense of the others. The idea has influenced anthropologists to look in similar directions (see, e.g., Kahn 1980; Wolf 1982), and the relation between the 'global' and the 'local' in cultural as well as economic spheres has become a widespread interest in the discipline. The problem, for mainstream anthropology, is that the political-economy view is outsider-centred. Their 'centre' is remote from the people who should be the objects (if not indeed the subjects) of study. Some writers in the 'subaltern studies' tradition (see, e.g., Guha and Spivak 1988) have put my general point here rather more strongly.

There is no doubt that the capitalist world system has had a global impact over the last few centuries, and little doubt that this impact is on the increase. Commentators have tended to view the phenomenon in Marxist or, more broadly, in evolutionist terms, where the capitalist system represents an evolutionary stage in which this type of society dominates those of the developing world. However, the idea of the 'world system' or 'globalization theory' can also been seen as a diffusionist notion. It is a modern (indeed a 'postmodern') version of grand diffusionism, where the global culture of the West stands in relation to the rest of the world as Elliot Smith and Perry believed Egypt had once stood (chapter 4). Ironically, there is a debate now emerging in archaeology about whether Wallerstein was correct to see the world system as developing only in the last few centuries, or whether it is more useful to consider the impact of prehistoric trade links too. There are also hints of this in the Kalahari debate, as we shall see shortly (cf. Shott 1992).

Three ethnographic debates

Several fierce debates have emerged in processual and Marxist anthropology. Here I want to look briefly at three, which to my mind provide illuminating illustrations of the interplay between the theoretical perspectives touched on in this chapter.

Friedman versus Leach: the political economy of the Kachin

Sir Edmund Leach was an intellectual eccentric who eventually became both an establishment figure and an inspiration to young anthropologists of his day. After training as an engineer, he studied under Sir Raymond Firth and did fieldwork in Sri Lanka (Leach 1961a), Burma (e.g., 1954), and elsewhere. He is usually thought of as one who turned against functionalism at an early date and introduced French structuralism into British anthropology. However, like Turner he advocated broadly a mixture of process and structure as constituting the foundations of social life, and it is his processualism which is our focus here.

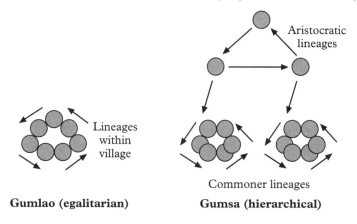

Aristocratic
lineages

Lineages
within
village

Commoner lineages

Gumlao (egalitarian)   **Gumsa (hierarchical)**

Figure 6.2 Marital alliance between Kachin lineages

Consider Leach's book *Political Systems of Highland Burma* (1954) and related work on the Kachin (notably Leach 1961b [1945/1951/1961]: 28-53, 54–104, 114–23). Before Leach, pre-functionalist ethnographic accounts of the Kachin described them as having an essentially uniform culture and social organization. The functionalist anthropology prevalent when Leach wrote his book assumed a balanced equilibrium, and it took for granted the existence of a single social system within which the ethnographer would work. In contrast to both, Leach focuses on the different structural arrangements in the kinship and political systems of two closely related groupings of clans, one system being egalitarian (*gumlao*) and the other a hierarchical version of the same thing (*gumsa*). A third, also hierarchical system impinges on these, namely that of the Tai-speaking Shan.

Another consideration with regard to kinship is that while *gumsa* is a hypogamous system (women marrying down), the Shan system is hypergamous (women marrying up). In *gumlao*, marriage is in a circle, with each man owing deference to his in-laws but no one clan having absolute priority over the others. This is transformed in the *gumsa* system into a relation of dominance, as men from superior groups give their sisters in marriage to members of lower-status groups. An idealized model is illustrated in figure 6. 2, where arrows indicate the direction of movement of women in marriage. Since bridewealth passes from the groom's family to the bride's, men in higher-status groups end up with fewer potential wives but greater wealth (indeed it seems that wealth was more important than status to those involved). Some marry Shan Chinese, and some become monks. Some Kachin even 'become' Shan.

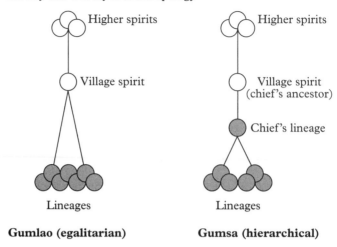

Gumlao (egalitarian)   Gumsa (hierarchical)

Figure 6.3 Relations between Kachin and their ancestral spirits

For Leach, kinship, class, history, and ideology work together in a complex framework, but not one which would readily be understood by the followers of Radcliffe-Brown or even Malinowski. Leach (1954: 292) summed up his efforts as follows: 'I am not concerned with *average* Kachin behaviour; I am concerned with the relationship between actual Kachin behaviour and ideal Kachin behaviour. And with this in mind I have tried to represent Kachin cultural variations as differing forms of compromise between two conflicting systems of ethics.'

In a now classic library re-study, Jonathan Friedman (1975; cf. 1996 [1979]) analysed Leach's ethnographic data in a structural Marxist perspective, and with particular attention to ecological factors which cause the oscillation and transformation of Kachin social structures. In Friedman's model, instead of the simpler Marxist notion of base and superstructure, we get a more complex four-tier model: the *ecosystem*, which constrains *productive forces*, which constrain *relations of production*, which in turn dominate both the ecosystem and the *superstructure*. Friedman emphasized relations between economics, kinship, and religion in arguing that surplus leads both to feasting and to the accumulation of wives, which entail respectively a gain in prestige and the birth of children, and in turn a higher rank, leading ultimately to the acquisition of prestations and more surplus. A wealthy lineage head would hold feasts for the entire village and thus be seen to have greater influence with the spirit world. This results in the setting apart of such a lineage, as it comes to be recognized as 'closer' to the spirits through its ancestor (as in figure 6.3). Thus the egalitarian *gumlao* system evolves into a *gumsa* one through a sequential combination of environmental, economic, kinship, and relig- ious factors.

In Friedman's model, the social processes described by Leach have been amplified, and Leach's structural-processual framework opened to a framework which emphasizes power and productive relations to a much greater extent. Leach was sceptical of Friedman's Marxist reading of his work, but its existence highlights the potential for multiple interpreta- tions. These may be especially appropriate in the analysis of dynamic social frameworks such as that of Burma in the period Leach described (which is until the Second World War). Marxist anthropology always worked best when it tackled real historical and ethnographic cases, and in this case its interplay with processualism was essential for its insight into Kachin society and social action.

Wilmsen versus Lee: Kalahari history and ethnography

The Kalahari debate concerns the degree to which the Bushmen or San of Southern Africa represent part of a regional or global economic system. It had been simmering for some time, but erupted with a vengeance in response to Marxist-influenced archaeologist-anthropologist Edwin Wilmsen's *Land Filled with Flies* (1989). Ecological-Marxist anthropol- ogist Richard Lee (e.g., 1979: 401–31) and others had long described relations between Bushmen and Bantu-speaking cattle-herders, but they had de-emphasized them and placed them in a context of 'social change'. The real problem is: when does 'traditional' life end and 'social change' begin?

The core of the debate consists of a series of articles and short com- ments published in the journal *Current Anthropology* (especially Solway and Lee 1990; Wilmsen and Denbow 1990; Lee and Guenther 1991) and one in *History in Africa* (Lee and Guenther 1993). More crucial, though, are the differing assumptions behind Lee's and Wilmsen's ethnographies. Lee often admits that his interest in Bushmen has come from his desire to reconstruct something of the foraging way of life of early humanity:

Foraging was a way of life that prevailed during an important period of human history. The modern foragers do offer clues to the nature of this way of life, and by understanding the adaptations of the past we can better understand the present and the basic human material that produced them both. (Lee 1979: 433)

Lee takes foraging for granted, as a basic and adaptive way of life, an assumption which is anathema to the hard-line revisionists. He also takes for granted the fact that Bushman societies are relevant units of analysis, in spite of the presence of members of other groups within their territories and at their waterholes. Although Bushmen and their cattle-herding neighbours do interact, they are seen as occupying different ecological niches.

Wilmsen (1989) argues that the political economy of the Kalahari is the best unit of analysis, and that this unit has been a meaningful construct since livestock were first introduced to the fringe areas of the Kalahari a thousand years ago. The apparent isolation of Bushmen observed by Lee and others, he says, is a product of the white domination of Southern Africa since the late nineteenth century:

> Their appearance as foragers is a function of their relegation to an underclass in the playing out of historical processes that began before the current millennium and culminated in the early decades of this century. The isolation in which they are said to be found is a creation of our view of them, not of their history as they lived it. (Wilmsen 1989: 3)

Traditionalists like Lee emphasize cultural continuity and the cultural integrity of Bushman groups. They see Bushmen as the inheritors of ancient indigenous environmental knowledge, hunting techniques, kinship practices, religious beliefs, and so on. Revisionists like Wilmsen de-emphasize these aspects in favour of greater concern with the integration of Southern African politico-economic structures taken as a whole. The irony is that both sides claim intellectual descent from Marx, and both sides see their approach as one which explains social processes.

Obeyesekere versus Sahlins: the death of Captain Cook

The third debate concerns an intriguing historical problem: why, on 14 February 1779, did Hawaiian warriors kill Captain James Cook upon his return to the islands? To date, each of the two main players, Marshall Sahlins and Gananath Obeyesekere, has contributed some half a dozen publications on the problem (see especially Sahlins 1981; 1985: 104–35; 1995; Obeyesekere 1992), and other protagonists and commentators on the debate are emerging (see, e.g. Borofsky 1997; Kuper 1999: 177–200).

Sahlins, a senior American anthropologist with a specialization in Polynesia, takes an essentially structuralist (or structural-processualist) point of view. He argues that Cook was the victim of mistaken identity and ritual sacrifice. Cook first arrived in the islands in January 1778 at the height of the annual celebrations for their fertility god Lono, and he came back a year later. The Hawaiians, in Sahlins' view, took him for Lono, and duly honoured him as their god. Shortly thereafter Cook set off to continue his expedition, but a storm forced him to turn back. This time his return was decidedly unexpected. More importantly, it was precisely at the wrong time of year for the god. A taboo was in effect, with the change in ritual cycle, and the king had gone inland. Cook's landing and his search for the king led to skirmishing between his marines and the islanders and the death of one of the local chiefs. This action was an apparent reversal of Hawaiian ritual, and 'Lono' had to die.

Obeyesekere, a Sri Lankan anthropologist of religion (based at Princeton), explains away Sahlins' argument as a Western imperialist myth. He argues that the Hawaiians treated Cook as a chief, not as a god. To Obeyesekere, Cook was a 'civilizer' who became a 'savage' when his expedition went wrong. What is more, to Obeyesekere, Sahlins is a myth-maker building his myth of Cook on a wrongful supposition that the Hawaiians had a structuralist mentality, whereas in fact they were pragmatic rationalists. Like Sahlins, Obeyesekere is interested in the relations between culture and historical process, but the focus is entirely different. In a sense, Obeyesekere's focus is on Western culture and the process of exploration and colonization, whereas Sahlins' focus is decidedly on Hawaiian culture and the Hawaiian ritual process.

What is at stake here is not just historical fact. Nor is it merely how to interpret the evidence to come up with a 'correct' retrospective ethnography of eighteenth-century Hawaii. The crux of the matter is two-fold: it relates first to the opposition between 'us' and 'them', which Obeyesekere is trying to break down, and secondly to the issue of who can speak for whom. Is Obeyesekere a legitimate, surrogate 'native voice' because he comes from a culture which was, like the Hawaiian one, the subject of colonial oppression? Or does he go too far in denying Sahlins, with his apparent mastery of the relevant sources, the ability to come up with a competent analysis?

These questions, taken much more broadly, form the theme of the postmodern critique which in the 1980s supplanted Marxism as the leading challenge to traditional lines of enquiry. Embedded in them is one of the central debates of anthropology in our time. Indeed, many would argue that it is *the* anthropological debate of all time. Can anthropology provide objective insights into alien cultures and their social action, or is the discipline forever doomed to implicit subjectivity which ought to be made explicit?

Concluding summary

Action-centred, processual, and Marxist perspectives represent the culmination of the 'social' tradition in anthropology. These perspectives, especially Marxism, have elements of all the preceding ones. Transactionalism, for example, has its roots in Malinowski's ideas on social organization, as well as in the sociology of Simmel and Weber. Different approaches within Marxism emphasize variously social evolution, diffusion (globalization), function, structure, and even reflexivity. On the last point, for example, Hindess and Hirst in their 'auto-critique' (1977: 7) suggest that theories exist only in the context in which they are expressed: their Marxist ideas are, in fact, a product of writing about them.

Plainly, transactionalism, processualism, and the various brands of Marxism are complex perspectives. Even the 'Manchester School' consisted of a blend of ideas and a variety of interests, from ritual to legal processes, from symbolic structures to relations between whites and blacks in the British colonies of south-central Africa.

In the remaining chapters we shall turn our attention away from 'social' to 'cultural' traditions. There is, of course, no absolute divide between them. The difference is one of emphasis: whether it is understanding society which should be our paramount goal, or understanding thought, the symbolic world, communication, or the place of the anthropologist and his or her worldview in relation to that of the alien 'other'.

FURTHER READING

The classic transactionalist monograph is Barth's *Political Leadership among Swat Pathans* (1959). Diverse Manchester ethnographies include Gluckman's *Custom and Conflict in Africa* (1955) and Turner's *Schism and Continuity in an African Society* (1957). An excellent example of structural-Marxist ethnography is Godelier's *The Making of Great Men* (1986 [1982]).

For a review of the Manchester School, see Richard Werbner's 'The Manchester School in South-Central Africa' (1984). Important edited collections respectively on transactionalism and Marxism include Kapferer's *Transaction and Meaning* (1976) and Bloch's *Marxist Analyses and Social Anthropology* (1975). For commentaries on the Kalahari debate, see, e.g., those by Kuper (1992) and Shott (1992). On the Hawaiian debate, see Borofsky (1997).

For a comprehensive review of theoretical developments from the 1960s to the 1980s, including those in Marxist anthropology, see Sherry Ortner's essay 'Theory in anthropology since the sixties' (1984). Bloch's *Marxism and Anthropology* (1983) provides a history of Marxist ideas in social anthropology. The review by O'Laughlin (1975) gives an overview of approaches in the Marxist tradition, while Legros' (1977) critique of evolutionist cultural ecology presents a good picture of the differences between Marxist and non-Marxist understandings of productive forces.

7   From relativism to cognitive science

Melford Spiro (1992), one of several critics of contemporary cultural relativism, defines three types: descriptive, normative, and epistemological. It is useful to follow his classification, and I shall outline each briefly here.

It is a truism that cultures differ one from another. With varying degrees of enthusiasm, anthropologists since the late nineteenth century have been 'cultural determinists', arguing that culture itself (and not merely biology) regulates the ways in which humans perceive the world. A corollary is that cultural variability will produce different social and psychological understandings among different peoples, and this position is called *descriptive relativism*. Virtually all schools of anthropology entail an acceptance of at least a weak form of descriptive relativism.

Normative relativism goes a step further in asserting that, because cultures judge each other according to their own internal standards, there are no universal standards to judge between cultures. Within normative relativism, we can distinguish two logically distinct forms: *cognitive relativism* and *moral relativism*. Cognitive relativism concerns descriptive propositions, like 'The moon is made of green cheese', or 'Pop music causes headaches.' It holds that in terms of truth and falsehood, all statements about the world are culturally contingent, and therefore non-culturally-contingent statements are simply not possible. In other words, all science is ethnoscience. Moral relativism concerns evaluative propositions, like 'Cats are more beautiful than dogs', or 'It is wrong to eat vegetables.' It holds that aesthetic and ethical judgements must be assessed in terms of specific cultural values rather than universal ones. It follows that in social and psychological terms, both appropriate behaviour and processes of thought (i.e., rationality) must also be judged according to cultural values. Boas and his followers, and to a lesser extent Evans-Pritchard and his, all espoused tenets of normative, and especially cognitive, relativism.

Epistemological relativism takes as its starting point the strongest possible form of descriptive relativism. It combines an extreme cultural-determinist position with a view that cultural diversity is virtually limitless. It is important here to distinguish between *generic cultural determinism* (which holds that there is a universal but uniquely human cultural pattern within which cultures vary, i.e., the 'psychic unity' of humankind) and *particular cultural determinism* (which holds that there is no such thing). Epistemological relativists espouse the latter. They argue that human nature and the human mind are culturally variable. Therefore, they claim, both generalizations about culture and general theories of culture are fallacious.

The main concerns of the present chapter will be with 'relativism' as the term was understood prior to the rise of postmodernism; with offshoots, notably cognitive anthropology; and with certain strands of antirelativism. The first great relativist in anthropology was Franz Boas, whose ideas were essentially of the descriptive relativist type. His follower, amateur linguist Benjamin Lee Whorf, embraced a form of cognitive relativism, as did later cognitive anthropologists and ethnoscientists. Early psychological anthropology of the 'culture and personality' school was characteristically associated with moral relativism. Epistemological relativism is strong in anthropology today, having emerged over the last thirty years or so in the hands of a diversity of thinkers in different countries. Clifford Geertz is perhaps the best-known proponent of it, but other interpretivist and postmodernist thinkers maintain more radical views. We shall return to radical epistemological relativism in chapter 10.

Franz Boas and the rise of cultural relativism

Classic cultural relativism emerged from the work of Franz Boas and his students. For the first half of the twentieth century it was the dominant paradigm of American anthropology. Some adherents (including Boas himself) stressed the richness of cultures then generally thought of as 'primitive', and several (again including Boas) used relativist ideology to argue the case against racism, anti-Semitism, and nationalist zealotry. Others developed their ideas through the study of the relation between language and culture, and still others, through psychological aspects of culture.

Boas was born in Westphalia in 1858. He studied physics and geography at Heidelberg and Bonn and took his Ph.D. at Kiel in 1881. It is said that his Ph.D. research, which was on the colour of water, led him directly to an interest in the subjectivity of perception. In 1883 he began fieldwork with the Inuit of Baffin Island with the intention of comparing their physical environment, measured 'objectively', with their own knowledge of it. He soon came to realize the importance of culture as a determining force of perception, and consequently he rejected the implicit environ-mental-determinist position with which he had started. He also began learning the complex language of the Baffin Island people, recorded folklore and other aspects of their culture, and eventually published accounts of his work in both German and English. Boas returned to Germany in 1884, and in the following year he began to study the cultures of the North West Coast of North America, first through museum collections in Germany and then, from 1886, through field studies on the North West Coast.

Boas taught at Columbia University in New York City from 1896 to 1936, and his department quickly became *the* centre of anthropological research in the United States. He objected to evolutionism, mainly on the grounds that the task of anthropologists should be to gain first-hand experience in other cultures and not to speculate about their past. He also objected to the idea of racial and cultural superiority implicit in evolution-ist writings. He countered this with an insistence on ethnographers con-ducting their fieldwork in the native language, and through use of the language, gaining an insider's view of the culture under study.

The title of his most famous book, *The Mind of Primitive Man* (Boas 1938 [first edition 1911]), perhaps now seems both evolutionist and sexist, but the book was written to oppose the incipient racism in America and in the world. Boas argues that the 'white race' is not intellectually superior, but just more advantaged than other 'races'. He cites the fact that many nations made contributions to the origins of world civilization. While seemingly accepting some aspects of evolutionism in his notion of 'the progress of culture', Boas rejects any biological basis for culture at all. In his view, language is independent of 'race', and culture is even more independent. He points also to the lack of comparability in data used to support evolutionism. He defines his 'primitive' people in a non-judgemental way: 'Primitive are those people whose forms of life are simple and uniform, and the contents and form of whose culture are meager and intellectually inconsistent' (Boas 1938: 197). He goes on to point out that different peoples are primitive or advanced in different respects. Australian Aborigines are poor in material culture but have a complex social structure. The Indians of California do superb artistic work, but their culture lacks complexity in other ways. He likens such differences to those between poor and rich in America and Europe. He adds that no people are untouched by foreign influences, and concludes that to assign a whole culture to a uniform category of 'primitive' or 'civilized' is pointless.

Most of Boas' work was of a more specific nature, on topics like art, mythology, and language, but he often addressed his anthropological arguments to the general public. His influence was great, partly because of his early monopoly on the training of postgraduate anthropology students in North America, and partly because he wrote prolifically and in plain English. Boas wrote few books, preferring short articles (of which he wrote over 600). The best and most influential of these are included in two collections, one published during his lifetime (Boas 1940) and the other compiled many years after his death by one of his admirers (Stocking 1974). Boas died on 21 December 1942 at a luncheon being held in his honour. He uttered his last words, 'I have a new theory of race . . . ', and before he could finish, collapsed and died in the arms of the person sitting next to him – the great French structuralist, Claude Lévi-Strauss.

Culture and personality

Culture was the abiding abstract interest of American anthropology from Boas to Geertz (with the latter steering clear of static abstraction in favour of a more dynamic approach). This does not mean that there has always been uniformity about what 'culture' is. In a famous overview, A. L. Kroeber and Clyde Kluckhohn (1952) cite over a hundred definitions by anthropologists, philosophers, literary critics, and others. They divide the anthropological definitions into six groups: descriptive (based on content), historical (emphasizing tradition), normative (emphasizing rules), psychological (dealing with learning or problem-solving), structural (having to do with pattern), and genetic (e.g., culture as a product of being human, or simply as that which non-human animals lack). To me, what comes out of their survey is the extraordinary range of perspectives on things which might make up culture. Ironically though, it is not the ideas of Boas or his followers that most anthropology students remember, but Tylor's (descriptive) definition of culture: 'that complex whole which includes knowledge, belief, art, law, morals, custom, and any other capabilities and habits acquired by man as a member of society' (Tylor 1871, I: 1).

While Tylor's definition has remained at the heart of considerations of culture in the abstract, the perspective which emerged as most crucial to its position as the quintessential anthropological concept was that of Ruth Benedict. The key text is her *Patterns of Culture* (1934), written no doubt under the guiding hand of Boas but with a greater emphasis on psychological aspects than in his work. Benedict's undergraduate education was in literature, and her early interest was poetry. Not long after her introduction to anthropology in 1919, she came to the conclusion that her colleagues were making all the wrong sorts of comparison. Just as poetry should be analysed in its cultural context, she argued, so too aspects of culture should be seen in light of the culture in its entirety. She favoured comparison not of kinship terminologies or techniques of pottery-making, but of whole cultures seen through an understanding of their particular 'dominant drives'. In *Patterns of Culture* Benedict compares three peoples: the Zuñi of New Mexico (studied by Ruth Bunzel, Frank Cushing, and others), the Kwakiutl of Vancouver Island (studied by Boas), and the Dobuans of Melanesia (studied by Reo Fortune). She comes to the conclusion that what is normal behaviour in one culture is not normal in another. Even psychological states are culturally determined.

The Zuñi are a ceremonious people. They value sobriety and inoffensiveness above all other virtues. They have cults of healing, of the sun, of sacred fetishes, of war, of the dead, and so on. Each has its own priestly officials, who perform various ceremonies according to the seasonal calendar. The details of these ceremonies are important. If anything goes wrong, it can have adverse consequences: if a priest says a rain prayer in the wrong way, it is likely to be hot and sunny.

All this is very different from what happens among most other Native North American peoples. Benedict contrasts the Zuñi to them, using a distinction invented by the nineteenth-century philosopher and literary critic, Friedrich Nietzsche. He had distinguished two elements of Greek tragedy: the 'Apollonian' and the 'Dionysian'. The Apollonian aspect is that of measure, restraint, and harmony; the Dionysian aspect, that of emotion, passion, and excess. Greek tragedy, according to Nietzsche, had both. American Indian cultures, according to Benedict, have one or the other.

Zuñi are described as Apollonian. They live an ordered life. Everything is done precisely. They do not get worked up, go into trance, or hallucinate. They just perform their rituals as they always have done. They distrust individualism. Supernatural power comes not from individual experience, but from prior membership in a cult. Even in courtship there are absolute and rather tedious rules about what to say and how to say it. Traditionally, there is not meant to be any deep feeling between husbands and wives; they just abide by the rules of proper behaviour. Nor, at least in Benedict's account, do the Zuñi distinguish sharply between 'good' and 'evil'. They say that things just are the way they are.

Kwakiutl are described as the opposite – an example of a Dionysian culture. In their religious ceremonies the chief dancer goes into deep trance. He foams at the mouth, trembles violently, and typically has to be tied up with four ropes (each held by a different person) to keep him from doing any damage. In the past, the most sacred of all the Kwakiutl cult groups was the Cannibal Society. According to accounts by Boas and others, the cannibals would sing sacred songs and dance, while they ate the bodies of slaves specifically killed for the purpose. In the absence of slaves, accounts claimed, the cannibals would just bite chunks out of the arms of the spectators, then vomit them up later.

Kwakiutl used to run their economy along similar Dionysian principles through the institution known as the potlatch. In the nineteenth century, the custom was that chiefs whose waters and lands produced well in a given year would hold great feasts to give away food and other items. Thereby they gained prestige over other chiefs and simultaneously spread their good fortune to members of other clans. In the period when pot-latching was at its most extreme (around the turn of the century), people, through their chiefs, bartered away enormous amounts of subsistence goods in exchange for copper bracelets and blankets. This was not so they could give them away as they previously had done, but so they could destroy them. The more one gives away, the higher one's prestige. And if one can destroy things, they reckoned, one gains even more prestige. Better yet, destruction insults the guests. The chiefs and their retainers even sang 'hymns of self glorification' as they destroyed their wealth.

Dobuans are different again. Their highest virtues, Benedict suggests, are hostility and treachery. For example, marriage begins with the treach-ery of a young man's prospective mother-in-law. A boy will sleep with several girls in sequence. Then one morning, when he wakes up, the mother of whomever he is sleeping with will be standing in the door of her hut. The mother will give him a digging stick and force him to go to work for her, and that means he is married! This does not actually matter very much, because, it seems, almost everyone on Dobu commits adultery. When it is found out, there are violent quarrels, broken cooking pots everywhere, and suicide attempts. There is also sorcery. If anyone has a good crop of yams, it is assumed he must have performed sorcery against those whose yams have not grown well. The Dobuans live in a state of perpetual fear of each other, and (says Benedict) they regard this as normal.

So, what is normal for the Zuñi is not normal for the Kwakiutl. What is normal in Middle America is not normal for the Dobuans, and vice versa. In Western psychiatric terms, we might regard the Zuñi as neurotic, the Kwakiutl as megalomaniac, and the Dobuans as paranoid. In Dobu, paranoia is 'normal'. Of course, in presenting here just the juicy bits from Benedict's account, I have perhaps portrayed her argument as more extreme than she might have preferred. Yet her premise, that culture determines both what is regarded as correct behaviour and what is re-garded as a normal psychological state, remains one of the strongest assertions of relativism in anthropology.

Using the same approach, Benedict herself went on to work with

Japanese immigrants in the United States during the Second World War (Benedict 1946). A number of others followed in her footsteps, notably Margaret Mead, a slightly younger contemporary at Columbia in the 1920s who published her first work in the field even before Benedict (Mead 1928; see also Mead 1930). Clyde Kluckhohn was another well-known figure, who applied Benedict's ideas on psychological aspects of culture in his ethnography of the Navajo (e.g., Kluckhohn 1944; Kluckhohn and Leighton 1974 [1946]). In the last couple of decades their work has come under fire, especially that of Mead on the supposed sexual freedoms enjoyed by Samoan adolescent girls (Freeman 1983). Mead had recorded on Samoa that premarital sex without loving attachment was regarded as normal, that adolescence was not marked by emotional stress, and that teenage rebellion did not exist there, and therefore that it is not a necessary result of the biological facts of puberty. Derek Freeman's alternative view suggests that all these generalizations are false. Yet to me what matters more is that Mead gained insights into American culture *through* her studies in Samoa and elsewhere. Although her writings were less explicit about 'personality' than Benedict's, Mead nevertheless became the most famous representative of the 'culture and personality' school. Her work marked the point of origin of psychological anthropology as we know it today (see, e.g., Bock 1980; 1988).

Primitive thought?

Do peoples who live in different cultures think differently? If so, are some ways of thinking more primitive than others? Can we say that some cultures are more primitive than others? The notion of 'primitive thought' has existed at least since the late nineteenth century, but in the twentieth century it has acquired new meaning. Among twentieth-century questions are: if 'primitive thought' exists, then does it exist only among 'primitive peoples', or is it found universally, perhaps deep within all cultures? Can 'primitive thought' be equated with 'rational thought', or is it different? Indeed is it *more* rational than the scientific thought of the Western world (as the most radical of the Boasians claimed)?

In order to explore these questions, we shall look next at the work of Lévy-Bruhl and Whorf, both active in the 1920s and 1930s. Their ideas are poles apart. Yet they touch on these questions in intriguing and enlightening ways. Then we shall take up briefly another side to relativism – within the 'rationality debate' which lasted roughly from the late 1960s to at least the early 1980s.

The anti-relativism of Lévy-Bruhl

The most important writer on 'primitive thought' was the French philosopher of the social sciences, Lucien Lévy-Bruhl. He rejected the notion of psychic unity and argued that primitive thought is qualitatively different from logical thought. It is not different because it is illogical, but because, in his view, it is *pre*-logical. Its 'pre-logical' nature is defined simply by the presumed absence of a separation of cause and effect. Although part of the *Année sociologique* school and in some respects a functionalist, Lévy-Bruhl's views are better characterized as evolutionist and anti-relativist.

Lévy-Bruhl wrote six books on 'primitive thought', as well as other books and articles on philosophical and political topics. The bibliographical details are not so important, but the French titles of his works on 'primitive thought' are interesting because they hint at his views with regard to the very concept of 'the primitive'. They include: *Les fonctions mentales dans les sociétés inférieures* (translated into English as *How Natives Think*), *La mentalité primitive* (*Primitive Mentality*), *L'âme primitive* (*The 'Soul' of the Primitive*), *Le surnaturel et la nature dans la mentalité primitive* (*Primitives and the Supernatural*), *La mythologie primitive* (not yet translated), and *L'expérience mystique et les symboles chez les primitifs* (not yet translated).

In *How Natives Think*, Lévy-Bruhl (1926 [1910]) divided human thought into just two categories, that of 'primitive mentality' and that of 'higher mentality'. The 'primitive' thinks logically enough in everyday situations, but cannot think logically in the abstract. For example, in 'primitive' cultures one's soul may be equated with one's shadow. The 'primitive', in general, is afraid of phenomena such as shadows because, says Lévy-Bruhl, he or she cannot distinguish between an object and what that object symbolically and mystically represents. A man from Aboriginal Australia does not have a notion of land ownership, since he cannot conceive of himself as being separated from his land. Or, when a South American Indian says she is a parrot, she does not mean (as we would now say) she is a member of the parrot totem. She means that there is an identity between herself and a bird. In the Indian's own view, apparently, she really is a parrot.

For Lévy-Bruhl, 'primitive thought' also differs from logical thought in that it is a product of collective, not individual, thinking. Like other French anthropologists of his time, he frequently referred to the *representations collectives* (collective representations) of peoples. Durkheim, Mauss, and Lévy-Bruhl alike opposed the idea that one can reduce collective action to the actions of a number of individuals, or a culture as a whole to the ideas of each individual bearer of that culture. Yet in

Lévy-Bruhl's case, this applied only, or at least predominantly, with reference to pre-literate cultures, as he regarded the mentality of those cultures with literacy as more individualistic. There is a consistency on this through Lévy-Bruhl's books; yet his private notebooks tell a different story.

Wherever he went, Lévy-Bruhl carried thin, black oilcloth, lined notebooks. Each section had a title, and at the bottom of each page was a note of the date and the place the notes were written. Happily, the notebooks of the last year of his life (1938 to 1939) survived the Second World War, and they indicate an interesting transformation of Lévy-Bruhl's theory. He did not give up the idea of primitive mentality, but he significantly altered its definition. On 29 August 1938, for example, Lévy-Bruhl jotted in his oilcloth pad:

let us rectify what I believed correct in 1910: there is not a primitive mentality distinguishable from the other by *two* characteristics which are peculiar to it (mystical and prelogical). There is a mystical mentality which is more marked and more easily observable among 'primitive peoples' than in our own societies, but it is present in every human mind. (Lévy-Bruhl 1975 [1949]: 100-1)

In other words, it is not the logic which is different, but the knowledge. Cultures are not different in kind, but only in degree.

Chronologically, Lévy-Bruhl's ideas were developed in parallel with those of Boas, Benedict, and Mead – all of whom held romantic attachments towards alien cultures. Lévy-Bruhl's writings challenged their romanticism. They also inflicted a philosophical debate into anthropology which anthropologists of the day were neither equipped to handle nor, in many cases, anxious to argue. Yet Lévy-Bruhl's ideas did make anthropologists think. Looking back on them today, we can see them in light of the work of more recent writers, like Lévi-Strauss. He in some ways follows Lévy-Bruhl (e.g., in distinguishing a profound difference between pre-literate and literate cultures), but in other ways represents an opposite position (e.g., in imputing psychic unity through the notion of *esprit humain*, sometimes translated 'collective unconsciousness').

Lévy-Bruhl still has some admirers, if very few followers. One who does write in the same vein is Christopher Hallpike. He has argued (e.g., 1979: 50-1) that Lévy-Bruhl's work would have been yet more valuable had Lévy-Bruhl been aware of the possibilities of cognitive psychology. Hallpike himself has likened 'primitive thought' to the thought processes of children constructing a correct understanding of the world. He takes his basic ideas from the Swiss psychologist Jean Piaget, but true to his anthropological understanding he develops the notion of 'primitive thought' through the analysis of collective representations.

The linguistic relativism of Whorf

The implication throughout Lévy-Bruhl's work (even in the notebooks) is that 'primitive peoples' are intellectually inferior to people like 'ourselves'. Taking these two categories as given, consider the alternatives.

(1) 'Primitive peoples' are intellectually the same as 'ourselves'.
(2) 'Primitive peoples' are intellectually different, but neither inferior nor superior.
(3) 'Primitive peoples' are intellectually superior to 'ourselves'.

The first two represent views which lie in-between the evolutionist position and the radical relativist one. The third, representing a radical relativism playing as inverse evolutionism, is more interesting than either, because it provides such a sharp contrast to the peculiar brand of evolutionism promoted by Lévy-Bruhl. It is a view best represented by Benjamin Lee Whorf, chemical engineer and amateur anthropological linguist of the Boasian tradition.

Before Boas it had been thought that languages were all pretty much alike. If one knew Greek or Latin grammar, one could describe any language in the world. The Boasians showed that in many respects this is not the case. Inuit and Amerindian languages are much more complex than Greek or Latin. Some have as many as seventeen 'genders', which can be used to make puns, and, no doubt, to confuse the never-ending stream of anthropologists who have gone to study them. Whorf came up with the idea that people who speak such languages have different ways of looking at the world from people who speak simpler languages, like English.

The 'Sapir–Whorf hypothesis', as this idea became known, bears the name of both Whorf and his mentor. (Edward Sapir was himself a student of Boas and a practitioner of both 'culture and personality' studies and anthropological linguistics.) In principle, the hypothesis suggests that there are not just two forms of thought, 'ours' and 'theirs', but a multiplicity of forms of thought, each associated with the language of its thinkers. However, in practice Whorf tended to talk about two main examples which can be taken as exemplary of wider patterns: thought as expressed in the English language, and thought as expressed in the languages of Native North Americans.

The similarities and contrasts between Lévy-Bruhl and Whorf come across well through a comparison of *How Natives Think*, part II (Lévy-Bruhl 1926 [1910]: 137-223), which deals with grammar and counting, and two essays in *Language, Thought, and Reality* (Whorf 1956 [written c. 1936]: 57-86), which deal with relations between expression and

thought in 'primitive communities'. Lévy-Bruhl and Whorf did not disagree about the data. Their ideas converge in that they both understood
the concrete complexity of grammar in the languages of so-called 'primitive' peoples. Where they differed significantly was in their deeper interpretation of that phenomenon.

The same example can be used to support either side of the argument.
Take this one (paraphrased from Lévy-Bruhl (1926 [1910]: 143)). It
illustrates the verbal prefixes and suffixes in the language of the Kiwai
Islanders of Melanesia:

rudo	action of two on many in the past,
rumo	action of many on many in the past,
durudo	action of two on many in the present,
durumo	action of many on many in the present,
amadurodo	action of two on two in the present,
amarudo	similar action in the past,
amarumo	action of many on two in the past,
ibidurudo	action of many on three in the present,
ibidurumo	similar action in the past,
amabidurumo	action of three on two in the present,
	and so on.

To Lévy-Bruhl, the concreteness of these forms reflected a 'primitive'
way of thinking – a lack of abstract thought. To Whorf, such constructions implied great linguistic sophistication. In this example, each word
may be divided into morphemes, that is, smaller units of meaning which
can be put together to form longer words (*ru-*, *-do*, *-mo*, *du-*, etc.). To a
Whorfian, the real concreteness is in these individual morphemes, and
the ability to put them together entails abstract thought. Another contrast
between the two is in their understanding of directionality in the relation
between language and thought. Both believed that language and thought
are related. To Lévy-Bruhl, language reflects thought. Among 'primitives', grammatical categories are built up on the basis of 'primitive
thought'. However, to Whorf, thought reflects pre-existing linguistic
categories. People think only through these categories, and never independently of them.

Whorf realized the possibility that the categories of the English language are not necessarily better than those of other languages. In fact, he
went further than that. He envied the Hopi for their ability to think in
ways 'in advance' of his own. He argued that Hopi grammar is better
suited to the expression of scientific ideas than English is (see especially
Whorf 1956: 59-60, 85). Specifically, the metaphysics underlying English
supposes two cosmic forms: space and time. Space is infinite, three-

dimensional, and static. Time moves in one direction, and it is divided into past, present, and future. The metaphysics underlying Hopi supposes two quite different cosmic forms: objective (manifested) and subjective (manifesting). The former includes the physical universe as experienced through the senses, and also past and present. The latter includes that which exists in the mind, including the Mind of the Cosmos itself, and also what English would characterize as the future tense.

Criticisms of Whorfianism

But is Whorfianism the answer? Did Whorf really explain the relation between language and culture, and the difference between different modes of thought? In fact Whorf has been criticized on several grounds. Let me take a few of the criticisms which have been suggested.

First, some of Whorf's published ideas on the relation between language and culture are just too simplistic. (Indeed Whorf, who disclosed some of his most radical statements in non-linguistic, non-anthropological journals, such as *Technology Review*, the promotional magazine of Massachusetts Institute of Technology, may have realized this.) It is easy to refute Whorf's simplistic notion that language determines thought. Peoples of similar culture sometimes speak very different languages. Speakers of Basque are similar in culture to their French- and Spanish-speaking neighbours. On the other hand, peoples who speak closely related languages can have quite different cultures. Navajo and Apache both speak languages of the Southern Athapaskan group, but the Navajo (culturally but not linguistically influenced by the Hopi) lived in permanent, scattered settlements and were, in early Euro-American contact times, largely peaceful. Their famous artwork is of Hopi origin. The Apache were more nomadic, with an economy based on hunting, gathering, some farming, and raiding. Neither group had a centralized political authority, but the Apache developed a hierarchy of leadership for purposes of raiding and warfare. Their cultures were different, but did they, or indeed do they, think similarly because they speak closely related languages? That question remains open.

Secondly, Whorf's ideas overemphasize linguistic difference. Whorf (along with Sapir, e.g. 1949 [1915-38]: 167-250) was among the first to make systematic studies of Amerindian languages which did not have Euro-centric categories as the foundation of the analysis, and therefore probably among the first outsiders to appreciate the great richness of expression in these languages. However, the pendulum has now swung the other way. Since the 1960s linguists have tended to emphasize universal aspects of language. For example, all peoples speak in sentences, and these are by definition made up of noun phrases and verb phrases. Thus Nootka may not be quite as different from English as Whorf thought it was; and, following his hypothesis, Nootka- and English-speakers may not be as different in their modes of thought.

Thirdly, what evidence do we really have that language determines thought? Whorf's evidence in favour of it is entirely inferential and based on language itself, with little or no attempt to test language against cognition. Proof of the Sapir–Whorf hypothesis would be hard to come by, though linguists are today working on it (see Lucy 1992).

Fourthly, if the thought patterns related through different languages are as different as Whorf suggests, then can a non-Hopi ever understand how a Hopi thinks? If not, then how can we ever compare modes of thought? Though 'weak' versions of the Sapir–Whorf hypothesis remain credible in the eyes of many, the 'strong' version championed by Whorf has never been sustainable. In its essence it denies the possibility of anthropological comparison.

The rationality debate

Since the late 1960s there has been a sporadic resurgence of interest in the question of 'primitive thought', or more accurately, in the question of rationality among 'primitive' peoples. A number of philosophers, sociologists, and anthropologists have participated in the debates, which have been played out at various conferences and in edited collections. The most important of these collections are Bryan Wilson's *Rationality* (1970) and Martin Hollis and Steven Lukes' *Rationality and Relativism* (1982). The former was put together mainly from papers originally published during the 1960s, while the latter consists mainly of specially written papers explicitly designed to supplement and amplify those in the Wilson volume. The former uses ethnographic data, mainly African and 'classic', whereas the latter explores the problem through pre-modern Western science as well.

Let me use just two papers from the latter volume as exemplars of approaches which move beyond a simple 'yea' or 'nay' answer to the question of rationality: those by Dan Sperber and Ernest Gellner.

Sperber (1982) classifies the broadly relativist traditions in social anthropology as either 'intellectualist' or 'symbolist' (see Skorupski 1976). Intellectualists argue that apparently irrational beliefs are not so irrational after all; rather, they are simply mistaken. For example, people believe that the earth is flat because they experience it as such. Symbolists argue that myths, rituals, and so on are only irrational at a literal (and superficial) level. As metaphors for moral values, or whatever, they may be

perfectly rational. Sperber's earlier *Rethinking Symbolism* (1975 [1974])
had been an attack on symbolist approaches (Victor Turner, Claude
Lévi-Strauss, etc.). Put simply, there he argued that symbolism is a
creative mechanism which produces meaning beyond established structures of understanding, and in so doing, helps to develop these very
structures. In his 1982 article he does much the same with regard to
extreme relativist views. Apparently irrational beliefs are not 'beliefs' at
all; they involve a different psychological state. What is more, they are not
irrational; they are (in his view) often simply ways of speaking about the
world. It is perfectly rational to speak about the world in the same way as
do other members of your own culture.

Gellner (1982 [1981]), a staunch anti-relativist, argues here that relativism and the existence of human universals are not incompatible. He
defines relativism as 'a doctrine in the theory of knowledge [which]
asserts that there is no unique truth' (1982: 183). He targets both cognitive and moral relativist statements, and argues both epistemological and
sociological cases against the equation of relativism with diversity. His
argument is complex. Essentially, he says that the problem of relativism is
whether there is only one world, whereas the problem of universals is
philosophically different. Moreover, the search for universals is itself not a
universal but is culturally specific (it is found not among all peoples, but,
for example, among the sort of people who might read this book). Yet
such a search *is* accessible to all human beings, and its diffusion (present-
day theorists would say 'globalization') is taking place.

In practice, most relativists in anthropology have been more interested
in cultural diversity than in universals. Lévi-Strauss, to the extent to
which he is the relativist some of his critics say he is, may be the exception
(see chapter 8). In these crucial articles, what both Sperber and Gellner
have done is to set aside the philosophical question of relativism by
showing its irrelevance to the weak relativist streak in anthropological
writing. The fact that other cultures view the world differently from one's
own is not, in itself, grounds for seeing all alien understandings as either
'irrational' or expressing valid alternative 'truths'. The existence of human universals does not make relativism untenable; nor does human
diversity make it tenable.

Towards cognitive science

After Whorf's untimely death in 1941, within anthropology there was a
lull in interest in the topics he studied. When interest in the linguistic
aspects of culture re-emerged in the 1950s, the theoretical emphasis in
linguistics had changed from the descriptive (pioneered by Boas and

Table 7.1. *Approximate correspondences between words for 'tree', 'woods', and 'forest' in Danish, German, and French*

Danish	German	French
	Baum (tree)	**arbre** (tree)
trae (tree, trees)	————	————
————	**Holz** (woods)	**bois** (woods, woodland)
	————	
skov (woods, woodland, forest)	**Wald** (woodland, forest)	————
		forêt (forest)

Sapir) to the structural. Ideas drawn from structural linguistics entered anthropology both through structuralism and through the more relativistic concerns of anthropologists interested in aspects of classification. Our concern here will be with the latter.

Structural semantics

Take these famous examples from the work of Danish linguist Louis Hjelmslev (1953 [1943]: 33-4): dark colours and clumps of trees. The terms for dark colours in Welsh differ from those in English, as Welsh has fewer terms. Welsh *gwyrdd* covers fewer shades than the English colour term *green*. Welsh *glas* covers some shades classified by English as *green*, all of *blue* and some of *grey*. *Llwyd* covers some of *grey* and some of *brown* (cf. Ardener 1989 [1971]: 9-12).

Similarly, when we compare words for 'tree', 'woods', and 'forest' in Danish, German, and French, we see a lack of exact correspondence, even between German and French, which have the same number of terms. This is illustrated in table 7.1. (Note here the distinction between English words in inverted commas, when English itself is an example, and in italics, when the English words are used as approximate glosses for foreign terms.) The French category *bois* (roughly 'wood', 'woods' or 'woodland') is wider than the German *Holz* (roughly 'wood' or 'small wooded area'). The French category *forêt* (meaning 'forest'), like its English equivalent, is narrower than the German *Wald* ('woodland' or 'small forest'). To say 'forest' in the French or English sense, a German would normally specify a *großer Wald* ('larger forest').

No language classifies everything. For colours, it would be impossible, since there is an infinite degree of natural variation in both the wavelength of light (red to violet) and the intensity of light (dark to light). Languages make meaning by making structure, and cultures do the same. Sometimes the structure is explicitly linguistic, as in the case of colour classification or words for things to do with trees. At other times, it is not, as for example in rules of etiquette or appropriate styles of dress.

Cognitive anthropology

American linguist Kenneth L. Pike made a great breakthrough in 1954 when he published the first part of an essay of 762 pages called *Language in Relation to a Unified Theory of the Structure of Human Behavior* (completed as Pike 1967). He took the idea of the relation between *sounds* (the phonetic) and *meaningful units of sound* (the phonemic) and postulated a more general relation between *units of any kind* (the etic) and *meaningful units of any kind* (the emic). Phonetics involves the study of all the sounds that humans can make. Phonemics (phonology) concerns sounds distinguished by contrasts with other sounds in a given language. Thus the theory which accounts for differences between sets of sounds in, say, Spanish and Portuguese, could be applied to differences between sets of words in Spanish or Portuguese, or indeed any other level of linguistic or cultural phenomena.

To put it another way, the etic is the level of universals, or the level of things which may be observed by an 'objective' observer. The emic is the level of meaningful contrasts within a particular language or culture. We can explain emic distinctions in terms of various frameworks or grids. Classic examples include Linnaean taxonomy; disease, in medical science; the measurement of the wavelength of light; the chromatic scale in music; and above all, the genealogical grid. While some radical relativists have questioned the universality of such grids, nevertheless their purported existence does highlight the difference between a postulated extra-cultural universal and one's own cultural framework taken (erroneously) as universal (see Headland, Pike, and Harris 1990).

The precise meaning of 'emic' has long been a subject of debate. Harris (1968: 568-604) saw it essentially as equatable with informants' statements, whereas Pike (1967: 37-72) emphasized instead the structured nature of the emic system. Just as informants cannot necessarily describe the grammatical rules behind their own use of language, so too they might be unable to describe the emic system which underlies their cultural understandings and practices. The discovery of that system is the task of the analyst, not the informant.

After Pike's pioneering work, anthropologists tried to formalize the relation between emic and etic categories. Complex methodologies were developed and debated. Following Ward Goodenough's (1956) famous paper on the relationship terminology of the inhabitants of the Truk Islands of Micronesia, several turned their attention to kinship. Emic structures are probably more transparent in relationship terminologies than in any other cultural domain. In them one can easily distinguish 'denotata' (the elements which make up a given class, in this case genealogical points of reference), from 'significata' or 'components' (the principles which distinguish the class), from 'connotata' (principles which, though not defining a class, are loosely associated with it), from 'designata' (the names of classes), from a class or classes of things themselves.

Using English as our example, take the class of kin which English-speakers call *uncle*. The designatum here is the word *uncle* itself. The denotata are genealogical points of reference FB, MB, FZH, MZH, and so on (that is, father's brother, mother's brother, father's sister's husband, and mother's sister's husband; denotata are customarily abbreviated in this way). One could define any class simply by listing all its members, but this is hardly satisfactory. Much more useful is an understanding of the principles of classification, and these are indicated in the significata or components. For the class designated *uncle*, the components are 'male' (to distinguish an uncle from an aunt), 'first ascending generation' (to distinguish an uncle from a nephew), 'consanguineal or consanguine's spouse' (to distinguish an uncle from a father-in-law), and 'collateral' (to distinguish an uncle from a father). By specifying each of these four components, we define what it means to be an *uncle*. Yet in addition to such signification, it is sometimes useful to consider the connotations (connotata) of being an uncle, for example, the characteristic features of 'avuncular' behaviour, whatever that might be in particular. These are not part of the componential analysis proper, but they do hint at its limitations.

Another limitation of componential analysis is the fact that we can have more than one correct analysis for any given set of terms. This is illustrated in table 7. 2, where two different analyses of the English terminology for consanguines (i.e., 'blood' relatives) are shown.

These two componential analyses differ in the technical understanding of the lineal/collateral or direct/collateral distinction and in the hierarchical relation between different distinctions of generation. The first representation (based loosely on that of Wallace and Atkins, 1960) is perhaps the most formally correct. Yet its precise distinction between 'lineals' (defined as ego and his or her ancestors and descendants), 'co-lineals' (siblings of lineals), and 'ablineals' (descendants of siblings of lineals)

Table 7.2. *Two componential analyses of English consanguineal kin term usage*

Componential analysis 1				
LINEALS		CO-LINEALS		ABLINEALS
male	female	male	female	
+2 grandfather	grandmother			
+1 father	mother	uncle	aunt	
0 EGO		brother	sister	cousin
−1 son	daughter	nephew	niece	
−2 grandson	granddaughter			

Componential analysis 2					
	DIRECT		COLLATERAL		
	male	female		male	female
Generation 2	+ grandfather	grandmother			
	− grandson	granddaughter			
Generation 1	+ father	mother		uncle	aunt
	− son	daughter		nephew	niece
Generation 0	brother	sister		cousin	

seems pedantic and counter-intuitive to me. The second (based on that by Romney and D'Andrade, 1964) was hailed in its time as a psychologically 'real' representation, that is, one which captures in its formal distinctions the thought processes of English-speaking people when they classify their kin. Yet for me as a native speaker of English, the placement of grandparents with grandchildren, of parents with children, and of 'generation 0' by itself, seems to make less sense than the placement of the generations from senior to junior.

The variant examples of table 7.2 show that there is always an element of indeterminacy in componential analysis, and that indeterminacy results from its reliance on lexical structures over actors' perceptions. Though this may be a limitation in some sense, it need not necessarily be very problematic, as long as we are prepared to accept (as postmodern relativists do) that different people, even in the same culture, think in different ways. In linguistics, many scholars hold to the view that the best grammatical analysis is the one which is simplest, whether it is most real

to the native speaker or not. There is a place for the alternative view that the best is precisely the one which is most meaningful to the native speaker (while also being formally correct, of course). If native speakers disagree about which one this may be, then so be it. The debate which ensued on this issue is called that of 'God's truth versus hocus-pocus', with the 'God's truth' side favouring the search for cognitive reality and the 'hocus-pocus' side maintaining a scepticism of this very possibility. The debate was played out in the pages of the *American Anthropologist* between 1960 and 1965, and the key papers are included within Stephen Tyler's edited collection, *Cognitive Anthropology* (1969: 343-432).

Ethnoscience

There are two quite different threads of relativist thinking in anthropology today. For convenience these might be labelled the modernist and the postmodernist perspectives. The modernist perspective follows from earlier concerns with formal properties of thought, such as those of the cognitive anthropologists of the 1960s. It therefore follows a formalist methodology (seeking form or pattern in modes of thought) and is most prevalent in the study of scientific thought in traditional cultures, such as in ethnozoology and ethnobotany. The postmodernist perspective rejects formalist methodology altogether in favour of an interpretivist one, which focuses on the interaction of individuals and the negotiation of cultural categories (see chapter 10).

The modernist strand alive today is the culmination of the Whorfian position. In the 1960s proponents of cognitive anthropology took up Whorf's concern of the relation between modern, Western science and the indigenous worldviews they studied. They called their field 'ethnoscience'. That term did not always designate anything at all different from 'cognitive anthropology' (which was how some still saw their enterprise), from 'componential analysis' (which remained their main methodology), or from 'the new ethnography' (a catchword coined in the 1960s to make the comparison between their work and 'the new archaeology' of Lewis Binford). Today however, 'ethnoscience' tends to designate a specialization more than a theoretical perspective – namely the specialized concern with indigenous knowledge systems such as ethnobotany, ethnozoology, ethnomedicine, and so on (see, e.g., Berlin 1992; Ellen 1993). For that matter, the old label 'new ethnography' has in recent times been applied to postmodernist perspectives.

The foremost proponent of ethnoscience in its broadest sense, Charles Frake, has explored both the esoteric and the mundane in his works on ecological systems, interpretations of illness, concepts of law, how to

enter a house, and how to ask for a drink in the Subanum, Yakan, and other cultures of the Philippines (see, e.g., Frake 1980). As these examples show, Frake's ethnoscience takes social action as well as the static categories of ethnoscientific discourse into account. Strategies and decision-making come into play. This is true even in the methodology he has espoused, as he makes explicit the eliciting techniques he employs. He shares this view with some of postmodern persuasion. Yet his approach, developed in the 1960s long before postmodernism came into anthropology, differs from postmodernism in its recognition of indigenous, culturally agreed categories, which are to be 'discovered' by an ethnographer through careful question-and-answer sessions.

While some in this tradition do take Western science as a baseline, others (including Frake) prefer to examine the modes of classification employed in traditional societies without necessary regard to such a baseline. Some have even examined Western science itself as a cultural tradition. Scott Atran's (1990) study of the 'folk biology' basis of natural history, from Aristotle to Darwin, is a good example. In its earliest days, ethnoscience was closely tied to linguistics, but in the hands of more recent practitioners it has gradually moved more towards cognitive psychology and now threatens to link up with interests not that far removed from those of the culture and personality school with which it has long been associated (cf. Bloch 1991; D'Andrade 1995: 182-243).

One approach which recognizes the existence of truth in science but nevertheless recognizes also social and cultural determinants within it, is the prevailing perspective of medical anthropology. Cecil Helman's (1994 [1984]) excellent overview of that field cites hundreds of studies in medical science and anthropology to illustrate the cultural, as well as the biological, construction of stress, pain, psychological disorders, and epidemiology. In the last instance, for example, North American psychiatrists are more prone to diagnosing 'schizophrenia' than those in Britain. Likewise, a North American doctor will diagnose 'emphysema' where a British doctor reads the same symptoms as 'chronic bronchitis'. Similar variations have been found in comparative research across Europe (Helman 1994: 270). This does not mean that modern medicine is fallacious (Helman himself is a practising physician), but that culture is everywhere – even in the 'rituals' which surgeons perform in the operating theatre (cf. Katz 1981).

Concluding summary

Boas founded a new anthropology based broadly on relativist principles, or at least on principles emphasizing culture difference and the moral

worth of different understandings of the world. Like the functionalists he challenged the old order, but the anthropology which emerged in Boasian America was (for a time) profoundly different from that of Malinowskian, Radcliffe-Brownian Britain. The strongest proponents of relativism were, in their different ways, those of the 'culture and personality school' and the proponents of the 'Sapir–Whorf hypothesis'. Yet the difference was as much one of interest (psychology or language) as of theoretical position.

One of the offshoots of Boasian anthropology has been the interest in cognitive aspects of classification. This interest highlights the sharp divide between the Boasian emphasis on culture as a way of thinking and the Radcliffe-Brownian emphasis on it as a minor adjunct to social structure. The Kroeber/Rivers/Radcliffe-Brown debate on kinship terms discussed in chapter 5 can be seen in these terms. Kroeber's position is in the tradition of Boas and Sapir, and foreshadows the central concerns with the 'emic' in the work of Pike, Goodenough, Frake, and the ethnoscientists of recent times. As we shall see in the next chapter, the structuralism of Lévi-Strauss was to combine elements of both cognitive and social-structural approaches. But, against Boas and his cultural particularism, it would place the emphasis once more on universals.

FURTHER READING

Important works in the Boasian tradition include Boas' *The Mind of Primitive Man* 1938 [1911] and *Race, Language, and Culture* (1940), Lowie's *Primitive Society* (1947 [1920]), Kroeber's *Anthropology: Culture Patterns and Processes* (1963 [1948]), and Kroeber and Kluckhohn's *Culture: A Critical Review of Concepts and Definitions* (1952). The classic text on 'culture and personality' remains Benedict's *Patterns of Culture* (1934). For critical commentaries on the Boasians and the 'culture and personality' school, see Stocking's collections (respectively 1986; 1996b). Boas, Lowie, Kroeber, Benedict, and Mead are all the subject of contemporary or more recent biographical works.

A good overview of relativist thought with reference to the 'rationality debate' is Hollis and Lukes' 'Introduction' to *Rationality and Relativism* (1982: 1-20). Gellner's (1985) *Relativism and the Social Sciences* is also relevant and includes his essay discussed here, 'Relativism and universals'. Two other books, each bearing the title *Modes of Thought* but published a quarter-century apart, together offer an insight into changes in the perception of such modes (Finnegan and Horton 1973; Olson and Torrance 1996).

The classic edited collection on 'cognitive anthropology' is the one by that title, edited by Stephen Tyler (1969). A relatively recent rethink of the Whorfian hypothesis is Lucy's *Language Diversity and Thought* (1992). See also D'Andrade's excellent overview, *The Development of Cognitive Anthropology* (1995).

8   Structuralism, from linguistics to anthropology

'Structuralism' refers to those theoretical perspectives which give primacy to pattern over substance. For a structuralist, meaning comes through knowing how things fit together, not from understanding things in isolation.

There are some similarities between structuralism and structural-functionalism: both are concerned with relations between things. However, there are important differences. Structural-functionalism finds order within social relations. Structuralists are generally as interested in structures of thought as in structures of society. Moreover, the structural-functionalism of Radcliffe-Brown was based mainly on inductive reasoning. One starts with data and sees what generalizations can be made about them. Structuralists often employ a method which is primarily deductive, that is, based on certain premises. Structuralists might follow these premises and see where they lead, rather as in algebra or geometry. They often prefer to work out logical possibilities first, and then see how 'reality' fits. Indeed, for a true structuralist, there is no reality except the relation between things.

Claude Lévi-Strauss has been interested in both the internal logic of a culture and the relation of that logic to structures beyond the culture – the structure of all possible structures of some particular kind. This is especially the case in his work on kinship (e.g., Lévi-Strauss 1969a [1949]; 1966a), arguably the most structured realm of culture. Yet, while Lévi-Strauss is both the best known and the most characteristic of structuralist thinkers, structuralist thought is applicable more widely. It came into anthropology through linguistics, and the work of Ferdinand de Saussure, among others, is significant in its anticipation of the structuralist anthropological enterprise. Structuralist thought has gone through anthropology to literary criticism too, but the last field will not concern us here.

If the French structuralism of Lévi-Strauss is characterized by a concern with the structure of all possible structures, then Dutch structuralism focuses more on regions, as in regional structural analysis (see also chapter 4). British structuralism, at least in the hands of its early propon- ents, focuses more on particular societies. These national traditions will be touched on at the end of this chapter.

Saussure and structural linguistics

Swiss linguist Ferdinand de Saussure is arguably the most important structuralist of all. However, the theory with which he is associated is not one he *wrote* on. Rather, we know it through his lectures, collected and published in his name in 1916 – three years after his death. His influence in the English-speaking world was slow to catch on. The lectures were published in English only in 1960. I shall draw here on a subsequently revised edition (Saussure 1974).

Saussure and his 'Course'

Saussure (de Saussure) was born in Geneva in 1857. He studied there (initially, physics and chemistry) and in Leipzig (comparative philology), and he taught philology in Paris before returning to his native city in 1891. In his lifetime he was best known for comparative and historical studies on Indo-European vowel systems. Some of this work seems to fore- shadow structuralism: later commentators (e.g., Culler 1976: 66–7) have picked up on the fact that even in historical reconstruction Saussure saw the relation between elements of language as the key to linguistic analysis. Like his near contemporary Durkheim, he had a foot in both diachronic and synchronic camps – indeed he virtually invented the distinction. While in his published work he maintained the traditional historical view of language, in his private lectures he anticipated Boas, Malinowski, and Radcliffe-Brown in stressing synchronic and relational elements of his subject.

The lectures Saussure gave in Geneva between 1906 and 1911 became known as the *Course in General Linguistics* or simply the *Course* (Saussure 1974 [1916]). This (along with some of the work of Edward Sapir) marks the earliest emphasis on synchronic, structural analysis in the study of language. It also marks the foundation of semiology or semiotics (the study of meaning through 'signs') and the dawn of structuralism. Saus- sure hints at the wider, semiological implications of his work, but his concern in the *Course* was explicitly with language. Indeed, he speaks disparagingly of the use of linguistics, for example, in reconstructing the racial history and psychological make-up of ethnic groups (1974 [1916]: 222–8).

Four key distinctions

Saussure made a number of distinctions now commonplace both in linguistics and in the social sciences: diachronic and synchronic, *langue* and *parole*, syntagmatic and associative (paradigmatic), and signifier and signified.

Saussure's distinction (e.g., 1974: 101–2, 140–3) between diachronic and synchronic studies of language was the most significant break with his contemporaries. In the *Course*, he gave at least equal prominence to the latter (language at a particular point in time), whereas linguists of his day tended to be concerned only with the former (language changes through time). In chapter 1, I described evolutionism and diffusionism as diachronic anthropological perspectives and most schools of anthropology as essentially synchronic, while allowing for an in-between set of interactive perspectives. However, for true Saussurians, there is no in-between. The synchronic/diachronic distinction is absolute.

Langue and *parole* (Saussure sometimes uses *langue* and *langage*) are the French words, respectively, for 'language' and 'speech' (e.g., Saussure 1974: 9–15). The French terms are often used in English to represent this distinction, especially in a metaphorical sense. *Langue* is 'language' in the sense of linguistic structure or grammar; and, by analogy, this can be the grammar of culture as well as of language. *Parole* means 'speech' in the sense of actual utterances; and by analogy, it refers also to the social behaviour of real individuals. A fieldworker, in either linguistics or anthropology, moves from the level of *parole* to that of *langue*, that is, from the speech or actions of Tom, Dick, or Harry to a general description of appropriate linguistic or social behaviour.

The third distinction is between syntagmatic and associative relations (Saussure 1974: 122–7). Following Louis Hjelmslev, most structuralists of recent decades have referred to the latter as 'paradigmatic'. Syntagmatic relations are literally those within a sentence. For example, the sentence 'John loves Mary' contains three words: the subject John, the verb 'loves', and the object (of John's love) Mary. If we substitute Sally or Suzie for Mary, we can say that an associative or paradigmatic relation exists between the words 'Mary', 'Sally', and 'Suzie'. Or take traffic lights: a commonly cited cultural example. The colours green, amber, and red stand in syntagmatic relation to each other, as do their respective cultural meanings: go, get ready, and stop. In contrast, a paradigmatic relation exists between the associated elements of these two syntagms or 'sentences'. Red and stop are part of the same paradigm: a red traffic light means to stop. This example illustrates the relational character of elements in a cultural grammar. Red does not mean stop in any absolute sense, but only within this particular framework. In a political context, for example, red means something else: Labour as opposed to (blue) Conservative or (yellow) Liberal Democrat on British politicians' rosettes; or Communist as opposed to (black) Anarchist, in flags carried by revolutionaries. (I should perhaps add that the usage of the term 'paradigm' in this paragraph is different from the Kuhnian usage explained in chapter 1; as Saussurians remind us, words also take their meanings from context.)

This leads to our final Saussurian distinction, that between signifier (the word or symbol which stands for something) and signified (the thing for which the word or symbol stands). These two elements together make up what Saussure (1974: 65–78) called the 'sign', whose salient characteristic is that it is 'arbitrary'. What he meant by this is that there is no natural relation between the phonological properties of a word and its meaning. If I speak Italian, I signify a four-footed, barking, family pet as *il cane*. If I speak French, I say *le chien*. If I speak German I say *der Hund*. If I speak English I say *the dog*. The phonetic makeup of the word, in each case, depends on which language I choose to speak. (Even the noise the animal makes is to some extent arbitrary: Italian dogs say *bau-bau*, French dogs say *oua-oua*, German dogs say *wau-wau*, and British and American dogs say *woof-woof* or *bow-wow*.) Likewise, symbolic elements of culture take their meaning both according to the given culture (say, French or British) and according to context within that culture. As Sir Edmund Leach used to say, a crown may stand for sovereignty (by metonymy – the part stands for the whole), or it may stand for a kind of beer (by metaphor – Brand X, 'the king of beers').

After Saussure

After Saussure, other linguists developed further ideas along the lines he suggested. The centre for such activity was Prague, where the Russian exile Roman Jakobson was based. Others in the 'Prague School' taught elsewhere, notably the Russian prince, Nikolai Trubetzkoy (see, e.g., Anderson 1985: 83–139). These 'functionalist' linguists, as they were sometimes called, developed complex theories of relations within phonological structures. Yet what is important for our purposes is their notion of 'distinctive features', which are analogous to what anthropologists have come to call structural or binary oppositions.

To simplify the basis of such theories, one can define the difference between two sounds in a particular language by the presence or absence of certain features. For instance, take the words *pin* and *bin* in English.

Table 8.1. *English voiced and unvoiced stops*

	Unvoiced	Voiced
Bilabial	p	b
Alveolar	t	d
Velar	k	g

P and *b* are produced in exactly the same part of the mouth (on the lips), and a deaf person reading lips cannot normally distinguish the two words. A foreigner with good hearing, but who speaks a language that does not make the *p/b* distinction, may not be able to 'hear' the difference either. More technically, English makes a distinction between the voiced bilabial stop, which linguists write /b/, and the unvoiced bilabial stop, written /p/. The difference is voicing. In saying 'bit', the English-speaker uses his or her voice on the initial sound, but does not do so in saying 'pit'. (Another subtle difference is the fact that the /p/ at the beginning of a word, in English, is also aspirated or breathed on, whereas the /b/ is not; but that need not concern us here.)

We can represent the structural relation between these two sounds along with other English 'stops' (consonants in which the flow of air in the mouth is stopped) as in table 8.1. The difference between *p* and *b* is replicated in the difference between *t* and *d*, which in turn resembles the difference between *k* and *g*. What distinguishes the first from the second in each pair is the absence of voicing. However, what distinguishes *p* from *t* from *k*, or *b* from *d* from *g*, is position in the mouth (front to back in each series, in terms of the point of articulation).

The recognition of the binary nature of voiceless/voiced distinction (i.e., the absence or presence of the feature 'voiced'), plus the recognition of the place of such a distinction in a wider system (in this case phonological) is what structuralism is all about. As we shall see, Lévi-Strauss' work in kinship, symbolism, mythology, and so on, is all based on similar principles. Fortuitously, Lévi-Strauss, a French Jew, spent the Second World War in exile in New York City, where members of the Prague School had also gone to escape Nazi persecution. Some of the early chapters of Lévi-Strauss' *Structural Anthropology* (Lévi-Strauss 1963 [1945 / 1951 / 1953 / 1958]: 29–97) bear a strong influence of the Prague School, and the first of these chapters (called 'Structural analysis in linguistics and in anthropology', pp. 31–54) was first published in 1945 in the first volume of the exiled Prague School's periodical, *Word: Journal of the Linguistic Circle of New York*.

Lévi-Strauss and structural anthropology

Lévi-Strauss was born in 1908, the son of an artist. He became an accomplished amateur musician, but his early academic training was in law and philosophy and his personal appraisal of his influences include geology, Freudian psychology, and Marxist theory. In 1934 he left France and went to Brazil to teach sociology, read the 1920 edition of Robert Lowie's *Primitive Society*, and ended up doing ethnographic fieldwork with the Bororo Indians.

The contrast between the famous final paragraph of *Primitive Society* (Lowie 1947 [1920]: 441) and Lévi-Strauss' anthropology is interesting. Lowie ends his book with a description of 'civilization' as 'that planless hodge-podge, that thing of shreds and patches' and looks forward to a day when 'the amorphous product' or 'chaotic jumble' will be put into a 'rational scheme'. The paragraph has been much debated, and in his preface to the 1947 edition Lowie (1947: ix) was to declare that it had 'no bearing on anthropological theory'. Yet Lévi-Strauss was to succeed where Lowie dared not, in finding (or creating) the most rational of all anthropological schemes. For Lévi-Strauss, the essence of culture is its structure. This is true both for particular cultures, with their own specific configurations, and for culture worldwide, in the sense that particular cultures exist as part of a system of all possible cultural systems. Nowhere is this more true than in *The Elementary Structures of Kinship* (Lévi-Strauss 1969a [1949]). Lévi-Strauss completed his manuscript in February 1947, exactly five months before Lowie's second preface.

Lévi-Strauss returned to France in 1939. He joined the Resistance, but his superiors thought it wiser for him, as a Jew, to leave for New York. There he met a number of the Central European linguists who were also in exile, borrowed ideas that they had developed within their discipline and applied them to anthropological data. However, it is worth remembering that much of his thought is derived directly from the tradition of Durkheim and Mauss (especially the latter, whose essay *The Gift* influenced his ideas on kinship as marital exchange). It is also important to see Lévi-Strauss as open to anthropological ideas from other countries, especially the American tradition from Boas (who, let us also remember, died in his arms), Lowie, and Kroeber. The complex web of influences on Lévi-Strauss' thinking to about 1960 is illustrated in figure 8.1.

Shortly after the War, Lévi-Strauss went back to France and established his tradition there. His Doctorat d'Etat thesis on 'the elementary structures of kinship' was published in French in 1949. The second edition appeared in French in 1967 and was finally translated for an English edition which came out two years later (Lévi-Strauss 1969a). He

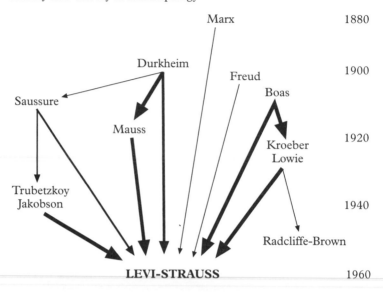

Figure 8.1 Influences on Lévi-Strauss until about 1960

followed *The Elementary Structures* with a widely read travelogue, based partly on his Brazilian fieldwork, *Tristes Tropiques* (1976 [1955]); two brilliant contributions to the study of classification, *Totemism* (1969b [1962]) and *The Savage Mind* (1966b [1962]); three collections of essays; works on language and on art; and four volumes known together as the *Mythologiques*. These latter, peculiarly titled works were published in French between 1964 and 1970 and in English between 1970 and 1981: *Le cru et le cuit* (translated as *The Raw and the Cooked*), *Du miel aux cendres* (*From Honey to Ashes*), *L'origine des manières de table* (*The Origin of Table Manners*), and *L'homme nu* (*The Naked Man*).

In the books on 'mythologics' or 'the science of myth' (as close as an English translation can come), Lévi-Strauss recounts and analyses 813 Amerindian myths, from Lowland South America to the North West Coast of North America. Their essence is contained in a fine, short work, based on radio talks Lévi-Strauss made in Canada in 1977, *Myth and Meaning* (1978a). As Lévi-Strauss spoke this one, rather than wrote it, and as its original is in English rather than French, it is much easier to follow than some of his other works. He wrote many of these in a rather dense academic French, and his translators have almost always attempted to render them as literally as possible. *Myth and Meaning* and *Tristes Tropiques* are easy to read, *The Savage Mind* is perhaps the most inspiring and indicative of his theoretical perspective, while *The Elementary Structures of Kinship* represents structuralist anthropology at its most extreme. In later years, Lévi-Strauss has produced further books on North West Coast mythology, as well as an intriguing text on human aesthetic sensibilities explored through the structural analysis of works of art and music (Lévi-Strauss 1997 [1993]).

Structuralism, pattern, and ideas

Structuralism in its widest sense is all about pattern: how things which at first glance appear to be unrelated actually form part of a system of interrelating parts. In structuralist theory, the whole is seen as greater than the sum of the parts, and most wholes can be broken down by appeal to the idea of distinctive features or binary oppositions. The presence or absence of one particular feature, in culture as in language, can explain a great deal. Structuralism in its 'purest' Lévi-Straussian sense shares this notion with structural (or functional) linguistics, and also with the cognitive anthropology which developed out of the Boasian tradition in North America in the 1950s and 1960s (see chapter 7). The distinctive feature of Lévi-Strauss' own contribution has been his search for the structure of all possible structures. His anthropology represents a culmination of the principle of psychic unity, or as Lévi-Strauss calls it, *l'esprit humain* – a term sometimes loosely translated as 'collective unconscious' (in opposition to Durkheim's 'collective consciousness').

Structuralism in anthropology concerns not merely social structure or structural form in their Radcliffe-Brownian senses, but also the structure of ideas. In Lévi-Strauss' work especially, structures are said to be built on a rational rather than an empirical foundation. That is, a Lévi-Straussian thinks out the logical possibilities for something, and only then looks for examples in ethnography. Take one of Lévi-Strauss' own analogies: the structure of crystals (Lévi-Strauss 1966a: 16). When a physicist studies the mathematical properties of a crystal, he or she is probably not concerned with specific real crystals (which will have flaws in them), but rather with some ideal, perfect crystal. The formation of real crystals is dependent on the effects of variations in heat and pressure, the presence of foreign bodies, and so on. One does not find an absolutely perfect crystal in nature; one finds it in the mind. Lévi-Strauss, therefore, is concerned with ideal structures of society, and in two senses: (1) in the sense of what is in *his* mind, and (2) in the sense of what is in the minds of the people with whom ethnographers work. Not surprisingly, other anthropologists did not take much to the first sense, but they have taken to the second. Yet it is the first sense which is more interesting here. In

Lévi-Strauss' vision, it is important for the anthropologist to hold a view of society which takes in every logical possibility.

It need hardly be said that Lévi-Strauss' output has been varied, complex, and often obscure to the uninitiated, but let me illustrate his contribution through three classic examples: elementary structures of kinship, the culinary triangle, and the Oedipus myth.

Elementary structures of kinship

In his early work (1969a [1949]) Lévi-Strauss was concerned with how rules of marriage affect, and even create, social structure. His 'alliance theory' (*alliance* being a French word for marriage) was set against the then current emphasis in British anthropology on 'descent theory', and true to form he sought to explain descent groups not as the basis of society but as elements in relations of marital exchange which exist between the groups.

As we saw in chapter 3, Lévi-Strauss argued in *The Elementary Structures* that the incest taboo is the essence of culture, and he virtually equated this taboo with the rules governing marriage. He then defined the relations between all human kinship systems, partly by exploring the nature of 'elementary' systems and partly by recourse to the ways in which ethnographic details of 'complex' systems can be seen as reflections of 'elementary' principles of kinship. Essentially, elementary structures are those with positive marriage rules (one must or should marry someone belonging to a particular class of kin, e.g., that of the cross-cousin), while complex structures are those with negative marriage rules (one must not or should not marry someone belonging to a particular class of kin, such as close relatives or members of one's own clan). It does not matter whether we are talking about 'real' or 'classificatory' cross-cousins, because in fact these are imaginary structures. Likewise, it matters little whether people really marry the way they are supposed to marry. Lévi-Strauss was concerned with the 'system of systems' which entails all logical possibilities, and with the formal, almost mathematical relationship of one system to another. He was not directly concerned with the operations of real kinship systems, because no society ever reaches the level of perfection described in his scheme – a point which was lost on his British and British-trained followers-turned-critics (cf. Lévi-Strauss 1966a; Korn 1973; Needham 1973). In more general terms, Lévi-Strauss' structuralism is mainly concerned with culture as an abstraction – not people's actual behaviour, but the idealized pattern it approximates.

Figure 8.2 shows the relations among kinship systems according to Lévi-Strauss' theory of alliance. I should add, though, that this is my

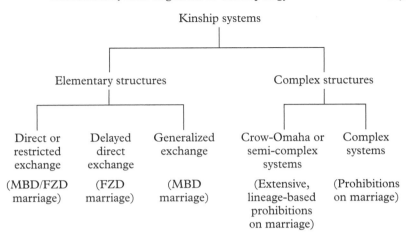

Figure 8.2 Lévi-Strauss' classification of kinship systems

preferred, simplified representation of the essence of his theory. Lévi-Strauss' own diagrams, representing relations between descent and residence (1969a: 216) and cycles of exchange (1969a: 465), are rather different.

Elementary structures include systems of direct exchange, where a group may 'take' wives from the same group it 'gives' wives to. The simplest type is one involving marriage between a man and his mother's brother's daughter (MBD) or father's sister's daughter (FZD), as in some parts of South America and Australia. Elementary structures also include systems of delayed direct exchange. Repeated father's sister's daughter marriage would, if it could be sustained in a real society, create such a structure. However, as Lévi-Strauss' chief critic among alliance theorists, Rodney Needham (1962), showed, such societies remain ethnographically rare if not non-existent. This is for rather technical reasons – among these the demographic unlikelihood of people keeping track of cross-cutting lineage and generational ties when no advantage to them or their society would be gained. In contrast, systems of generalized exchange, such as those involving marriage to the category of the mother's brother's daughter, are very common in parts of Asia. Here it is not necessary to keep track of generation, because one may repeat the marriage of one's parents. For example, if I as a male member of Group A marry a woman of Group B, my son (also Group A by patrilineal descent) may marry a woman from Group B too (such as his actual mother's brother's daughter or anyone classified as such).

Complex structures comprise those systems of Europe, Japan, most of

Africa, and so on, where no such 'elementary' patterns are to be found: one marries anyone, provided he or she is not a close relative. However, some societies, especially in Native North America and West Africa, have such an extensive array of negative marriage rules that their systems, from an individual though not a lineage point of view, come to resemble those of generalized exchange. For example, among the Samo of Burkina Faso, a man must not marry a member of his own patrilineal group, or his mother's, his father's mother's, or his mother's mother's patrilineal group. These 'semi-complex' or 'Crow-Omaha' systems (called after two Native North American peoples) thus lie in-between the more typically complex and the elementary ones (see Héritier 1981: 73–136).

Lévi-Strauss' work on kinship had a profound effect on British anthropology in the 1950s and 1960s, as Leach, Needham, and others sought to apply his methods to the study of particular kinship systems based on alliance. The British structuralists antagonized both Lévi-Strauss, through their rejection of his abstract search for universal patterns, and the structural-functionalists, through their emphasis on alliance over descent (see, e.g., Barnard and Good 1984: 67–78, 95–104). While few in Britain or North America accepted Lévi-Strauss' emphasis on universal structures of kinship in the human mind, the empirical basis of his theory was widely debated (cf., e.g., Hiatt 1968; Lévi-Strauss 1968).

The culinary triangle

One of the most indicative of Lévi-Strauss' excursions into the universality of the human mind is that of our second example: the 'culinary triangle', based on Jakobson's 'consonant triangle' and 'vowel triangle'. Lévi-Strauss first published on the idea in an article in 1965, and this was followed by several discussions, notably in the conclusion to the third volume of the *Mythologiques* (Lévi-Strauss 1978b [1968]: 471–95).

Lévi-Strauss claims that whereas the relations between consonants *p*, *t*, and *k*, and between vowels *u*, *i*, and *a*, can be defined according to relative loudness and pitch, similar relations between states of food substances and between styles of cooking can be defined according to degree of transformation and the intervention of culture. The argument is obscure but interesting. In the 'primary form', the two axes, normal/transformed and nature/culture, distinguish raw from cooked from rotted food (see figure 8.3). In the 'developed form', these same axes distinguish roasted from smoked from boiled food. In terms of means, roasting and smoking are natural processes, while boiling is cultural in that it needs water and a container. In terms of ends, roasting and boiling are natural (boiling is a process similar to rotting), while smoking is cultural (cooked, as opposed

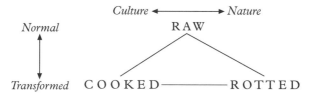

PRIMARY FORM

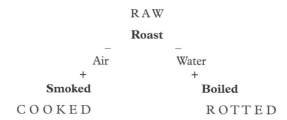

DEVELOPED FORM

RAW

Roast

Air   Water
+   +
Smoked   **Boiled**
COOKED   ROTTED

Figure 8.3 The culinary triangle

to raw or rotted). Boiling and roasting of meat are further contrasted in that boiling conserves all the juices (and therefore is naturally plebeian), and roasting destroys some of the meat (and in hierarchical societies, it is associated with high status – the wealthy can afford to be wasteful). While the culinary triangle is one of the most famous examples of structuralist interpretation in anthropology, unfortunately Lévi-Strauss' attempts to generalize about egalitarianism and hierarchy have only lead to puzzlement and ridicule (see Leach 1970: 28–34).

Leach (1976b: 55–9) once analysed aspects of costume and colour symbolism in the same way, but there is a crucial difference between his thinking and that of Lévi-Strauss. Lévi-Strauss' argument is intended to apply universally, whereas Leach's is both comparative and culture-specific. In India, for example, a bride traditionally wears a multi-coloured sari, and a widow wears a white sari. In the West, a bride traditionally wears a white dress, and a widow wears a black dress. The cultural rules are different, though in each case colour symbolizes an activity. Moreover, we cannot say merely that white is for marriage or life, and black is for death in Western culture taken as a whole. In some Christian churches, a priest or minister wears white or coloured garments when engaged in ritual activities, and black in non-ritual contexts. In other Christian churches, the equivalent person may wear black when engaged in ritual activities and ordinary, multi-coloured clothes otherwise. The wearing of white or black in these cases is not only culture-dependent; it is also dependent on very specific culturally significant activities. This is where British structuralism, which emphasizes cultural diversity as well as cross-cultural commonalities of social and symbolic structures, parts company with Lévi-Straussian structuralism with its emphasis on cultural universals embedded in the psychic unity of humankind.

The Oedipus myth

Our third example is Lévi-Strauss' analysis of the myth of Oedipus. There are, of course, a number of different versions of the story, and there are related myths which, in true *Mythologiques* fashion, can be further analysed as permutations of the key myth. Leach (1970: 62–82) does this in his well-known rendition. Here I will recount the version implied by Lévi-Strauss (1963 [1955]: 213–18), with his Latinized Greek names for the protagonists, and simply outline his central explanation.

The main characters are all related (see figure 8.4). Cadmos is the son of the king of Phoenicia. His sister, Europa, is carried off by Zeus, king of the gods, so Cadmos is sent to look for her. However, the Delphic oracle tells him to stop and follow a cow, then to build a city where the cow stops. So he does. Where the cow stops, he founds the city of Thebes. Later, Cadmos kills a dragon. He sows the teeth of the dragon onto the ground, and up come the Spartoi (or *sparti*, which means 'sown'), born from the teeth. Five of the Spartoi help Cadmos to build Thebes. Then they kill each other.

Cadmos subsequently has other exploits, marries a goddess, and has five children, among them Polydorus, who becomes king of Thebes. Polydorus has a son called Labdacos, who succeeds him. Labdacos has a son called Laios, and Laios marries Jocasta. Laios is told by an oracle that he will have a son who will kill him, so, when Oedipus (his son) is born, Laios leaves him exposed, tied to the ground by his foot, on top of a hill. Eventually, a shepherd finds Oedipus and takes him in, and Oedipus is adopted by Polybus, king of Corinth. Later Oedipus is told by the oracle that he will kill his father, so he vows never to return to Corinth again. Instead, he goes to Thebes.

On the way to Thebes he meets Laios (his true father), has a quarrel, and kills him. Later he meets the Sphinx, who has a habit of asking passers-by her riddle, and then killing them if they do not know the answer. None of them do, except Oedipus. The riddle is 'What is it that speaks with one voice, yet becomes four-footed, then two-footed, then three-footed?' The answer, Oedipus knows, is 'man' – who starts as a 'four-footed' baby, then walks on two feet, and finally, in old age, with a

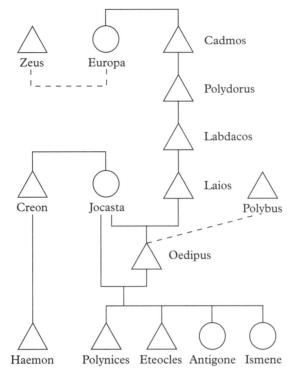

Figure 8.4 Kin relations among characters in the Oedipus myth

stick. So instead of the Sphinx killing Oedipus, Oedipus kills the Sphinx. (In some versions, the Sphinx kills herself.)

Oedipus' reward for killing the Sphinx is the hand in marriage of the widowed queen of Thebes, who is really his mother Jocasta. Oedipus means 'swollen foot'; and Jocasta realises he is 'the child grown into an adult' – the answer to the Sphinx's riddle. Realising too that she has committed incest with him, she kills herself. Then Oedipus blinds himself to become 'the old man' of the riddle. He goes off and is eventually swallowed into the earth, and Thebes comes under the rule of a new king, Creon, Jocasta's brother: Jocasta and Oedipus had had four children – Polynices, Eteocles, Antigone, and Ismene; Antigone and Ismene have gone off to lead Oedipus into the countryside and when they return, they find their brothers quarrelling – Eteocles is defending his crown, and Polynices is outside the city attacking it; eventually, both brothers die, and their mother's brother Creon becomes king. Now, Eteocles has killed his brother Polynices, whom Antigone was very fond of, so Creon, the new king, forbids Antigone to bury her brother Polynices because he,

Table 8.2. *Lévi-Strauss' analysis of the Oedipus myth*

I	II	III	IV
Cadmos seeks Europa who is ravished by Zeus			
		Cadmos kills the dragon	
	The Spartoi kill each other		
			Labdacos='lame'
	Oedipus kills Laios		Laios='leftsided'
		Oedipus kills the Sphinx	
			Oedipus='swollen foot'
Oedipus marries Jocasta despite taboo			
		Eteocles kills Polynices	
Antigone buries Polynices despite taboo			

having tried to take the crown from Eteocles, is now a traitor. There is an elaborate state funeral for Eteocles, but Polynices is condemned to lie unburied. Antigone, however, manages to sneak out and bury Polynices secretly. (In retribution, Creon has Antigone buried alive, walled up in a cave, though she manages to hang herself. Her beloved cousin Haemon, and his mother, commit suicide too, and the story goes on.)

Lévi-Strauss (1963 [1955]: 214) attempts to explain the complexities of the Oedipus myth with a simple diagram, the main features of which are shown in table 8.2. Column I gives details of violations of taboos, specifically taboos of incest and the burial of kin, or in Lévi-Strauss' words 'the overrating of kinship'. Column II gives details of 'the underrating of kinship', the same thing 'inverted': fratricide and parricide. Column III concerns the killing of monsters, by men. The dragon was a male monster who had to be killed in order for humankind to be born from the earth. The Sphinx was a female monster who was unwilling to allow humans to live. In Lévi-Strauss' words, this column represents the 'denial of the autochthonous origin of man' (in other words, the denial of aboriginal association of humankind with the earth). Column IV concerns the meaning of the names of some of the characters. All the meanings are related to difficulties in walking straight or standing upright. They imply that the humans who bear these names are still attached to the earth. The Spartoi were born of the earth without human aid; and in contrast, Oedipus was exposed at birth and staked to the ground. Therefore his foot became swollen, and he was, though born of woman, not fully separated from the earth. So this column, Lévi-Strauss says, indicates 'the persistence of the autochthonous origin of man'. In other words, column IV is the opposite of column III. What is more, column III stands in relation to column IV as column I stands in relation to column II.

The point of all this is that myths are made up of elements known as 'mythemes' (by analogy with phonemes), which myth-makers arrange and rearrange to create meaning, often unconsciously. Myths do not just tell stories; they express symbolic truths, sometimes specific to cultures or culture areas and sometimes universal. The same mythemes may be found in different myths, and may be transposed in myths which occur in different cultures. In any given telling, they may be 'read' either dia-chronically (here, top to bottom, one column at a time or through all the columns) or synchronically (across the columns, showing relations from column to column). Lévi-Strauss himself has always been content to see myth analysis for its own sake, though it has the potential to provide clues to other aspects of culture. It has indeed found use too in the analysis of dreams and dream sequences (e.g., Kuper 1979b).

Structuralism and national traditions of anthropology

While it is easy to think of Lévi-Strauss as the paradigmatic structuralist and his universalistic concerns the epitome of structuralist theory, his thought has both paralleled and influenced structuralist anthropologists working from different premises. Many do not accept his emphasis on psychic unity, favouring either regional or culture-specific foci.

Dutch structuralism emerged from studies of language, culture, and society, by Dutch academics and civil servants in the early twentieth-century Dutch East Indies (now Indonesia). This form of structuralism, described in chapter 4, emphasizes structures which are unique to culture areas or regions (e.g., J. P. B. de Josselin de Jong 1977 [1935]). J. P. B. de Josselin de Jong and other early Dutch structuralists developed their ideas partly independently of Lévi-Strauss, and even anticipated him, especial-ly in studies of kinship. Later Dutch anthropologists utilized Lévi-Straus-sian methods and replicated Lévi-Straussian studies of mythology and symbolism, generally within a regional framework. Such a regional ap-proach was characteristic of anthropology, especially in Leiden, for sev-eral decades.

Although Lévi-Strauss, rather like Lévy-Bruhl, has often commented on distinctions between 'elementary' structures and 'complex' ones, 'cold' societies and 'hot' ones (with reference to the relative 'heat' of historical change), and societies with mainly 'concrete' and those with 'abstract' thought, his entire approach is predicated on reasoning from the general to the specific. British structuralists have tended to work the other way round, and that is why even those Britons who have been much influenced by Lévi-Strauss' work have found themselves expressing fundamental disagreements with his methodology. This is somewhat true with Leach, but even more so with Rodney Needham (e.g., 1962) in his work on kinship. In the 1970s and 1980s as Professor of Social Anthropology at Oxford, Needham went on to write prolifically on language, religion, symbolic classification, emotion, and what might best be called anthropological philosophy. Sadly, after his disagreements with Lévi-Strauss Needham hardly ever, in this later, non-kinship work, referred to him. Some of Needham's works still carried structuralist theory with them (e.g. Needham 1979), while others obscured it or cast it aside in favour of an emotional variety of interpretivism almost unique to Needham's anthropology (e.g., 1981).

In other countries structuralism caught on in various ways between the 1950s and 1970s, but the Dutch and British traditions have remained the prime exemplars respectively of the regional and culture-specific versions. Belgian anthropology has some parallels with anthropology in Holland. Belgian structuralist Luc de Heusch has applied a regional-structural methodology to the study of political processes, kinship transformations, myth, sacrifice, and symbolism in Central Africa (e.g., de Heusch 1982 [1972]) and in Africa more widely (de Heusch 1985). Roy Willis, a British anthropologist and translator of both de Heusch and Lévi-Strauss, has done similar work in Central Africa (see Willis 1981) and has postulated a common structural basis (but with crucial culture-specific differences) for animal symbolism in African societies outside that region (Willis 1974). As we saw in chapter 6, Sir Edmund Leach and Marshall Sahlins also applied a structuralist approach to the study of social transformations. These writers have all added a historical dimension to Lévi-Strauss' structuralism, giving rise to theories of social transformation which both influenced and drew from processualist and Marxist anthropology from the 1950s to the 1980s.

Meanwhile back in France, Louis Dumont, a student of Mauss and one-time colleague of Evans-Pritchard at Oxford, developed a distinct but seminal, regional-structural understanding of social hierarchy in India (see especially Dumont 1980 [1967]). His work has had its followers, and its critics, in all countries in which the study of the Indian subcontinent is a particular focus. Meanwhile in the United States, studies in ethnoscience and cognitive anthropology developed through interests in human universals, linguistic models, and culture-specific semantic structures which parallel 'structuralism' proper in other countries. Lévi-Strauss himself has frequently praised Americans outside the structuralist tradition as we usually think of it, for their contributions towards his own theories. In Australia and South America too, the intrinsic structuralist thought of the indigenous populations has lent itself well to the development of structuralist ideas among local anthropologists.

Other French anthropologists developed different strands of thought, most broadly structuralist but others less so. Furthermore, the structure of French academia itself, based on research 'teams' (équipes) rather than broad-based teaching departments, fostered the creation of diverse ethnographic and theoretical micro-traditions. Lévi-Strauss and Dumont were key foci, but so too were, for example, Marxist theorists such as Maurice Godelier and Claude Meillassoux (chapter 6).

Concluding summary

Structuralism emphasizes form over content, and in a sense denies that there can be content without form. Structures in language at any level (e.g., phonological, morphological, syntactic) have potential analogies in culture of almost any sphere (e.g., kinship, cooking, mythology). Because of this, structuralism made an easy transition from the linguistics of Saussure and the Prague School to the anthropology of Lévi-Strauss and his followers.

While the influence of Lévi-Strauss has always remained paramount, structural anthropology is a complex tradition. Theoretical stances have always been defined partly by national concentrations of interest, though national boundaries have never been able to contain good ideas (or indeed bad ideas), and structuralism throughout its history has been both an international and a transdisciplinary phenomenon.

FURTHER READING

Culler's *Saussure* (1976) and Leach's *Lévi-Strauss* (1970) are good introductions to the respective ideas of Saussure and Lévi-Strauss. The best source on Saussure's key ideas, however, is the *Course* itself (Saussure 1974 [1916]).

The two volumes of Jakobson's selected writings (1962, 1971) give an idea of Jakobson's influence on Lévi-Strauss. Steiner's *The Prague School* (1982) is another useful source.

There are numerous biographical and analytical studies of Lévi-Strauss, such as those by Boon (1973), Badcock (1975), Sperber (1985 [1982]: 64–93), and Henaff (1998 [1991]). See also *Conversations with Claude Lévi-Strauss* (Lévi-Strauss and

Eribon 1991 [1988]), Lapointe and Lapointe's bibliography (1977), and Pouillon and Maranda's (1970) two-volume collection of papers dedicated to Lévi-Strauss. The A. S. A. conference volume, *The Structural Study of Myth and Totemism* (Leach 1967), also makes interesting reading. It includes Lévi-Strauss' famous analysis of the story of Asdiwal (a North West Coast myth recorded in four versions by Franz Boas), as well as several critiques of Lévi-Strauss' work.

A readable introduction to structuralism in anthropology generally is Leach's *Culture and Communication* (1976b). For a broader understanding of structuralism through key texts, see de George and de George's *The Structuralists: From Mauss to Lévi-Strauss* (1972). For references to poststructuralist and interpretivist critiques of structuralism, see chapters 9 and 10.

9   Poststructuralists, feminists, and (other) mavericks

The poststructuralists, feminists, and mavericks described in this chapter have in common a desire to move away from the more formalist ideas of functionalism and structuralism towards a looser, yet more complex, understanding of relations between culture and social action. The growing interest in power is represented in many of the works touched on here as well.

Poststructuralism occupies an ambiguous position in anthropology. On the one hand, it is in essence a critique of structuralist thought played out mainly in structuralist terms. That is, the poststructuralists, who have practised mainly outside social anthropology (in philosophy, literary criticism, history, and sociology), have offered critiques of Lévi-Strauss and other declared structuralist writers. At the same time, poststructuralists have pointed the way to the explanation of action, the scrutiny of power, and the deconstruction of the writer as a creator of discourses. Thus poststructuralism touches on the interests of transactionalists, Marxists and feminists, and postmodernists alike. In a loose sense, poststructuralism is a form of postmodernism, as structuralism is the primary form of 'late modernism' in anthropology (see chapter 10).

Feminism has its main roots in substantive, as opposed to grand theoretical, issues of sex roles and gender symbolism. However, over the last twenty years it has achieved the status of a theoretical paradigm not only in the substantive area of gender studies, but also more widely in anthropology. It has moved from a concern centrally with women and women's subordination *per se* to a more general commentary on power relations, symbolic associations, and other facets of society at large, as well as a discourse on issues such as reflexivity, the gender of the ethnographer, and therefore the place of the ethnographer in anthropological fieldwork. Thus it too has close links with much in the postmodern agenda, though not all feminists claim to be postmodernists nor all postmodernists, feminists.

It is often all too easy to think of anthropology as definable in terms of grand ideas, competing paradigms, and schools of thought. While these represent a substantial portion of 'anthropological theory' as it is commonly understood, there is nevertheless a place for the maverick. This is true above all on the fringes of structuralist thought, as thinkers have tried to integrate ideas of structure with those of action. Victor Turner and Sir Edmund Leach would certainly be contenders for the status of 'maverick eclectic' (see chapter 6), as would Rodney Needham (chapter 8), David Schneider and Ernest Gellner (chapter 10). For me though, Gregory Bateson and Mary Douglas stand out as especially relevant for treatment here. What they have in common with each other and with much in the poststructuralist and feminist movements is their use of structural (but dynamic) models to explain social action as embedded in culture.

Poststructuralism and anthropology

Poststructuralism, like structuralism, is a mainly French perspective and one which transcends the disciplines. Its adherents sometimes draw heavily on structuralism; indeed, the boundary between the two perspectives is not always a clear one. For me, the most salient feature of poststructuralism is a reluctance to accept the distinction between subject and object that is implicit in structuralist thought, especially that of Saussure.

The idea of 'poststructuralism' is most closely associated with the literary critic Jacques Derrida, whose writings include some direct criticism (and 'deconstruction') of Saussure and of Lévi-Strauss (see, e.g., Derrida 1976 [1967]). Others, more loosely definable as 'poststructuralists', include Marxist writer Louis Althusser, psychoanalyst Jacques Lacan, and sociologist-anthropologist Pierre Bourdieu. Finally, there is philosopher-historian Michel Foucault, who, along with Bourdieu, has had a profound effect on social anthropology over the last twenty years or more.

Derrida, Althusser, and Lacan

Although less important for anthropology today than the ideas of Bourdieu or Foucault, those of Derrida, Althusser, and Lacan have all had a marked impact in their own spheres of interest. Within anthropology, their impact has been most marked in feminist and late Marxist theory.

Derrida (e.g., 1976 [1967]; 1978 [1967]) broke with structuralism in an attempt to expose what he saw as the fallacy of any analysis which accepts the totality of a text as a unit of analysis. Any text, he argues, will entail contradictions. The Saussurian notion of 'difference' (referred to by post-Saussurian structuralists in terms of distinctive features or binary oppositions) is transformed into a complex concept where meaning is both 'different' (through *différence*, 'difference') and 'deferred' (through *différance* [*sic*], Derrida's neologism for this phenomenon). The double meaning of the French verb *différer* ('to differ', or 'to defer until later') captures for Derrida the contradictions entailed both in any synchronic analysis of meaning and in the Saussurian priority of speech over writing. Derrida's break with structuralism is also, in a sense, a break with modern Western thought in general and its quest for universal understandings. Texts refer simply to other texts, not to anything beyond that. The notion of 'intertextuality', or relations between texts, has implications for anthropology, especially in the aftermath of Clifford and Marcus' famous edited volume *Writing Culture* (1986), which will be discussed at length in the next chapter. Derrida's method of deconstructing texts has also influenced feminist attempts to understand cultural differences in the perception of male and female.

Of more direct influence on feminism and feminist anthropology, though, is the work of Lacan (1977 [1966]). His work stresses among other things the importance of language in defining identity, and the complexity of sexual identity through complementary images of male and female, and mother and child. Two famous notions of his have given both inspiration and cause for alarm in feminist circles: that 'woman does not exist' (in that there is no ultimate female essence) and 'woman is not whole' (in that a woman lacks a penis, which in turn symbolizes both all that is lacking in male ideology and the social status of women).

Althusser's writings, especially his *Reading 'Capital'* (Althusser and Balibar 1970 [1968]), present a curious mixture of structuralism and Marxism. He argues for a distinction between a 'surface' reading of Marx and a 'symptomatic' reading, the latter being a deeper and truer understanding of Marx's intention. By the latter sort of reading, it is argued, we can gain better insight into the nature of modes of production. This liberating idea was important for Marxist anthropology because it gave anthropologists greater scope to bend Marx's words while maintaining the premise of being true to Marx's intentions. In *For Marx* (1969 [1965]), Althusser considers the ways in which discourse and power enable modes of production to be reproduced through the generations. Here again, his work has proved useful to anthropologists trying to cope with relations between kinship, gender, and production (see, e.g., Meillassoux 1972; 1981 [1975]). Although perhaps more literally a structuralist than a poststructuralist, Althusser pushed at least some Marxist anthropologists towards a confrontation with (Marx's) texts and away from the latent Lévi-Straussian concerns of the structural Marxists (see chapter 6).

Bourdieu's practice theory

Pierre Bourdieu is Professor of Sociology at the Collège de France. Early in his career, as part of his military service, he taught in Algeria (incidentally, the birthplace of both Derrida and Althusser). This led to his ethnographic research on the Kabyles, a Berber people who live in the northern mountainous-coastal area of that country. He has long maintained two diverse research interests: education and social class in French society, and kinship and family organization in Kabyle society. Some of his work, especially in the former, involves a critique of the abuse of power by state authorities. However, he is best known in anthropological circles for his theoretical interest in 'practice', as exemplified in comments on Kabyle patrilateral parallel-cousin marriage, rituals, and the seasonal cycle. The diverse foci perhaps reflect his own 'practice' as both a sociologist of his own society and an anthropologist of an alien one (Reed-Donahay 1995).

The key texts in practice theory are *Outline of a Theory of Practice* (Bourdieu 1977 [1972]) and *The Logic of Practice* (Bourdieu 1990 [1980]). The argument is the same in both. Objective understanding misses the essence of practice, which is an actor's understanding. Structuralists from Saussure to Lévi-Strauss remain at the level of the model, while Bourdieu calls for engagement in the domain of performance. Likewise, distinctions like system/event, rule/improvization, synchronic/diachronic, and *langue/parole* are jettisoned in favour of a new order based on what he calls *habitus* (a Latin word meaning, loosely, 'habitat' or 'habitual state', especially of the body). In Bourdieu's view, the analysis of this should enable the anthropologist to understand the nature of power, symbolic capital, Mauss' 'gift', and more.

Bourdieu is essentially arguing against a static notion of structure. Crucially, habitus lies between the objective and the subjective, the collective and the individual. It is culturally defined, but its locus is the mind of the individual. Habitus is a kind of structure of social action by culturally competent performers. It is analogous to Noam Chomsky's (1965: 3–9) notion of linguistic 'competence', the idea that a native speaker has in his or her mind an intuitive model which generates 'performance' in the speech act. Instead of social institutions, habitus is made up of 'dispositions', which members of a culture know intuitively how to handle. Individuals make choices as to which dispositions to follow and when, according to their understanding of them within the habitus and their own place in the system of events.

Bourdieu variously defines habitus as 'the durably installed generative principle of regulated improvisations' (1977: 78) or 'the system of structured, structuring dispositions . . . always ordered towards practical functions' (1990: 52). Such systems function, he says:

> as principles of the generation and structuring of practices and representation which can be objectively 'regulated' and 'regular' without in any way being the product of obedience to rules, objectively adapted to their goals without presupposing a conscious aiming at ends or an express mastery of the operations necessary to attain them and, being all this, collectively orchestrated without being the product of the orchestrating action of a conductor. (Bourdieu 1977: 72; cf. 1990: 53)

Bourdieu's concern is to move social science away from an emphasis on rules, towards a theory of practice. Yet structure is still there, not so much a constraining structure, but an enabling structure (for those who know how to use it), one of choice.

However, individuals do not all have equal access to decision-making processes. This is where power comes in. Bourdieu's theory of power, implicit in his theory of practice, is that those people who can impose their 'practical taxonomy' of the world on others, by definition, wield power (see, e.g., Bourdieu 1977: 159–97). This may be done through teaching the young, through cultural domination, or through the 'symbolic violence' of, for example, entrusting servants with one's property (and thereby instilling in them one's own values). Bourdieu has been criticized, though, for not going far enough in recognizing individual consciousness. According to Jean Comaroff (1985: 5), Bourdieu's actors 'seem doomed to reproduce their world mindlessly, without its contradictions leaving any mark on their awareness – at least, until a crisis (in the form of culture contact or the emergence of class division) initiates a process of overt struggle'.

Such criticisms notwithstanding, Bourdieu has become one of the most widely cited and most admired figures in our discipline. Indeed Comaroff herself, in toying with the interplay between event, culture, structure, transformation, and consciousness, is building on Bourdieu's strengths as much as she is probing his weaknesses. Virtually all fieldworkers today aim to couple their Malinowskian or Boasian methodological basics (participant-observation, use of the native language, search for connections, and gathering of details over a long period) with a quest for the habitus which might explain the actions of their informants. In a sense, Bourdieu has succeeded where the Marxists failed. He has turned anthropological studies as a whole towards an interest in practice, while maintaining an implicit recognition of cultural diversity as at least one essence of the human condition.

Foucault's theory of knowledge and power

Michel Foucault was Professor of the History of Systems of Thought at the Collège de France. He wrote widely on the history of medicine (especially psychiatric medicine), penology, and sexuality. He argued consistently against a straightforward structuralist approach, though his theoretical focus changed in the course of his career. In the 1960s Foucault emphasized the absence of order in history and articulated the significance of Saussurian *parole* over *langue* (e.g., Foucault 1973 [1966]; 1974 [1969]). In other words, structures are not pre-existing, and discourse should be paramount over cultural grammar. What is more, order is created by the historian or social scientist who writes about an event, not by the actor in a given time and place.

In the following decade, Foucault came to focus on the ways in which power and knowledge are linked (e.g., 1977 [1975]). Power is not something to possess, but rather it is a capability to manipulate a system. In other words, neither social nor symbolic structures are to be taken for granted; nor should they be seen as culturally agreed schemata which each member of society understands in the same way. A related notion has been his idea of 'discourse'. While in linguistics, 'discourse' has generally held the meaning of 'continuous' speech (e.g., what might be analogous to a paragraph or longer segment in writing), in Foucauldian usage it is widened. Here it represents a concept involving the way people talk or write about something, or the body of knowledge implied, or the use of that knowledge, such as in the structures of power which were Foucault's overwhelming concern.

Power is a strong and growing interest in anthropology, and Foucault's influence is very wide. His idea of discourses of power is applicable in feminist theory and has also had great impact in studies of colonial and postcolonial domination of the Third World and Fourth World by the West (see, e.g., Cheater 1999). As Bruce Knauft has put it: 'The trend in anthropology has been to invoke Foucault as a dependable and general-purpose critic of Western epistemological domination' (Knauft 1996: 143). Foucault's ideas have struck a chord particularly with the likes of James Clifford, George Marcus, and others part of or influenced by the *Writing Culture* phenomenon. As with Bourdieu's impact, that of Foucault has altered the direction of anthropology in both fieldwork interests and high theoretical analysis.

Feminism in anthropology

The feminist critique concerns both gender relations in particular societies and the idea of gender as a structuring principle in human society generally (H. L. Moore 1988: vii). While the former may be regarded as essentially a substantive issue, the latter is a theoretical one and therefore merits the same treatment as, for example, Marxism, poststructuralism, or postmodernism – all perspectives with links to feminism in anthropology.

From gender studies to feminist anthropology

In her magnificent overview of feminist anthropology, Henrietta Moore (e.g., 1988: 1) goes to great lengths to point out that although the impetus for feminist anthropology may have been the neglect of women as objects of ethnographic scrutiny, the real issue is one of representation. Women were long represented as 'muted' (as Edwin Ardener put it), as profane, as objects of marital exchange, and so on, and not as prime actors in the centre of social life.

Female anthropologists have been present since the early part of the twentieth century, but through most of that century they did fieldwork as 'honorary males' in small-scale societies. Gradually the significance of females in society became known in the discipline, as more female ethnographers took to describing female roles in activities such as subsistence and (women's) ritual. By the early 1970s, male bias came to be widely recognized: including that of cultures being studied, that of anthropology itself, and that of Western culture generally (H. L. Moore 1988: 1–2). Feminist anthropologists took as their task the deconstruction of these various forms of male bias. So feminist anthropology grew from 'the anthropology of women', the crucial difference being that it is the notion of gender relations and not merely what women do which is central to the feminist enterprise (see H. L. Moore 1988: 186–98). As Moore puts it: 'Feminist anthropology . . . formulates its theoretical questions in terms of how economics, kinship and ritual are experienced and structured through gender, rather than asking how gender is experienced and structured through culture' (1988: 9).

One of the key figures in the early development of feminist anthropology was a man. Edwin Ardener (1989 [1975]: 127–33) argued that dominant groups in society maintain control over expression. Therefore 'muted groups', as he called them, remained in relative silence. Women are the most significant such group in any society, both numerically and otherwise. Even where women are literally vocal, their expression is inhibited by the fact that they do not speak the same 'language' as the dominant group: women and men have different worldviews. Ardener further suggests that anthropology itself is male dominated, but for subtle reasons. Anthropologists are all either male or (in the case of female anthropologists) trained in a male-biased discipline, itself the product of a male culture.

Feminist writers in anthropology have pointed out problems in privileging women as ethnographers of women (see, e.g., Milton 1979; Strathern 1981; 1987a). Moore (1988: 5–10) analyses these problems, which she groups into three kinds: ghettoization, the assumption of a 'universal woman', and ethnocentrism or racism. The first set of problems stems from the idea of the anthropology of women as almost a subdiscipline. For Moore it is a critique of the discipline as a whole, an all-embracing theoretical perspective, and not a specialized branch of the subject.

Moore's second set is related to the erroneous assumption that women are everywhere much the same, as if biological difference itself were enough to create universal cultural differences between men and women. The category 'woman', she argues, needs more careful scrutiny than that, and the mere fact that an ethnographer and her subject may both be women is not enough to assume that they see the notion of 'woman' in the same way. In short, feminist anthropology should rely on ethnography and not on bland but bold assumptions.

The third set of problems is related to the feminist notion of experience. Just as 'economics, kinship and ritual are experienced . . . through gender' (Moore 1988: 9), so too are ethnicity and race. People have multiple identities, but these are not separate but interrelated. A black woman from London, for example, is not just a black, a female, and a Londoner. Her identity is made up of an intricate and simultaneous contextualization of all these statuses and others. Such a view contrasts, if subtly, with the notion of a complex of multiple but separate identities as understood in the traditional functionalist anthropology, for example, of Radcliffe-Brown:

The human being as a person is a complex of social relationships. He is a citizen of England, a husband and a father, a bricklayer, a member of a particular Methodist congregation, a voter in a certain constituency, a member of his trade union, an adherent of the Labour Party, and so on. (Radcliffe-Brown 1952 [1940]: 194)

Gender as a symbolic construction

Anthropologists writing on gender have approached the subject with two perspectives (which are not necessarily mutually exclusive): gender as a symbolic construction, and gender as a complex set of social relations (H. L. Moore 1988: 12–41). The former view is associated, for example, with Edwin Ardener's 'Belief and the problem of women' (1989 [1972]:

72–85), and Sherry Ortner's 'Is female to male as nature is to culture?' (1974).

Consider Ortner's essay. She argues that women everywhere are associated with nature. Her grounds are that the biological fact that women, not men, give birth, bestows on them that universal association. Since every culture (she says) makes a symbolic distinction between nature and culture, men will therefore be associated with culture. She argues further that women's reproductive role tends to confine them to the domestic sphere. Thus women (and to some extent children) represent nature (and the private), while men represent culture (and the public). It is important to note, though, that it is not *her* belief that women are associated with nature in any intrinsic way. Rather it is a cultural-universal belief founded on the structural opposition between nature and culture. Thus Ortner sets herself apart from her analysis.

While Ortner's essay does not represent the basis of all feminist anthropology, it was a major catalyst for debate. Many feminists have indeed been critical of her model, and some have been able to counter it with ethnographic cases which do not fit. Foremost among these are the 'simple societies' described by Jane Collier and Michelle Rosaldo (1981). They point out that hunting-and-gathering societies in Southern Africa, Australia, and the Philippines do not associate childbirth or motherhood with 'nature'. Nor do they associate women simply with reproduction and its aftermath. These societies are essentially egalitarian, and women share child-rearing with men.

Gender as a complex set of social relations

Collier and Rosaldo's perspective is characteristic of the idea of gender as a complex of social relations. This sort of perspective tends to emphasize the social over the cultural, and often seeks the boundary between egalitarian and male-dominant societies. The problem of supposed universal subordination of women is obviously inherent in it, for if there are egalitarian societies then women are not always subordinate. In an overview of women, culture, and society, Rosaldo (1974) argued simply that association with the domestic sphere, rather than with nature, made women subordinate.

Marxist feminists have pushed this case most strongly (see, e.g., Sacks 1979). Eleanor Leacock (1978) went further than others in asserting that previous writers had ignored history, especially the fact that colonialism and world capitalism have distorted relations between men and women. In this well-argued paper, she suggests that the public/private distinction was absent among foragers in pre-contact times, and women's subordina-

tion only came about with the growth of private property. Her research on the history as well as the ethnography of the Montagnais-Naskapi of Labrador showed many changes in political authority since the earliest, seventeenth-century, reports. Further research has shown that the same is true in other parts of the world too, notably in Aboriginal Australia.

There have been many attempts to explain universal male dominance, and some have combined the idea of gender as a symbolic construction with that of gender as embedded in social relations. One of the most interesting for its extreme stance is that of Salvatore Cucchiari (1981). Like Knight (see chapter 3), Cucchiari argues that it is possible to reconstruct the prehistory of gender relations. Very simply, his model supposes that in the beginning not only was there equality between the sexes, but also a lack of gender distinction (and bisexuality as a norm). The earliest differentiation was between categories 'Forager' and 'Child Tender', not 'male' and 'female'. However, as people became aware of 'proto-women's' exclusive abilities to bear and nurse children, these proto-women were made a sacred category. Child Tenders became proto-women. From this developed exclusive heterosexuality (as an ideal), sexual jealousy, and sexual control – leading ultimately to universal male dominance.

While most feminists would hold back from such speculations, the search for origins remains permissible in the anthropology of gender. Such big questions as the origin of gender hierarchy link up with feminist interests in exposing power relations of all kinds, with gender differentiation taken as the basis for many. Feminism in anthropology has also helped to reorient much in kinship studies, especially in light of Marxist critiques (see Meillassoux 1981 [1975]). On another front, there is much in broadly feminist anthropology to challenge the image of male dominance as portrayed in traditional ethnographies, and new methods of ethnographic portrayal have resulted in quite different pictures of social life, for example those of Lila Abu-Lughod writing on Bedouin women (e.g., Abu-Lughod 1986). Indeed, that same ethnographer, citing feminist critiques and perspectives of 'halfies' (defined as those 'whose national or cultural identity is mixed by virtue of migration, overseas education, or parentage'; 1991: 137), argues that the critique makes the concept of culture itself problematic. She suggests that anthropologists should write 'against culture' in order to battle against the hierarchies it implies.

Embodiment

Coming out of both feminist theory and Foucault's interests has been a new focus on the body as a source of identity, which logically confounds

the separation of sex and gender. The sex/gender distinction actually reproduces some distinctions it serves to question (Yanagisako and Collier 1987).

'Embodiment', even beyond its gender aspects, is an area of increasing interest. In particular, Thomas Csordas (1990; cf. 1994) has built on Merleau-Ponty's (1962) notion that embodiment is indeterminate. His view is much more radical than the notion of the 'anthropology of the body' which emerged in the 1970s. The body is more than the sum of its parts. What is more, one can have 'multiple bodies', for example, physical and social (see Douglas 1969); or individual, social, and body politic (respectively body as self, body as symbol, e.g., of nature, and external control of the body; Scheper-Hughes and Lock 1987).

Andrew Strathern and Pamela Stewart (1998) compare embodiment to communication as modes for the understanding of ritual. In their terms, the embodiment perspective emphasizes the putative effects of ritual on the performers, while the communication perspective emphasizes the social context and the context involving the spiritual powers to which the rituals are directed. Their definition is quite straightforward: 'In the broadest sense, we take the term embodiment to refer to the anchoring of certain social values and dispositions in and through the body . . .' (1998: 237). Others have utilized the concept to explore aspects not only of power and gender, but even species. Thus for Donna Haraway (1988; 1991), both gender and feminism are about embodiment, while embodiment is further both individual and collective, the latter in the sense that it defined the collectivity, for example, of all female human (or primate) bodies.

Two maverick eclectics

My focus in this last section is on just two scholars, whose maverick status is heightened by the fact that neither ended their careers in conventional anthropological writings nor even within anthropology departments. All the same, Gregory Bateson and Mary Douglas are both brilliant exemplars of anthropological theory's contribution to social thought. They remain significant for our discipline, while nevertheless neither leading from the front nor following the trends of their times.

Structure and conflict: Bateson on national character

Bateson was one of the most fascinating figures of twentieth-century scholarship. He neither built up an institutional following nor even gained the conventional recognition of close colleagues and students. Yet he was

influential because everyone from Radcliffe-Brown to the postmodernists admired his ability to make sense of what to others was simply the vagary of culture.

Gregory Bateson's father, William Bateson, was a founder of modern genetics, and Gregory's early interests were also in biology. He studied zoology and anthropology at Cambridge, and in 1927 he went off to do anthropological fieldwork with the Iatmul of New Guinea. There he met Margaret Mead, whom he eventually married and with whom he later carried out field research on Bali. Like W. H. R. Rivers, Bateson practised as a psychiatrist, working especially with alcoholics and schizophrenics. He spent much of his later life studying dolphins. He was also heavily involved in the Green movement, and in radical approaches to education at all levels.

Beginning with his ethnographic study of the *naven* ceremony of the Iatmul (Bateson 1958 [1936]), Bateson cultivated a sense of understanding the bizarre through the analysis of form in relation to action. The ceremony lent itself well to such a broadly structural approach, involving as it did transvestism, ritual homosexuality, and the purposeful and (in the ritual context) permissible violation of taboos which (in other contexts) regulate kinship and gender relations. My main example here, though, is drawn from Bateson's essay 'Morale and national character', based on a comparison between aspects of German, Russian, English, and American culture during the Second World War (Bateson 1973 [1942]: 62–79). Let us look at just one of his comparisons: that between the English and the Americans as he (an Englishman working in America) perceived them.

Basically the problem is this: if you put an American in a room with an Englishman, the American will do all the talking. What is more, the American will talk mainly about himself (let us assume, as Bateson did, that these two characters are both male). The Englishman will regard the American as boastful and will resent it. The American will resent the fact that the Englishman appears to have nothing to contribute to the conversation. If the Englishman does talk about himself, he will understate things. He will try to be modest, but in doing that the American will only see in him a false modesty or arrogance. So, both the American and the Englishman are behaving in the way they think is appropriate. However, the Englishman sees the American as boastful, and the American sees the Englishman as arrogant.

Why is this? Bateson's answer rests on two sets of oppositions: dominance v. submission, and exhibitionism v. spectatorship. The dominance/submission opposition, he says, has a clear association with parenthood (dominance) and childhood (submission), while the exhibitionism/spec-

Table 9.1. *Bateson's solution to a problem of national character*

Activity	English interpretation	American interpretation
exhibitionism	dominance (parentlike behaviour)	submission (childlike behaviour)
spectatorship	submission (childlike behaviour)	dominance (parentlike behaviour)

tatorship opposition is variable in the manner in which it is mapped onto dominance and submission. This is illustrated in table 9.1.

By way of further explanation, Bateson suggests this. In England (at least in the upper-middle-class household of the early twentieth century), when the father comes home from work he talks to his children. The children sit and listen. Therefore exhibitionism (doing all the talking) indicates a parentlike role; in other words, dominance. Spectatorship (doing the listening) indicates a childlike role; in other words, submission. In America, says Bateson, the opposite is true. When the father comes home from work, he listens to his children who tell him, and their mother, what they have been up to at school. The parents sit and listen. Thus in America, exhibitionism is associated with childlike behaviour, and spectatorship is associated with parentlike behaviour. These associations are carried through into later life. So, when the adult, male American meets his English counterpart, he tries to show off all his knowledge, abilities, wealth, or whatever. The American, subconsciously perhaps, perceives himself as being submissive and childlike. He treats the Englishman as a parent-figure, which in both cultures is a means of being polite. For the Englishman, exhibitionism is a sign of dominance, and he incorrectly believes the American is trying to be dominant.

Implicit in all this is a distinction between two concepts which Bateson called by the Greek words *eidos* and *ethos*. Culture is made up of both (see, e.g., Bateson 1958 [1936]: 123–51, 198–256). In Bateson's usage, eidos is what we more generally call 'form' or 'structure' (cf. Kroeber 1963 [1948]: 100–3). The sets of oppositions he describes in his study of national character (spectatorship v. exhibitionism; dominance v. submission) are part of the eidos of American and of English culture. Ethos refers to the customs, the traditions, also the feelings, the collective emotions, either of a given culture or of a given event which is defined according to cultural norms. More specifically it refers to their distinctive character or spirit. These concepts are related, and at least in his national-character study ethos seems to depend for its cross-cultural definition on the relation between the eidos of one culture and that of another.

The methods Bateson used seem particularly suited to the analysis of conflict and potential conflict, and he developed a similar approach to understanding conflict between, for example, male and female among the Iatmul, and East and West in the nuclear arms race. Similarly, Canadian anthropologist Elliott Leyton (1974) has analysed conflict in Northern Ireland in terms of direct, eidotic oppositions between aspects of the ethos of Nationalist and Unionist cultures (or Catholic and Protestant) in Northern Ireland. Anthropologists from Northern Ireland have criticized Leyton since then for oversimplifying, as certainly Bateson did on Americans and Englishmen, but the point of this kind of analysis is that conflict is often better understood in terms of structures and processes of interaction than in terms of ethnographic detail alone.

Structure and action: Douglas on grid and group

Mary Douglas' approach is essentially structuralist but played out within a dynamic framework. Like Bateson and Bourdieu, she is interested in the relation between individual actions and the cultural frameworks within which action is interpreted. Douglas read philosophy, politics, and economics at Oxford, and subsequently studied anthropology there under Evans-Pritchard (see chapter 10). She did fieldwork with the Lele of Kasai Province, in the Congo, and taught for many years at University College London. She later became Director of the Russell Sage Foundation in New York and taught at Princeton and Wisconsin, before retiring to London.

Douglas' early work was quite straightforward, with special interests in economics and religion. The latter led her to studies of purity and pollution among the Lele, among the ancient Hebrews, and in Britain. Her first famous book (though not her first book) was *Purity and Danger* (1966). There she examined concepts such as these and hinted at the form of analysis which she was soon to develop in *Natural Symbols* (1969): *Natural Symbols* and most of her many subsequent publications have utilized the framework she calls 'grid/group analysis' (see also, e.g., Douglas 1978; 1982; 1996).

Grid/group analysis is a method of describing and classifying cultures and societies, aspects of culture or society, individual social situations, individual actions, or even individual preferences. The principle is that virtually anything one might want to classify in relation to its alternatives can be measured along two axes, which are called respectively 'grid' and 'group' (figure 9.1). However, Douglas and her followers are not so much concerned with quantitative measurement as with structural opposition,

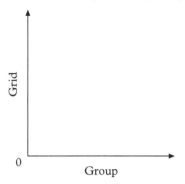

Figure 9.1 The grid and group axes

in other words the presence or absence of high grid or high group constraints.

The *grid* dimension is the measure of 'insulation' or 'constraint' imposed not by group cohesion, but by individual isolation. To be low on the grid scale is to have freedom to act or the scope to interact with others as equals; to be high is to be insulated or constrained in decision-making by the social system. The *group* dimension is the measure of group cohesion, whether people in a group do everything together (high group) or act individually (low group). Douglas' interest lies in determining and accounting for the relative presence or absence of high-grid and high-group features, rather than the establishment of precise co-ordinates along the axes. Thus there are only four logical possibilities, each represented by a different 'box' (figure 9.2). She conventionally labels the boxes with the letters A to D, though unfortunately her usage differs from publication to publication (with no fewer than three different labelling systems). The one shown here is the system used in her booklet *Cultural Bias* (1978), the publication which remains the best introduction to the theory.

Douglas asserts that her method can be used for the study of everything from witchcraft to food preferences (to take examples respectively from her early and recent writings). One which I think brings out the theory particularly clearly is the working environment of research scientists (see Bloor and Bloor 1982). It matters little whether we are talking about astronomers or zoologists, but let us suppose all the scientists are in the same field, say medical research. The differences between them are those of their respective structural positions in their subculture, or their 'sociology' (as Douglas sometimes puts it). They may differ also in the way they

B	C
High grid **Low group**	**High grid** **High group**
Isolation, by choice or compulsion	Strongly incorporated, with hierarchy
A	**D**
Low grid **Low group**	**Low grid** **High group**
Active individualism, often with competition	Strongly incorporated, without hierarchy

Figure 9.2 The grid and group boxes

see their work environment, their 'cosmology'. Let us call the protagon-ists Alice, Ben, Carlos, and Deborah (respectively Boxes A, B, C, and D).

Alice is an independent researcher. She goes to work whenever she wants and takes holidays when she chooses. She gets paid according to the amount of work she does, and works on whatever project she wants to. She is not constrained by outside forces; therefore she is *low grid*. She is also *low group* because she is not constrained by group conformity. She belongs to various professional associations, and also to different clubs outside her profession. Sometimes she chooses solitude; sometimes she joins in group activities. Either way, she does not follow the crowd. She is equally free to associate with different groups or with none.

Ben is high grid, low group. He works for a drug company and is on a five-year contract to discover a cure for a rare disease. He has to submit reports to the company every week, detailing what he has been doing. He has to keep accurate records of his activities on a minute-by-minute basis, and is expected to put in exactly forty-eight hours a week. He is therefore constrained by the forces of his high grid predicament. He is also low group. This could mean that he has nobody else working with him. The constraints of time keep him from joining groups, either formal or infor-mal. Unlike Alice, Ben is not low group by choice, but is forced there by the kind of work he does. While all the other boxes have their natural incumbents, Box B is 'unfriendly' (Douglas' term) to almost any person-ality type, and Ben is not happy.

Carlos is high grid, high group. He works in a hierarchical university department. Like Ben, he is constrained by the fact that he has a strict timetable. Yet unlike Ben, he is very much a member of the group. His level within the system does not matter, as he is constrained by the system itself. Even if he is the Dean of Medicine, he is constrained by the money he gets from the university or the research councils, and he never gets enough. Being high group, he has lots of activities related to the main group he belongs to: his department. Supposing he is the head of the department, he might have to chair meetings, organize research and teaching, see visiting scientists, perhaps treat patients, and supervise the activities of his staff. Characteristically in a high-group situation, Carlos would mix business with pleasure. He might be expected to referee the inter-departmental football matches every Saturday, or to invite each of his staff to dinner, one a month, in rotation.

Deborah is low grid, high group. She also works in a university department, but it is one which is run on an egalitarian, democratic basis. She might be the professor, or she might be a junior assistant. It does not really matter, because in this case professors and assistants take turns teaching each other, doing experiments together, and washing the test tubes and coffee cups. She is in a low-grid situation because her group is egalitarian and democratic. Unlike Alice, she is also in a high-group situation, one full of group-oriented constraints. Alice belongs to lots of different societies. Deborah only belongs to her strongly group-oriented department. Like Carlos, she spends lots of time in departmental activities, and whatever the group (her department) all want to do, everyone does.

Mary Douglas and her students have compared a variety of situations in this manner. Her method works best when like is compared to like, as in the case just described. However, her early assumptions about comparing whole societies has not borne fruit. Nor is it particularly meaningful to think in terms of hermits and taxi drivers being Box A, prisoners being Box B, soldiers being Box C, and members of religious cults or hippie communes being Box D – though these are all associations she has described. It may be useful, though, to compare different hippie communes, each as being, in a relative sense, higher grid or group than the next. In other words, if within Western society all hippie communes are relatively low grid and high group, then a small set of boxes for hippie communes (A to D) might be envisaged as lying all within a larger Box D in a grid/group diagram of Western society as a whole.

Grid/group analysis was an interesting idea, and it remains one for many social scientists outside mainstream anthropology. Yet it may also have been an idea (like hippie communes) whose time had come and gone before it took off. It remains to be seen whether some new focus within her paradigm can be made. There may well be hints of poststructuralism and postmodernism hidden in the paradigm, which surely could yield insights into relations between, for example, fieldworkers and their subjects.

Concluding summary

Mavericks, poststructuralists, and feminists possess a diversity of perspectives. Yet these perspectives have in common both roots in structuralist thinking and challenges to mainstream structuralist anthropology, especially in attempts to integrate structure with action and account for relations of power. Functionalism and structuralism had represented both safe perspectives and safe periods for anthropology, indeed in the latter case a period in which anthropology served as a major source for ideas in other disciplines, including literary criticism. Poststructuralist, feminist, and (as we shall see in the next chapter) interpretivist and postmodernist ideas have all challenged the authority of ethnographic reporting and the methods of analysis characteristic of structural anthropology and its predecessors.

If Bateson and Douglas are anthropologists whose thoughts and interests drifted away from the narrow anthropological perspectives of their times, the poststructuralists are just the opposite: practitioners of other disciplines whose insights have offered inspiration for emerging developments within our discipline. Interpretivism in some respects represents the opposite of structuralism – a rejection of meaning as embedded in structure in favour of the intuitive and interactive creation of meaning. In other respects it represents a logical development from poststructuralism, with its breaking down of traditional constructions and opening up of new agendas for anthropology through links with literary criticism and social theory. The last two decades have seen great changes in anthropological perceptions, but they are no greater than the changes which took place in the 1920s or in the 1950s, and the next chapter offers a survey of recent developments in the historical context of a wider interpretive anthropology.

FURTHER READING

Useful commentaries on the leading figures discussed in this chapter include those of Brockman (1977) on Gregory Bateson, Fardon (1998) on Mary Douglas, Jenkins (1992) on Pierre Bourdieu, and Smart (1985) on Michel Foucault.

Among good introductions to poststructuralism is the one by Sarup (1988), which also introduces postmodernism. Ortner's essays 'Theory in anthropology since the sixties' (1984) and 'Resistance and the problem of ethnographic refusal' (1995), along with Knauft's *Genealogies for the Present* (1996), provide excellent overviews of the impact of feminism, poststructuralism, etc. on anthropology.

The best overview of feminist anthropology is H. L. Moore's *Feminism and Anthropology* (1988), and her *A Passion for Difference* (1994) covers a wealth of issues related to current debates. See also Strathern's essay, 'An awkward relationship' (1987a).

10 Interpretive and postmodernist approaches

After Radcliffe-Brown's death in 1955, British anthropology went in four different directions. Some in the next generation simply continued Radcliffe-Brown's line of enquiry (notably Fortes and to some extent Goody). Others, such as Firth, came to emphasize individual action over social structure – an approach drawn partly from Malinowski's early fieldwork-based version of functionalism (chapter 5). This line of thought developed into theories such as processualism and transactionalism (chapter 6). Still others took to at least some of Lévi-Strauss' structuralist ideas (chapter 8), often adapting them to new interests in social process. Finally, a large number came eventually to follow Evans-Pritchard in his rejection of the idea of anthropology as a science, in favour of an interpretive approach which placed anthropology firmly within the humanities.

In the United States, Clifford Geertz began to propound his own style of interpretivism. Anthropology in his hands (and in Evans-Pritchard's) turned the linguistic analogy sideways. Cultures were no longer metaphorical 'grammars' to be figured out and written down; they were 'languages' to be translated into terms intelligible to members of other cultures – or more often than not, the anthropologist's own culture.

In France, outside anthropology, structuralism was under attack as the last bastion of 'modernism'. Philosophers and literary critics there and their followers in North America developed new, 'postmodern' ways of looking at the world. To a great extent, this followed from the idea that the world itself had undergone a quiet revolution. The world had moved beyond modernism, with its hierarchy of knowledge, to a postmodern phase where there was no place for grand theory of any kind (except, a cynic might say, postmodernism itself).

These ideas filtered into anthropology in the late 1970s and early 1980s. There were also developments within our discipline which made it more open to postmodernist ideas. The interpretivism already present served as a foundation – as did latter-day attacks on the alleged colonial mentality and imperialist foundation of anthropology. In the same time period, feminist anthropology grew and further challenged androcentric models, reflexivity became a byword of ethnographic method, and writing and reading took on theoretical significance in the new, literarily aware anthropology. All this culminated in the publication of *Writing Culture* (Clifford and Marcus 1986), and in the eyes of some the discipline was born again.

This chapter focuses on these various strands of thinking. While Evans-Pritchard may be thought of as a thoroughly modernist practitioner of the discipline, his ideas nevertheless foreshadow interpretivism. The eventual move towards postmodernism in the hands of Edwin Ardener and others at Oxford, Evans-Pritchard's old university, lies within the Evans-Pritchardian tradition, or at least possesses a spirit which Evans-Pritchard would have recognized as his own (see chapter 9). At the other extreme, *Writing Culture* signalled a focus on the 'poetics and politics' of writing ethnography. What these strands have in common is a vision of anthropology as a rejection of scientific method, a recognition of the importance of writing, and an attempt to gain insight through human understanding rather than formal methods of research and analysis. In spite of their diversity, it is therefore quite appropriate to see all these threads of interpretive and postmodernist thinking as part of one great movement within the discipline – a movement that all of us have been influenced by, however much some may wish to distance themselves from it.

Evans-Pritchard's interpretive approach

E. E. Evans-Pritchard studied under C. G. Seligman and Bronislaw Malinowski at the London School of Economics. He made six major field expeditions to the Sudan and British East Africa, notably with the Zande (Azande), Nuer, Anuak, Shilluk, and Luo. His accounts of Zande witchcraft (Evans-Pritchard 1937) and Nuer politics and kinship (1940; 1951a) served both to epitomize the British anthropology of their time and to inspire succeeding generations – albeit more on a theoretical than an ethnographic level. In recent years, some of his Nuer work, based on less than a year with the people, has been the subject of criticism for overstating the importance of the lineage in political affairs (e.g., Kuper 1988: 194–201). However, *Witchcraft, Oracles, and Magic among the Azande* (Evans-Pritchard 1937) and *Nuer Religion* (1956) have fared better. Both of these were attempts to understand and relate the inner thoughts of his subjects.

Witchcraft, Oracles, and Magic is an ethnography of Zande thought processes. The author argues that Zande are so obsessed with witchcraft that to understand their belief in it and how that belief is used to explain cause and effect is to understand their society. If a grain storage bin falls and kills someone sitting under it, one cause may well be that termites have eaten the supports, but the question of why it fell at that time on that person must be answered by whose witchcraft is involved (Evans-Pritchard 1937: 69–72).

Nuer Religion concerns, among other things, the definition of *kwoth*. Like Latin *spiritus*, Greek *pneuma*, and Hebrew *ruah*, it also designates 'breath'. In its metaphorical senses, it can refer to spirits of several kinds, including the Nuer entity Evans-Pritchard translates as 'God'. Throughout *Nuer Religion*, the author engages his reader in an exercise to picture and feel the essence of Nuer belief through the words, the symbolism, and the rituals which characterize the system described by the title of that book. It is worth remembering, though, that 'Nuer religion' is not itself a Nuer concept; it is an anthropologist's one (see Evans-Pritchard 1956: 311–22). Evans-Pritchard's monograph, together with a similar one by his colleague Godfrey Lienhardt (1963) on the religion of the neighbouring Dinka, formed the foundation of anthropological studies of belief. They also focused attention on translation, both real and metaphorical. It is interesting that whereas Evans-Pritchard speaks of 'God' and 'spirits' and often uses the Nuer term, Lienhardt prefers the English 'Divinity' and 'divinities' – precisely in order to get away from the directness of the more familiar English terms. It may also be worthy of note that both these Oxford anthropologists converted to Roman Catholicism; and this, it has been said, might have played some part in the formulation of their similar approaches to the interpretation of religious belief and practice.

Evans-Pritchard practised his anthropology within the general theoretical framework of Radcliffe-Brown. However, he rejected Radcliffe-Brown's notion of the discipline as a science and argued the case for anthropology as an art (e.g., Evans-Pritchard 1965). This marks the crucial difference between Evans-Pritchard's vision and the mainstream British tradition from which it diverged. Especially in his later years, Evans-Pritchard developed the idea of anthropology as 'translation of culture', and this became a catch-phrase in the works of many of his students. What anthropologists are supposed to do is get as close as possible to the collective mind of the people they study, and then 'translate' the alien ideas they find into equivalent ideas within their own culture. This is, of course, not the same thing as actual, linguistic translation. Like Radcliffe-Brown's sea shells and Lévi-Strauss' crystals, it is an analogy (see chapters 5 and 8). Evans-Pritchard rejected the Lévi-Straussian idea of a 'grammar' of culture in favour of a 'meaning' in the more subtle everyday discourse of culture. The difficulties of translation (whether to go for a literal one, or an idiomatic one) have precise analogies in ethnography. If we translate Nuer or Zande ideas too literally, then no one outside of Nuerland or Zandeland will understand them. If we translate too idiomatically, then we will fail to capture the essence of Nuer or Zande thought. Anthropology, according to this view, is forever caught in the translator's dilemma.

In his 1951 textbook *Social Anthropology*, derived from a series of six lectures presented on BBC Radio, Evans-Pritchard reviews the scope of social anthropology, its history, methods, and theory, and its potential for applied work. At several points Evans-Pritchard (e.g., 1951b: 62, 116-17) criticizes the 'natural science' analogy and offers instead the vision of anthropology's object as the totality of moral and symbolic systems, which in his view are quite unlike any systems found in nature. They are not governed by natural laws, though they do entail social structures and cultural patterns. Was Evans-Pritchard a structural-functionalist masquerading as an epistemologist? Was he, until his bid for freedom in the 1950s, a philosopher-historian strapped into the straitjacket of functionalist dogma? Or did he simply change his mind, from history to functionalism to epistemology, in the course of his career?

Mary Douglas (1980: 29-38) suggests that Evans-Pritchard's career represented a single, coherent research programme and that he was always an interpretive thinker. Another view is that he broke with functionalism in the 1940s and consolidated his perspective in the 1950s (e.g., Kuper 1996 [1973]: 124-6). In support of Douglas' position, one can cite much in *Witchcraft, Oracles, and Magic* and point to the fact that the text of *Nuer Religion* is made up of papers written and presented up to a decade before its publication. However, Evans-Pritchard's ethnographic work is not all that different from that of any of his contemporaries. The ways in which it differs do not mark him out as having a unique methodological approach or understanding of society, but rather indicate a desire for innovation, especially in his concern with systems of belief. Radcliffe-Brown regarded Evans-Pritchard as one in the same mould as himself and feared that Meyer Fortes would be the rebel. Fortes, though, continued the Radcliffe-Brownian tradition at Cambridge, where it competed with Leach's structuralism and processualism for the favour of the students. Whatever elements of Evans-Pritchard's writing predate *Nuer Religion*, the publication of that book marks a departure from structural-functionalism towards a new kind of reasoning about the nature of religious belief. Evans-Pritchard recalls Durkheim more than he does Radcliffe-Brown, but the emphasis is more on seeing the spirit world as a Nuer sees it and explaining it as if to a Western theological audience, and rather less on demonstrating a relation between belief and social structure.

One of Evans-Pritchard's strongest statements against functionalism lies in his 1950 lecture, 'Social anthropology: past and present', published in his first series of collected essays (1962: 13–28). He argues that the failing of social anthropology since the Enlightenment has been to model the discipline on the natural sciences, and suggests that it is better seen as among the historical sciences or more generally as a branch of the humanities. The fact that historians' issues are generally diachronic, whereas anthropologists' are synchronic, does not bother him. The synthesis of events and the integrative description both aim at is enough for him to assert a methodological similarity. He says that the description of structural form is not antithetical to either history or anthropology. Likewise, 'History is not a succession of events, it is the links between them' (1962 [1961]: 48).

Evans-Pritchard's main influence was at Oxford, where he held the Chair of Social Anthropology from 1946 to 1970. Indeed, he still casts his spell over the Institute of Social and Cultural Anthropology there. It is his bust and not Radcliffe-Brown's or Tylor's which graces that institute's library, and his work which the Oxford tradition has carried forward. In the 1970s, when Oxford anthropology was polarized between Needham's latent structuralism and Ardener's incipient postmodernism, both sides took comfort in Evans-Pritchard's inspiration (see, e.g., Needham 1972: xiv, 14–31; Ardener 1989 [1971]: 35–9). Needham's struggle with the relation between the English word 'belief', the inner state it describes, and the cross-cultural applicability of the concept, is to a large measure attributable to the text of *Nuer Religion*.

Geertz's interpretivism

While Evans-Pritchard showed the way towards interpretivism, it is nevertheless a little harder to justify the appellation 'ism' to his approach than it is to that of Clifford Geertz. Evans-Pritchard's anthropology was, as much as anything, a reaction against the structural-functionalist enterprise, whereas Geertz's marks a positive move towards an understanding of the minutiae of culture as an end in itself.

Geertz, now based at Princeton, was trained at Harvard and has taught at Berkeley and Chicago. He did fieldwork on Java and Bali and in Morocco. His ethnographic work has been diverse in scope and approach. *The Religion of Java* (1960), for example, was fairly conventional, whereas *Kinship in Bali* (Geertz and Geertz 1975) challenges the idea of kinship as an autonomous system which can be understood cross-culturally and argues for its inclusion in a symbolic domain. *Agricultural Involution* (1963), in contrast to both, is in the broad framework of

Stewardian ecological anthropology, while some of his other work on social change in Indonesia lies in the realm of social history. In *Islam Observed* (1968), Geertz turns his attention to comparison, in an attempt to understand Islam in the context of two countries where he has ethnographic experience: Indonesia and Morocco. Unlike Evans-Pritchard (1965 [1963]: 13–36), he does not hold up 'the comparative method' as an impossibility!

The core of his interpretivist anthropology, though, lies in the introductory essay to his book *The Interpretation of Cultures*, which was completed and published in 1973 – the year of Evans-Pritchard's death. There Geertz (1973: 3–30) sums up his approach as one of 'thick description'. Anthropology is about picking through the strata embedded in a particular culture, and revealing them through layers of description. It is not about cognition as anthropologists in America then understood it; nor is it necessarily about large-scale comparison. Critics (e.g., Kuper 1999: 109–14) have pointed out the ambiguity of Geertz's definition of 'thick description' (as detailed and layered) as well as the thinness of some of his own ethnography (in that the sources of his own generalizations are seldom made clear). Yet Geertz's interpretivist challenge is, if in these ways problematic, nevertheless both deeper in ethnographic detail and richer in metaphor than Evans-Pritchard's.

In his two major collections, Geertz (1973; 1983) pushes for an image of society as 'like a text' – for Kuper (1999: 112) 'a metaphor running away with itself'. Geertz also argues for anthropology as the understanding of the 'local' in a tense interaction with the 'global', for an emphasis on the minutiae, even the trivia of culture, and for culture as a symbolic system, but a system within which social action takes place and political power is generated. He deconstructs common anthropological notions such as 'culture', 'worldview', 'art', 'custom', and 'customary law', with a fluency of style that is virtually unmatched. If he were a bad writer, he would undoubtedly have had less influence, but the effect of Geertz's subtle and skilful breaking-down of anthropological conceit and positivist tendencies has been profound. His collected essays are probably as much read outside the discipline as by anthropologists themselves, and (for better or worse) to many are paradigmatic of the discipline as a whole.

In some of his recent work, Geertz has ventured yet further into interpretivism through re-interpreting the ethnography of others. In his award-winning *Works and Lives* (Geertz 1988), he examines the writings of Evans-Pritchard, Malinowski, Lévi-Strauss, and Benedict. Through the analysis of the imagery and metaphors of his chosen authors, Geertz argues that anthropology is simply 'a kind of writing'. This is a major postmodernist challenge to the discipline, and one which is commonplace in the work of both American and French writers over the last two decades (see Clifford and Marcus 1986; Sperber 1985 [1982]). Jonathan Spencer (1989) has argued that Geertz and his followers are mistaken in the view that anthropological texts are merely pieces of writing. Spencer puts the case that anthropology is also 'a kind of working', and demonstrates the logic of putting both the ethnographer, and the diversity of points of view among informants, into the text. Yet whether Geertz's emphasis on writing is exaggerated or not, he has usefully focused attention on anthropology as a creative endeavour.

Today, Geertz remains as one of anthropology's most influential figures, both within and beyond the discipline. His interpretivism undoubtedly paved the way for postmodern anthropology. Some say he is not just a precursor but part of the movement. Before getting into the nuances of postmodernism proper, though, a focus on further foundations, especially with regard to new concepts and interests beyond those of Geertz himself, is worthwhile.

Concepts of changing times

The postmodernist challenge in anthropology has yielded new concepts and areas of new research associated with them. Among the most important are reflexivity and orientalism. Let us consider these with regard to the related concepts of reflexivism (which entails a theoretical emphasis on reflexivity), occidentalism, and globalization.

Reflexivity and reflexivism

All anthropologists do comparison of one kind or another. Those who work far from home might compare more to classic anthropological cases like Nuer or Trobriand society. Others argue that a better kind of comparison is that to societies which are similar, technologically, geographically, or linguistically (see chapter 4). Those who work in societies closely related to their own, either culturally or geographically, tend to make comparisons to their own society more explicit in their writings. At the extreme, there is explicit comparison of one's own culture, described through one's *self* as exemplar, and through the 'self' as vehicle imposed upon the culture purportedly described. In this case, the culture under description can become mere background for the anthropologist's exploration of his or her own cultural and social identity. This is a case of extreme reflexivity.

Reflexivity has formed a major part of the incipient postmodern project within anthropology since the 1970s. Perhaps the first explicit publication in this mould is Judith Okely's essay, originally published in an early issue of the *Journal of the Anthropological Society of Oxford*, 'The self and scientism' (Okely 1996 [1975]: 27–44). However, the roots of reflexivity are yet deeper. Malinowski's fieldwork diary, much commented on by Okely, is the best-known example. Although Malinowski apparently meant it only to record his own private musings, it found its way into print twenty-five years after his death (Malinowski 1967), and it contrasts sharply with his formal ethnographic accounts. In the diary he reveals his sexual fantasies, his heavy use of drugs, his distaste for some aspects of Trobriand culture, and his boredom in the Trobriand Islands. Malinowski's student Jomo Kenyatta, later the first president of Kenya, included reflexive comment in his ethnography of his own people (Kenyatta 1938), but most of the Malinowskians and the Boasians steered clear. Lévi-Strauss included much autobiography in *Tristes Tropiques* (1976 [1955]), though he too separated this from both his ethnographic and his theoretical commentaries. What makes the efforts of most post-modern writers fundamentally different is their assertion that reflexivity itself is ethnography, or at least a central part of it, and that ethnography is at least the major part of anthropological theory itself (see Rabinow 1977).

Reflexivity has strong links with feminist anthropology. Feminist anthropology and gender studies share much of their subject matter, but their approaches are somewhat different. Henrietta Moore (1988: 188) has written that the anthropology of gender is about 'the study of gender identity and its cultural construction', whereas feminist anthropology is about 'the study of gender as a principle of human social life' (see chapter 9). For the last couple of decades, anthropologists interested in the study of gender have moved decidedly away from this 'gender studies' approach to one emphasizing the position of woman as ethnographer as well as that of woman as informant or object. By the middle of the 1980s it was not uncommon for the anthropologist to put herself forward as the main subject of anthropological discourse, as reflexivity gained favour within postmodernist and especially (loosely) feminist circles, and ultimately found favour in anthropology at large (see, e.g., Okely and Callaway 1992). The danger of losing the 'other' for the emphasis on the 'self' became all too easy, as extreme reflexivity became at worst a fetish and at best a theoretical perspective (reflexivism) in its own right.

A further twist is found in the kind of study where the analyst, drawing on her own experiences, speaks for a wider community of oppressed people or attempts to give 'voice' to the oppressed through herself. Writers in this tradition sometimes take their inspiration from the post-structuralist, feminist literary theory of Gayatri Chakravorty Spivak and her 'subaltern studies' associates (see, e.g., Guha and Spivak 1988). Some of Lila Abu-Lughod's writings on Bedouin women (e.g., Abu-Lughod 1990) are in this vein. The idea is that there is something shared among 'subaltern' or subordinate groups, whether subordination is on the basis of gender, class, ethnicity, or history of colonial injustice. Sherry Ortner (1995), on the other hand, points to the Geertzian 'thinness' of work following this approach: a thinness derived from a reluctance to tackle internal politics and problems of representing the 'other' or indeed the (subaltern) self.

Other trends in the last decade have been towards moderation, either allowing personal reflexivity to mingle with reflections on theory, or pursuing the reflective experiences of the traditional objects of ethnography. The former is exemplified by Kirsten Hastrup's (1995) brilliant critique of anthropology's assumptions and directions. The latter includes Pat Caplan's (1997) record of her friendship with 'Mohammed', one of her informants, through the thirty years she has worked with the Swahili of Tanzania. Much of Caplan's text is made up of quotations, and the 'voice' of the informant is heard along with the confessions of the ethnographer. But there is 'fact' as well, especially on spirit cults; and a fine balance is achieved between ethnography and autobiography.

There is still another kind of reflexivity, though perhaps it is less recognized as such. This is the kind of reflexive study which examines not an individual but a collective self: anthropology as a whole, or perhaps a group of anthropologists who share a common interest or ethnographic region. What I have in mind is the kind of study which examines this collective self in interplay, not with individual informants, but with a culture built both of real happenings and of images portrayed through ethnography. A good example is Alcida Ramos' (1992) study of Yanomami ethnography. She remarks that anthropologists who have worked with the Yanomami groups in Brazil have variously presented them as being fierce, erotic, intellectual, or just plain exotic. In some ways, sometimes, they are all these things, but the imagery which has been built up around them is powerful. Ramos notes that media hype has exaggerated ethnographic description to such an extent that some ethnographers, notably Napoleon Chagnon, have been led to tone down new books and new editions of old books which have fuelled that flame.

Orientalism, occidentalism, and globalization

An important component of postmodern anthropology is the interest in power, derived from Foucault among others (see chapter 9). A related concern has been the identification of power as a manifestation of colonial and postcolonial discourses through 'orientalism'. The concept was introduced by Edward Said, a Palestinian literary critic long resident in the United States. In *Orientalism* (1978) and later works, Said attacks the West for creating a notion of the East, the Orient, in order to dominate it, by trade, colonialism, and other forms of exploitation. The West, he says, more polemically, also needs the Orient in order to define itself: what is *not* East is West. Many of his more salient ideas were, in fact, anticipated by anthropologists (e.g., Asad 1973; cf. Goody 1996), who have also pointed out that anthropological studies, at least in colonial times, were embedded in unequal relationships between the West and the Third World. Said is implicitly critical of our discipline and its orientalist discourse, though his main grudges are directed at literary figures, philologists, and archaeologists.

However, recently some anthropologists have turned Said's argument on its head, not so much to negate it as to point out that it is only half the story. James Carrier of the University of Durham has edited a volume called *Occidentalism* (Carrier 1995a), in which nine mainly American anthropologists (some, including Carrier, trained in sociology) comment on the notion of 'the West'. Most of the contributors note that 'oriental' peoples are as likely to have biased and generalized visions of the West as 'occidental' peoples are of the East. Indeed, as Carrier points out in his preface, when he moved from sociology to anthropology, from a training concentrating on the nuances of social complexity in industrial capitalist societies of the West to a specialization in Melanesian society, he was startled by the lack of sophistication in the ways in which anthropologists talk about their own societies.

It struck me at the time as a professional double standard, and it repelled me. These were conscientious scholars who devoted great effort to uncovering the nuances, complexities, and inter-connections of the societies that they studied. Yet they would casually characterize Western society in terms so simplistic that they would not be tolerated of an anthropologist speaking about a village society. (Carrier 1995b: vii–viii)

Carrier goes on to suggest that three trends are prevalent in anthropology today with regard to occidentalism: a tendency towards self-reflection, a growing interest in the 'invention of tradition', and an increasing concern with the ethnography of the West itself (1995b: viii–ix).

The relations between Occident and Orient, whether imagined or real, are now bound up with the process of globalization, also an increasing object of anthropological enquiry. In one of six volumes stemming from the 1993 Decennial Conference of the Association of Social Anthropologists of the Commonwealth, Norman Long (1996) speaks of 'globalization', 'localization', and even 're-localization'. Globalization involves processes of movement in population (e.g., migrant labour), skills, capital, technology and technical knowledge, and also symbolic representations (e.g., notions of 'modernization' and 'globalization' itself, and new concepts of 'citizenship' such as that of the European Union). Localization involves the interplay between local forms of knowledge and external pressures, while re-localization involves the assertion, rediscovery, or invention of locally based knowledge, especially knowledge which can be used in agrarian economic and social development. Long argues for actor-centred research on these issues.

In the same volume, Aihwa Ong (1996) hints at the fallacy in seeing all aspects of globalization, modernization, and industrialization as the same thing, and explicitly opposes the yet bigger fallacy of equating any of these simply with Western culture. Take modernization: China has been in the process of modernizing for a very long time; and the process of modernization and even industrialization in Japan began, not with Commodore Matthew Perry's visit in 1853 (as American school children are taught), but as an ultimate consequence of the expansion of trade from China throughout East and Southeast Asia over a long period.

The true 'postmodern condition', to my mind, is reflected in Marc Augé's (1995 [1992]) intriguing study of the globalized 'non-space' of refugee camps, international hotels, motorways, and airport lounges. As a theme promoted by both evolutionist and postmodernist anthropology as well as a topic visible to anthropologists whenever they do fieldwork or even attend conferences, globalization is a popular and timely concern. The irony is that in theoretical terms it might as easily be seen as most akin to the least trendy of all theoretical perspectives, diffusionism.

Postmodernism and postmodern anthropology

Postmodernism constitutes a critique of all 'modern' understandings. Postmodernists define what is 'modernist' as what is all-encompassing; they reject both grand theory in anthropology and the notion of completeness in ethnographic description. On the latter score, they oppose the presumption of ethnological authority on the part of the anthropologist. Thus reflexivity, and ultimately embodiment, came to the fore. In a wider sense, postmodernist anthropology takes its cue from critical studies of 'orientalist' writing and levels its critique at the creation of the 'other' (and consequent definition of the 'self') as the driving force of all previous positions in the discipline. Postmodernism is also a logical development of both relativism and interpretivism, so much so that it is difficult to isolate these perspectives except superficially – by chronology, vocabulary, or style of writing.

The return to relativism

In a provocative article, Sjaak van der Geest (1990) has suggested that relativism itself is a dogma, not the absence of one. Anthropologists propagate relativism against the cognitive certainties both of those from alien cultures which they study and of non-anthropologists from their own cultures. Yet anthropology has, within the last decade, returned from mildly relativistic notions that each culture has its own value system or semantic structure to stronger views reminiscent of those of Benedict and Whorf. Only now these are couched in the jargon of postmodernism and devoid of any theory of culture as a whole. All this highlights the fact that 'relativism' is not really a monolithic concept (see also chapter 7). The term designates a myriad of theoretical fragments carved from the rock of Boasian anthropology. Yet Boasianism, in one form or another, remains a touchstone to many in American anthropology, both those who oppose relativist dogma and those who espouse insights brought more recently from newer trends in thinking about the relation between anthropology and its objects of study.

Postmodernism came into anthropology long after its early use in studies of art and the practice of architecture. In those fields, from the late 1950s, the term characterized a rejection of formal principles of style and the admission of unlikely blends and especially of local variation. In the social sciences, including anthropology, the term recalls the definition put forward by Jean-François Lyotard, Professor of Philosophy at the Université de Paris VIII (Vincennes), in his report to the government of Quebec on the 'postmodern condition': 'Simplifying to the extreme, I define *postmodern* as incredulity toward metanarratives' (Lyotard 1984 [1979]: xxiv).

In anthropology, following from this, postmodernism involves a rejection both of grand theoretical truth and of the wholeness of ethnographic reality. In other words, to a postmodern anthropologist there is no true, complete statement that can be made about a culture. Nor, for many, can we even come up with an approximation. Therefore, grand theory (what Lyotard calls 'metanarrative') is doomed – except, it seems, the metanarrative of postmodernism itself!

'Writing culture'

Anthropology's premier postmodernist text is *Writing Culture* (Clifford and Marcus 1986), based on a conference on 'The Making of Ethnographic Texts', held in Santa Fe, New Mexico in 1984 (see also Marcus and Clifford 1985). Eight practising anthropologists, a historian of anthropology (James Clifford), and a literary critic (Mary Louise Pratt) presented papers there, and all but one of these appears in the celebrated volume (the missing paper was by Robert Thornton). The unifying theme of *Writing Culture* is a consideration of literary methods within anthropological discourse, though the authors hold a range of views from moderate to radical on the subject. A number of contributors also examine the intrusion of power relations in the ethnographic process. It is worth touching very briefly on each.

James Clifford, in his introduction, attacks the idea of ethnography as a representation of the wholeness of culture and stresses the incompleteness of ethnographic expression, even in the hands of indigenous scholars. He argues for an appreciation of ethnography as writing, but rejects the extremist view that it is only writing or that the recognition of ethnography as a kind of 'poetry' precludes objectivity. His substantive contribution, on 'ethnographic allegory', is decidedly literary in character, and focuses on 'the *narrative* character of cultural representations' (Clifford 1986: 100). George Marcus also offers a literary analysis, but in his case invoking world-systems theory to unmask the 'authority' of the author; and in his afterword he comments briefly on the challenge he believes the Santa Fe conference has given the discipline.

Mary Louise Pratt discusses some diverse ethnographies; she advocates the 'fusion' of object and subjective understandings and the re-examination, on the part of ethnographers, of their enterprise in light of historical precedent and literary genre. Vincent Crapanzano looks at the problems of translation in three quite different texts, including an eighteenth-century one, a nineteenth-century one, and one by Geertz (on the Balinese cockfight). Renato Rosaldo looks at modes of authority in two texts, including Evans-Pritchard's *The Nuer*; and Talal Asad takes as his object of 'translation' an essay by Ernest Gellner on 'translation' in the British anthropological tradition, notably in *Nuer Religion*.

Michael Fischer looks at the dynamism of ethnicity, which, he says, must be re-invented in each generation. Paul Rabinow takes on textual construction in Geertz's interpretivism and Clifford's 'textual meta-anthropology', along with other examples, to illustrate that representations are social facts. Stephen Tyler, a convert from cognitive anthropology, here speaks with the strongest postmodern voice. He comments on the death of scientific thought and celebrates the fragmentary nature of a would-be postmodern ethnography. The latter, he says, aims at a 'discourse', that is, a dialogue, as opposed to the former monologue of the ethnographic 'text'. However, he laments that no postmodern ethnography exists, while asserting at the same time that 'all ethnography is post-modern in effect' (Tyler 1986: 136).

Since *Writing Culture*, a number of anthropologists, both those involved in that project and others, have continued the discourse. Notable examples are Marcus and Fischer's (1986) attempt to justify the experimental and critical nature of recent anthropological writing; Clifford's (1988) treatise on twentieth-century ethnography, literature, and art; Michael Taussig's (1993) highly original study of imitation and the construction of alterity in the self/other opposition; and some of Rabinow's (1997) collected essays. The tempered search for connections figures prominently in the work of Marilyn Strathern (e.g., 1991; 1992), one of the leading anthropologists in Britain today. She argues, among other things, that partial connections are necessary because the amount of data anthropologists have to hand is too great to treat in any other way. American sociologist Norman Denzin (1997) sums up postmodern ethnography as a 'moral discourse'. He says that ethnographers should move beyond the traditional, objective forms of writing about peoples to more experimental and experiential texts, including autobiography and performance-based media; towards greater expression of emotion; to fictionalization, thereby expressing poetic and narrative truth, as opposed to scientific truth; and also towards lived experience, praxis, and multiple points of view.

Postmodernists often stress the arbitrary in culture, descriptions of culture, and theorizing about culture. When commenting on postmodernism itself, postmodernists tend to invoke reflexivity. As Crapanzano (1992: 88) puts it, 'Not only is the arbitrariness of the sign in any act of signification paradigmatically proclaimed but so is the arbitrariness of its syntagmatic, its syntactic, placement. ' In other words, whereas some poststructuralists (notably Bourdieu) oppose Saussurian distinctions altogether, here Crapanzano, a decided postmodernist, expands the Saussurian notion of arbitrariness to cover not only signs themselves, but even signs in relation to other signs. For postmodernists, one's vantage point is arbitrary. Therefore the distinction which Saussure, and virtually every linguist and anthropologist since have recognized, that between observer and observed, is called into question.

For reflexivists and other, less self-centred late interpretivists, the nomothetic and the ideographic (see Radcliffe-Brown 1952: 1) blend to form an unbounded mix. Ethnography and theory, and observer and observed (or collective self and collective other), become almost indistinguishable in the course of an anthropological text. It is perhaps no accident that the ethnography of Europeans by Europeans, or of Americans by Americans, form good examples of this genre. Michael Herzfeld (a Harvard-based Englishman who writes on Greeks) epitomizes the soft postmodern tradition in anthropology. His *Anthropology Through the Looking Glass* (Herzfeld 1987) ranges from critiques of more formal and positivistic anthropological theory and exaltations of earlier wisdom, to discussions of contradictions within Greek culture and, more important-ly, contradictions within the anthropological distinctions between self and other and observer and observed. It presents itself as a search for connections which override the contradictions. Herzfeld here draws heavily on the definitive third edition of the *New Science* of Gimbattista Vico (for an English translation, see Pompa 1982 [Vico 1744]: 159–267), an eighteenth-century Italian philosopher, little read in his time, who tried to understand the relations between entities such as history and social evolution, nationhood and religion.

Recent work on the theory of tropes, including metaphor, metonymy, synecdoche, and irony is equally relevant to the postmodernist quest, and James Fernandez (e.g., 1986) of the University of Chicago is the leading proponent of this idea. I read his ethnography of the Fang of Gabon as a search for the deep emic, and therefore within the grand anthropological tradition which includes Malinowski and Boas (as well as Geertz). The spirit of David M. Schneider, great Chicago interpreter of the divergent symbolism of American and Yapese kinship, seems to be there too (see especially Schneider 1980 [1968]; 1984). Often borrowing new ideas from linguistics (e.g., Lakoff and Johnson 1980), Fernandez and the contribu-tors to his edited collection on tropes (Fernandez 1991) see culture as a constant and complex play of tropes. However, whereas George Lakoff and Mark Johnson argued that people map the unfamiliar onto the familiar to create new understanding, Naomi Quinn (1991), for example, argues essentially the reverse. Metaphors are based on culturally agreed understandings, and more often than not they add complexity rather than clarity. For her, as for generations of anthropologists before her, it is culture that is central.

Problems with postmodernism

In one of his many brilliant polemics, the late British philosopher-anthro-pologist, Ernest Gellner (1992: 22–79), attacked relativism and post-modernism as subjectivist and self-indulgent. Postmodernism is the most prevalent form of relativism today, and Gellner saw it as especially prob-lematic in its misplaced attacks on, for example, the stated objectivism of European colonial ethnography. For postmodernists, ethnography in the colonial era represented a tool in the hands of oppressive colonial govern-ments and multi-national corporations. For the anti-postmodernist, post-modernism's attempt to liberate anthropology is misguided, its attacks on earlier anthropological traditions misplaced, and its subjectivity down-right nonsensical. The postmodernist, says Gellner, sees anthropology as a movement from positivism (to postmodernists, a belief in objective facts) to hermeneutics (i.e., interpretation). Yet the postmodernist movement is really a replay of the romanticist one two centuries before, in their overthrow of the classical order of Enlightened Europe. Gellner goes on to attack the contributions to *Writing Culture* for their lack of precision. He concludes: 'In the end, the operational meaning of postmodernism in anthropology seems to be something like this: a refusal (in practice, rather selective) to countenance any objective facts, any independent social structures, and their replacement by a pursuit of meanings, both those of the objects of inquiry and of the inquirer' (1992: 29).

Rabinow and Clifford bear the brunt of Gellner's criticisms, but he blames Geertz for the origins of the obsession with hermeneutics and takes his philosopher's knife to Geertz's (1984) defence of relativism.

Geertz has encouraged a whole generation of anthropologists to parade their real or invented inner qualms and paralysis, using the invocation of the epistemological doubt and cramp as a justification of utmost obscurity and subjectivism (the main stylistic marks of 'postmodernism'). They agonize so much about their inability to know themselves and the Other, at any level of regress, that they no longer need to trouble too much about the Other. If everything in the world is fragmented and multiform, nothing really resembles anything else, and no one can know another (or himself), and no one can communicate, what is there to do other than express the anguish engendered by this situation in impenetrable prose? (Gellner 1992: 45)

Let me sum up the interpretivist and postmodernist enterprises. To soft postmodernists (including Geertzian interpretivists), society is like a text, to be 'read' by the ethnographer as surely as his own text will be read by his readers. Other postmodernists seem to see culture as 'shreds and patches' (to borrow Lowie's phrase) – each shred and each patch, a play on another one. To some, culture is a series of word plays or 'tropes'. Ethnography is much the same thing, and anthropological theory is little more. According to most adherents of these schools, there should be no grand theory and no grand analogy – except that culture is in some unspecified way 'like a text'. The question I would raise about all interpretivist approaches, to a greater or lesser degree, is what they think anthropology would be like if *their* metanarrative were true? Everything is relative; there is no truth in ethnography. Anthropology should dissolve into literary criticism, or at best into that brand of literary criticism that has taken over a big piece of anthropology's subject matter – cultural studies (see, e.g., Bratlinger 1990).

Yet there seems to be a subtle battle among interpretivists and postmodernists generally. One side sees ethnography as an end in itself, or rather an attempt to understand, but one which never quite reaches the level of understanding previously claimed for it. These anthropologists try to understand the human condition through detail, even the detail of ethnographic activity. Radical reflexivists are happy to write more about themselves doing ethnography than about the ethnographees, their subjects. This is the most extreme of all ideographic approaches: ethnography (writing about people) and ethnographic method (doing fieldwork) merge into one. While anthropology as a whole has taken on board and greatly benefited from recent discussions of reflexivity, it is nevertheless important to distinguish this strong version of the phenomenon from the simple awareness of the role of the ethnographer as a social actor as well as a gatherer of data.

The other side sees ethnography as a means to an end, a means to build a wider understanding of human nature. For these anthropologists, interpretivist in temperament and influenced by the more positive aspects of the postmodern critique, there is hope. They may borrow freely from evolutionism and functionalism, from structural Marxism or from biological anthropology. Theirs is a discipline of nomothetic inquiry. In the last section here, I will examine the possibilities for an anthropology in the latter image.

Mixed approaches: towards a compromise?

Robert Layton (1997: 157–215) characterizes present-day anthropology as polarized between socio-ecology and postmodernism. I believe that this characterization, while it has much truth, is too extreme. More and more, anthropologists are showing that they are happy to mix approaches and take from different theoretical traditions. This has been going on at least since the 1950s.

My preference is to look at new developments since the 1950s in terms of three strands of thinking: structural, interactive, and interpretive. These strands are not mutually exclusive. On the contrary, in the hands of diverse theorists and ethnographers, they are intertwined, overlapping, intersecting. While Lévi-Straussian structuralism is concerned unambiguously with structure, transactionalism overwhelmingly with interaction, and Geertzian interpretivism at least primarily with interpretation, there is nevertheless great potential to aim for an understanding which draws on two or even three. Some recent writers, such as Anthony Cohen (e.g., 1985; 1994), have blended interpretive and interactive interests. Edmund Leach (1954), Victor Turner (1957), and Pierre Bourdieu (1977 [1972]) have emphasized both structure and action in their analyses of social process. Roy Willis (1974), Rodney Needham (1979), and a number of others, have mixed structure and interpretation. Some of Ladislav

Holy and Milan Stuchlik's work makes good use of all three within a single paradigm (e.g., Holy and Stuchlik 1983). The simple answer, then, is that the future of anthropology may lie in the blending of approaches. Sociologists, and some anthropologists, like to think in terms of the three great social theorists – Marx, Durkheim, and Weber. They are like primary colours. You can mix them, or rather mix different strands of their thinking, to come up with almost any theoretical position.

Of course, things may not be quite as simple as this. Italian anthropologist Carla Pasquinelli (1996) has suggested a different interpretation, specifically on the concept of 'culture'. She points out that this concept is quintessentially 'modern' in that it is what modernists employ to define the pre-modern 'other'. It arose within evolutionist theory and remained powerful right through what she sees as the three phases of anthropological thinking: the material phase (concerned with customs and traceable from Tylor to Boas), the abstract phase (concerned with patterns, e.g., Kroeber and Kluckhohn), and the symbolic phase (concerned with meaning and typified by Geertz). However, she argues, Geertz's position is liminal, as he sees culture as 'local knowledge', dispersed and fragmentary (i.e., postmodern), while nevertheless seeking, through 'thick description', the totality of culture which Tylor championed (i.e., modern). The break comes with James Clifford (e.g., 1988), who overthrows the object (culture) in favour of the subjectivity of narrative (i.e., of the ethnographer).

But can there be anthropology without an object? If we are not studying culture or society, what then is cultural or social anthropology? This, in my view, is the dilemma postmodernism has left for the present generation (cf. Strathern 1987b; Fox 1991). At the risk of stating the obvious, throughout this book I hope I have shown that cultural anthropology remains a field of diverse viewpoints. The present generation can take its pick between innovative work within the evolutionist school, it can still lift ideas from structuralist or processualist theories to suit new purposes, or it can accept wholeheartedly the postmodern condition if it is prepared for the consequences. The blending of old ideas, of all sorts, seems the safest bet.

Concluding summary

Interpretivism and postmodernism fit into anthropology in a very straightforward way, as aspects of a time-honoured set of analogies between language and culture. An understanding of that relationship, and its historical transformation, lies at the root of new developments in anthropology and in other social sciences.

Anthropological theory has paralleled linguistic theory in uncanny ways through its history. This is not simply fortuitous. Rather it has been recognized and utilized by generations of anthropologists through linguistic and related analogies. Analogy expresses form, but anthropology also shares some content with linguistics, both in that language is an aspect of culture and in that debates on language and writing have become prominent in anthropology itself. It is commonplace to talk of the 'linguistic analogy', though it might be more accurate to think of a set of linguistic analogies which have competed both against each other and against other analogies (the biological analogy, for example) through much of the history of anthropology.

Lévi-Strauss (1963 [1952]: 67–8) once drew attention to three levels of relations between linguistics and cultural anthropology: the relation between a language and a culture, that between language and culture in the abstract, and that between the two disciplines. I would choose a different set of relations to cover the whole realm of linguistic ideas within cultural anthropology: society or culture as grammar, ethnography as translation, and society and ethnography as 'discourse'.

The analogy of grammar was implicit in the work of Radcliffe-Brown and his followers, though they tended to speak more of anthropology as like biology and societies as 'organisms' than of anthropology as like linguistics and culture as 'language'. Later it was made explicit by Lévi-Strauss and structuralist anthropologists generally. For them culture and society have at their root a form which is analogous to the grammar of language. This may be a specific cultural grammar, or (in much of Lévi-Strauss' work), it may be a universal grammar held in common between all cultures.

The analogy of translation was implicit, and occasionally explicit, in the work of Evans-Pritchard. It is still more explicit in the work of Geertz with his notion of religion as a cultural system (Geertz 1966) and in his collections on 'interpretive anthropology' (1973; 1983). For Evans-Pritchard alien cultures are like foreign languages, to be 'translated' into terms familiar in the 'language' of one's own culture. For Geertz, culture is embodied in the symbols through which people communicate. Geertz has moved away from cognitive anthropology and its concerns with thought in the abstract, towards an understanding of action from the actor's point of view. In this he shares much with his early mentor, sociologist Talcott Parsons (e.g., 1949 [1937]), also with processual and action-oriented anthropologists, notably Victor Turner (e.g., 1967), and to some extent with the proponents of the 'embodiment' perspective to the study of ritual.

The discourse analogy, borrowed from Foucault (e.g., 1974 [1969]), features prominently in social anthropology, especially but not exclusively in the work of those who see themselves as part of the postmodern project. Anthropology itself is a discourse. The older, modern anthropologies are discourses partly representing the interests of the segments of society from which they stem. Yet it would be too simplistic to define functionalism, for example, simply as a discourse produced by the British colonial enterprise (cf. Asad 1973). Rather, it is more meaningful to view anthropology throughout its history as a discourse on the human condition, played out in a dialogue between those under the scrutiny of anthropologists on the one hand, and the anthropologists themselves on the other. This view would unite postmodern and modern anthropology in a common enterprise – indeed one consistent with the definition of anthropology given in the first edition of the *Encyclopaedia Britannica* (1771: I, 327): 'ANTHROPOLOGY, a discourse upon human nature'.

FURTHER READING

Douglas' *Evans-Pritchard* (1980) is the best guide to the basics of that thinker's anthropology. See also Pals' *Seven Theories of Religion* (1996), which contains interesting essays on both Evans-Pritchard and Geertz. Geertz's own *Works and Lives* (1988) makes stimulating reading on the ideas of a number of the other major anthropologists. The most important of Geertz's works though are his two collections of essays (1973; 1983). See also Shankman's essay 'The thick and the thin' (1984).

Knauft's excellent *Genealogies for the Present* (1996) reviews the debates in postmodernist anthropology and other recent trends. Lechte's *Fifty Key Contemporary Thinkers* (1994) is a useful guide to the ideas of structuralist, poststructuralist, and postmodernist thinkers, mainly outside anthropology but who have influenced our discipline. There are many guides to postmodernism in general, among the most interesting is Smart's *Postmodernism* (1993). On cultural studies and theoretical ideas within related fields, see Milner's *Contemporary Cultural Theory* (1994).

H. L. Moore's essay 'Master narratives: anthropology and writing' (1994 [1993]: 107–28) offers a stimulating and highly readable review of the problem of writing. See also James, Hockey, and Dawson's edited volume *After Writing Culture* (1997) for further British approaches to the problems highlighted in *Writing Culture* (Clifford and Marcus 1986). A similar edited collection touching on reflexivity is Okely and Callaway's *Anthropology and Autobiography* (1992).

11   Conclusions

This book has dealt with the 'content' of anthropological theory. Yet anthropological theory is not a vessel to be emptied of old ideas and filled with new ones, or stuffed with more virulent paradigms to strangle the weak ones. Anthropological theory undoubtedly has 'form' as well as content, and in this final chapter we shall focus initially on the question of what form this might be, then return to the issue of the relation between form and content, first with some reflections on the future of anthropological ideas and then with a concluding summary.

National traditions and the future of anthropological theory

It is commonplace to think of anthropology in terms of national traditions, and often useful to do so. I think it is especially useful when trying to envisage the roots of and relations between the Boasian and Malinowskian/Radcliffe-Brownian traditions, and also the relation between anthropology and sociology (which at least had the potential to become part of our discipline, or ours part of theirs). Each new development is partly the product of individual thinking, of course, but also very much the product of the circumstances in which these thinkers found themselves. Some of these circumstances were, in fact, single events or clusters of events occurring at around the same time. Among dates to remember, I would pick out 1748 (which marks the publication of Montesquieu's highly influential book, *The Spirit of the Laws*), 1871 (the date of publication of numerous important works, and that of the founding of the Anthropological Institute), 1896 (when Boas established anthropology at Columbia University), and 1922 (Rivers' death, the publication of important works by Malinowski and Radcliffe-Brown, and the approximate date each of them began teaching in earnest their functional theories). Figure 11.1 illustrates this vision of the history of anthropology, together with the development of sociology and the false start of the mainly German philological tradition.

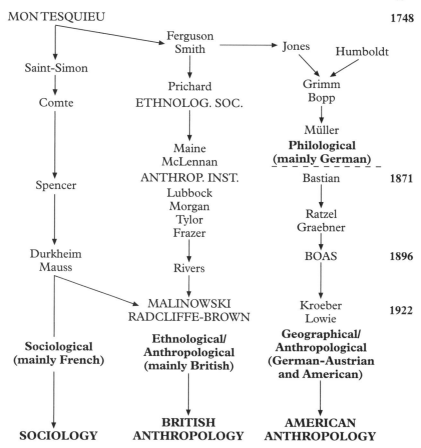

Figure 11.1 Three traditions

That said, it is not always easy to define traditions in anthropology along national lines. Fortes more than once remarked that modern social anthropology contains 'two distinct lines of descent':

I see one as going back through Radcliffe-Brown, Lowie, and Rivers, to Morgan and Maine in particular, and the other as going back through Kroeber, Malinowski, and Frazer, to Tylor and to some extent Boas. I see the first line as the source of our structural concepts and theories, the second as the source of our speciality in the study of facts of custom, or culture. (Fortes 1969: 14)

This confounds the notion that American anthropology is the tradition concerned with culture, while British anthropology is the tradition concerned with society (Radcliffe-Brown, Rivers, Maine, Malinowski,

Frazer, and Tylor were British; and Lowie, Morgan, Kroeber, and Boas were American). Fortes went on to say that in the metaphorically 'double descent system' which makes up anthropology, each anthropologist belongs to both descent groups and takes from each according to the task at hand.

Integration of all theoretical approaches is one logical possibility. However, it is not likely that a single agreed paradigm will emerge, at least in the short term. What is likely is that there will be an integration of ideas on the part of individuals. This has been in practice for many years, beginning with people such as Edmund Leach (with his blend of structuralist and action-oriented ideas). Nowadays many anthropologists fall, at times, within the scope of more than one paradigm, and some blend two or more. Very broadly three contemporary approaches or emphases may be noted: interpretation, action, and structure. The relation between paradigms associated with such approaches has already been noted (in chapter 10), but others may be possibilities. For example, another set sometimes discussed is that of structure, event, and history (see Augé 1982 [1979]). In their different ways, regional comparison and Marxism may be said to have elements of both structure and history, whereas other approaches could potentially mix event with either of these two (see Holy and Stuchlik 1983).

Today there are a great number of theoretical perspectives for anthropologists to choose from, and these are each made up of many lines of influence. The possibilities for combining them are enormous. This is a positive and truly postmodern tendency. The danger is that the narrower postmodernist project might hold sway, with non-postmodernly correct positions being rejected simply because they make explicit their pre-postmodern origins. However, the acceptance of a diversity of approaches – with the utilization of theoretical ideas according to topic of concern – is at least as old as the early relativism of Franz Boas. Indeed, even before that, anthropologists were free to accept other influences and combine perspectives. For example, Morgan and Tylor happily incorporated diffusionist elements into their specific unilinear-evolutionist schemes.

Anthropologists also operate at different levels of theory: in grand theory, in middle range theory, and increasingly in specific theoretical debates. Anthropology as a whole (including biological as well as cultural anthropology) retains a long-standing concern with two quite different problems: the understanding of human nature and the study of cultural diversity. In the eighteenth-century Enlightenment the former was the main interest. With the development of anthropology proper, in the nineteenth century, cultural diversity became prominent in the hands of the polygenists. Later it came to be what unilinear evolutionism was trying to explain. With Boas and the early relativists, diversity was extolled as a wonder of humanity, and it has seen some resurgence in recent years. Since the 1970s, relativism has come back and swamped both the old functionalist interests in social laws and the structuralist (including structural-Marxist) interests in cultural universals.

Further thoughts on histories of anthropology

Can there ever be a true history of a discipline? Or, the converse, is all history 'Whig history'? I think there are good grounds for favouring the latter, inherently relativistic, view, or at least for admitting that whenever anthropologists put pen to paper they will come out with a somewhat Whiggish version of events. 'Whig history' is a phrase coined by Sir Herbert Butterfield around 1931, when he said that historians have all too often seen history as a conflict between progressives and reactionaries, where the progressives (Whigs) eventually win and bring about changes effecting the present situation. Whig history is thus subjective and 'presentist', and that is why true historians do not like it (see, e.g., Stocking 1968 [1965]: 1-12). Good history, they say, is 'historicist', in a very precise sense of that word.

Yet much of the history of anthropology, especially that written by practising anthropologists, is presentist because that history is relevant to today's concerns. It is also, in the hands of several practitioners, *mythical* in the sense that Malinowski (1948 [1925]: 79, 120) used the word. By this I mean that history gives anthropologists a 'mythical charter' by which to view their own place in the discipline. I would not deny that my own history of the discipline is somewhat 'mythical', 'presentist', and 'Whiggish'. Such a heretical view is acceptable to me because in this book I do not claim to be presenting *the history* of anthropology, but only one possible history among many. More accurately, I am presenting snippets of history chosen and juxtaposed to show the complex connections among the different ideas which make up, not the history of anthropology, but anthropological theory.

There are other possible histories, and there can be more complex uses of history to illustrate ideas. The simple 'great man' view is found in many books, for example, in Adam Kuper's *Anthropology and Anthropologists* (1996 [1973]) or Jerry Moore's *Visions of Culture* (1997). In contrast, L. R. Hiatt chooses a unique method of historical portrayal in *Arguments about Aborigines* (Hiatt 1996). He focuses on aspects of Aboriginal society (gender relations, conception beliefs, political organization, land issues, etc.) and the ways in which each has been interpreted by successive generations of anthropologists.

In *A Century of Controversy* Elman Service (1985) focuses on the specifics of anthropological debate, with issues like the status of kinship terminologies or the nature of culture coming to the forefront. Murray Leaf, in *Man, Mind, and Science* (1979), virtually sets aside anthropological debate in favour of a history of anthropology seen in terms of philosophical questions. Robert Layton's recent book, *An Introduction to Theory in Anthropology* (1997), lies in-between. Layton touches on both debates and philosophical questions (as well as questions of ethnographic interpretation), but largely ignores pre-functionalist anthropology and downplays national traditions. Jack Goody's *The Expansive Moment* (1995) and Henrika Kuklick's *The Savage Within* (1991) present social histories of British anthropology, but they differ profoundly in method and the interpretation of that history. James Urry, in *Before Social Anthropology* (1993), blends several approaches, as his is a collection of his own diverse essays on the history of British anthropology.

This list is certainly not exhaustive, but it gives some idea of the range of possibilities that have, to date, been realized. I hope also that it confirms my feeling that there is no such thing as *the* history of anthropology, any more than an ethnographer today could claim to be writing *the* ethnography of his or her 'people'.

Concluding summary

I do not accept that old anthropological theories die with their proponents. Rather, I hold that in general they are either incorporated into new theoretical trends, or they return in some later generation in a different guise. The foundations of our discipline were there in the Enlightenment, especially in the notion of the social contract (the seventeenth- and eighteenth-century basis of all social science), but the discipline itself emerged in the nineteenth century. The arguments of early theorists remain worthy of close scrutiny, partly because they illustrate so well the character of incipient and past anthropology. They are important equally because anthropologists of later times, and even today, define their own positions in relation to those of earlier writers – either in opposition to them or, not uncommonly, in the augmentation and transformation of their theoretical notions.

Evolutionism is often thought of as a nineteenth-century theory. But then, what about the preconceptions of the late twentieth century? Evolution is not entirely unrelated to the commonplace idea of progress or to the notion of social development. 'Progress', in fact, was a very nineteenth-century concept, and it is retained in our thinking today. The word 'development', with its present-day meaning of helping out people in poorer countries to be economically, at least, more like people in richer countries, is only about forty or fifty years old. Yet in some respects, this concept represents a re-invention of Victorian evolutionary theory. It suggests similar ways of thinking about relations between technology, economics, and society to those pursued by nineteenth-century reformers and social theorists. What many nineteenth- and late twentieth-century anthropologists have in common is a desire to understand causal relationships within a framework of 'progress' or 'advancement'. Some late twentieth-century anthropologists have even taken up the search for human cultural origins, and this represents a promising development – given especially the much greater sophistication of relevant cognate disciplines, such as archaeology, linguistics, and human genetics.

Diffusionism in its pure and extreme forms is long dead, but ideas which grew from diffusionist schools, such as an interest in historical particularities and the notion of the culture area, have, if anything, increased in importance in the last few decades. Regional studies within various theoretical traditions are also increasing in prominence, as anthropological studies focus more on similarities and differences between closely related cultures. The increase in regional focus stems directly from the sheer number of ethnographic studies done by modern anthropologists.

Relativism has been a prominent feature of anthropological traditions, especially in North America, since Boas. In a sense, all anthropology is relativistic, as by its very nature the study of variety in human culture does, or at least should, lead to an appreciation of cultures in their own terms. This does not mean that all anthropologists are relativists in any pure sense. On the contrary, both 'pro' and 'anti' positions on relativism are prominent today, and the new relativism of reflexivity and discourse analysis stems not only from a renewal of interest in Boasian ideas, but equally from the influence of interdisciplinary postmodernist foci.

Functionalism, like diffusionism, is a word few anthropologists would be associated with today. However, functionalist methodology remains the basis of anthropological fieldwork. As Edmund Leach used to say, all anthropologists are functionalists when in the field, because they need to see how social institutions are related and how individuals interact with one another. When anthropologists return from the field to their respective universities, he claimed, they reformulate their ideas in frameworks which go beyond functionalism. In Leach's own case, this resulted in a mixture of structuralism and processualism. For others, it results in different mixes, but the functionalist basis of anthropology itself, like its relativist basis, is still there.

Structuralism achieved great notoriety, thanks especially to the work of Lévi-Strauss, which was influential well beyond the boundaries of anthropology. Within anthropology, Marxist thought frequently had a strong structuralist element. Regional comparison as a theoretical paradigm took much from Lévi-Straussian structuralism and from the Dutch school which preceded it. To some extent too, interpretivist and postmodern perspectives build on structuralism and functionalism precisely by making explicit their rejection of the tenets of these earlier paradigms. They depend, at least in anthropology (perhaps less so in literary criticism, for example), on their own structural opposition to structuralism itself.

Processual and interactive approaches had their heyday in the immediate post-functionalist era, but they too have strengthened with each challenge to the conservatism of static approaches of all kinds. Probably they will never die, as all anthropologists now realize that they must take account of the nuances of social interaction and social change. Processual approaches offered a good antidote to overly formal ideas within functionalism and structuralism. They also enabled function-minded and structurally inclined anthropologists to look more closely at the nuances of social life through their studies of relations between different social or symbolic structures.

Early British interpretive approaches, such as the diverse ones of Evans-Pritchard, Needham, and Ardener at Oxford, built upon functionalism and structuralism while rejecting the analogies on which they are based. They sought structures which are intuitive, and encouraged scepticism of formal approaches and universalistic comparisons. Postmodernist, poststructuralist, feminist, and Marxist approaches all amplify this through their emphasis on the relation between the culture of the anthropologist and the culture of the informant, and more particularly on the relationship between anthropologist and informant as people, each with their own understanding of the other. An added dimension is that the anthropologist, knowing this, must reinterpret his or her own actions and consciousness of purpose in the very process of engagement with the 'other'.

Finally, it is worth reiterating the fact that anthropology is a discipline very conscious of its past. Anthropological theory has a complex history, but its structure can be seen through the influences of individuals, the interplay within and between national traditions, and the development of new foci of interest, new ideas from within and from beyond anthropology itself, and (every few decades) new grand perspectives. Yet there are many ways in which to envisage that history and these relationships. I have put them together in the way that I read them. Others may read, interpret, construct, or deconstruct them differently.

Appendix 1
Dates of birth and death of individuals mentioned in the text

Albert, Prince (Franz Albrecht, Prinz von Sachsen-Coburg-Gotha),
    1819–61
Althusser, Louis, 1918–90
Ardener, Edwin, 1927–87
Aristotle, 384–322 BC
Asad, Talal, 1927–
Atran, Scott, 1952–
Avebury, Lord, see Lubbock, Sir John, Bt.

Bachofen, J. J., 1815–77
Bailey, F. G., 1924–
Barnes, J. A., 1918–
Barth, Fredrik, 1928–
Bastian, Adolph, 1826–1905
Bateson, Gregory, 1904–80
Bateson, William, 1861–1926
Benedict, Ruth Fulton, 1887–1948
Bentham, Jeremy, 1748–1832
Binford, Lewis R., 1930–
Boas, Franz, 1858–1942
Boissevain, Jeremy, 1928–
Bopp, Franz, 1791–1867
Bourdieu, Pierre, 1930–
Buffon, Georges-Louis Leclerc, comte de, 1707–88
Bunzel, Ruth, 1898–1990
Burke, William, 1792–1829
Burnett (Burnet), James, see Monboddo, Lord
Butterfield, Sir Herbert, 1900–79
Buxton, Sir Thomas Fowell, Bt., 1786–1845

Caplan, Pat, 1942–
Carrier, James G., 1947–

Chagnon, Napoleon A., 1938–
Childe, V. Gordon, 1892–1957
Chomsky, Noam, 1928–
Clifford, James, 1945–
Cohen, Anthony P., 1946–
Colson, Elizabeth, 1917–
Comaroff, Jean, 1946–
Comaroff, John, 1945–
Comte, Auguste, 1798–1857
Cook, Captain James, 1728–79
Crapanzano, Vincent, 1939–
Cushing, Frank, 1857–1900

Darwin, Charles, 1809–82
De Groot, Huig, see Grotius, Hugo
De Heusch, Luc, 1927–
De Saussure, Ferdinand, see Saussure, Ferdinand de
Denzin, Norman K., 1941–
Derrida, Jacques, 1930–
Douglas, Mary, 1921–
Dryden, John, 1631–1700
Dumont, Louis, 1911–98
Durkheim, Emile, 1858–1917

Eggan, Fred, 1906–91
Einstein, Albert, 1879–1955
Elkin, A. P., 1891–1979
Elliot Smith, Sir Grafton, 1871–1937
Engels, Friedrich, 1820–95
Epstein, A. L. (Bill), 1924–
Epstein, T. S. (Scarlett), 1922–
Evans-Pritchard, Sir Edward E., 1902–73

Fardon, Richard, 1952–
Ferguson, Adam, 1723–1816
Fernandez, James W., 1930–
Firth, Sir Raymond, 1902–
Fischer, Michael M. J., 1946–
Fortes, Meyer, 1906–83
Fortune, Reo F., 1903–79
Foucault, Michel, 1926–84
Fox, Robin, 1934–

Frake, Charles O., 1930–
Frank, Andre Gunder, 1929–
Frazer, Sir James, 1854–1941
Freeman, J. Derek, 1916–
Freud, Sigmund, 1856–1939
Friedman, Jonathan, 1946–
Frobenius, Leo, 1873–1938

Geertz, Clifford, 1926–
Gellner, Ernest, 1925–95
George I, King of Great Britain and Elector of Hanover,
    1660–1727
Gluckman, Max, 1911–75
Godelier, Maurice, 1934–
Goodenough, Ward H., 1919–
Goody, Jack, 1919–
Graebner, Fritz, 1877–1934
Granet, Marcel, 1884–1940
Grimm, Jacob, 1785–1863
Grimm, Wilhelm, 1786–1859
Grotius, Hugo (Huig de Groot), 1583–1645

Hare, William, d. 1860
Harris, Marvin, 1929–
Hastrup, Kirsten, 1948–
Helman, Cecil, 1944–
Herder, Johann Gottfried von, 1744–1803
Herskovits, Melville J., 1895–1963
Hertz, Robert, 1881–1915
Herzfeld, Michael, 1947–
Heyerdahl, Thor, 1914–
Hiatt, L. R., 1931–
Hjelmslev, Louis, 1899–1965
Hobbes, Thomas, 1588–1679
Hodgkin, Thomas, 1798–1866
Holy, Ladislav, 1933–97
Home, Henry, see Kames, Lord
Humboldt, Alexander von, 1769–1859
Humboldt, Wilhelm von, 1767–1835
Hume, David, 1711–76
Hunt, James, 1833–69
Hunter, Monica, see Wilson, Monica

Ingold, Tim, 1948–

Jakobson, Roman Osipovich, 1896–1982
Jones, Sir William, 1746–94
Josselin de Jong, J. P. B. de, 1886–1964

Kaberry, Phyllis M., 1910–77
Kames, Lord (Henry Home), 1696–1782
Kapferer, Bruce, 1940–
Kardiner, Abram, 1891–1981
Kenyatta, Jomo (Johnstone Kemau), 1889–1978
Kluckhohn, Clyde, 1905–60
Knauft, Bruce M., 1954–
Knight, Chris, 1942–
Knox, Robert, 1791–1862
Krige, Eileen Jensen, 1904–95
Kroeber, Alfred Louis, 1876–1960
Kropotkin, Peter, 1842–1921
Kuhn, Thomas, 1922–96
Kuper, Adam, 1941–
Kuper, Hilda Beemer, 1911–92

Lacan, Jacques, 1901–83
Lamarck, Jean-Baptiste de Monet, chevalier de, 1744–1829
Lang, Andrew, 1844–1912
Layton, Robert, 1944–
Le Blanc, Marie-Angélique ('Wild Girl of Champagne'),
     b. c. 1721
Leach, Sir Edmund R., 1910–89
Leacock, Eleanor, 1922–88
Lee, Richard B., 1937–
Lévi-Strauss, Claude, 1908–
Lévy-Bruhl, Lucien, 1857–1939
Lewis, Oscar, 1914–70
Leyton, Elliott, 1939–
Lienhardt, Godfrey, 1921–93
Linnaeus, Carolus (Carl von Linné), 1707–78
Locke, John, 1632–1704
Long, Norman, 1936–
Lowie, Robert H., 1883–1957
Lubbock, Sir John, Bt. (Lord Avebury), 1834–1913
Lyotard, Jean-François, 1924–

Maine, Sir Henry Sumner, 1822–88
Malinowski, Bronislaw, 1884–1942
Marx, Karl, 1818–83
Mauss, Marcel, 1872–1950
Max Müller, F., see Müller, Friedrich Max
McLennan, John Ferguson, 1827–1881
Mead, Margaret, 1901–78
Mendelssohn, Felix, 1809–47
Mitchell, J. Clyde, 1918–
Monboddo, Lord (James Burnett), 1714–99
Montelius, Oscar, 1843–1921
Montesquieu, Charles-Louis de Secondat, baron de la Brède et de,
     1689–1755
Moore, Henrietta L., 1957–
Morgan, Lewis Henry, 1818–81
Müller, Friedrich Max, 1823–1900
Murdock, George Peter, 1897–1985

Nadel, S. F., 1903–54
Needham, Rodney, 1923–
Newton, Sir Isaac, 1642–1727
Nietzsche, Friedrich, 1844–1900
Nilsson, Sven, 1787–1883

Obeyesekere, Gananath, 1930–
Okely, Judith, 1941–
Ortner, Sherry B., 1941–

Pasquinelli, Carla, 1939–
Perry, Commodore Matthew, 1794–1858
Perry, William James, 1887–1949
Peter ('Wild Peter of Hanover'), c. 1710–85
Piaget, Jean, 1896–1980
Pike, Kenneth L., 1912–
Prichard, James Cowles, 1786–1848
Pufendorf (Puffendorf), Samuel, Freiherr von, 1632–94

Radcliffe–Brown, A. R., 1881–1955
Ratzel, Friedrich, 1844–1904
Redfield, Robert, 1897–1958
Rivers, W. H. R., 1864–1922
Rosaldo, Michelle Z., 1944–81

Rosaldo, Renato, 1941–
Rousseau, Jean-Jacques, 1712–78

Sahlins, Marshall, 1930–
Said, Edward W., 1935–
Saint-Simon, Claude-Henri de Rouvroy, comte de, 1760–1825
Sapir, Edward, 1884–1939
Saussure, Ferdinand de, 1857–1913
Schapera, I., 1905–
Schmidt, Pater Wilhelm, 1868–1954
Schneider, David M., 1918–95
Seligman, C. G., 1873–1940
Service, Elman R., 1915–96
Simmel, Georg, 1858–1918
Smith, Adam, 1723–90
Smith, William Robertson, 1846–94
Spencer, Herbert, 1820–1903
Spencer, Jonathan, 1954–
Spiro, Melford, 1926–
Spivak, Gayatri Chakravorty, 1942–
Srinivas, M. N., 1916–
Steward, Julian H., 1902–72
Stewart, Dugald, 1753–1828
Stocking, George W., Jr, 1928–
Strathern, Andrew, 1939–
Strathern, Marilyn, 1941–
Stuchlik, Milan, 1932–80

Tax, Sol, 1907–95
Thomsen, Christian Jürgensen, 1788–1865
Trubetzkoy, Nikolai Sergeyevich, 1890–1938
Turner, Victor W., 1920–83
Tyler, Stephen A., 1932–
Tylor, Sir Edward Burnett, 1832–1917

Urry, James, 1949–

Van Gennep, Arnold, 1873–1957
Vico, Giambattista, 1668–1744
Victor ('Wild Boy of Aveyron'), b. c. 1788
Victoria, Queen of the United Kingdom and Empress of India, 1819–
    1901

Wallace, Alfred Russel, 1823–1913
Wallerstein, Immanuel, 1930–
Weber, Max, 1864–1920
Werbner, Richard P., 1937–
Westermarck, Edward, 1862–1939
White, Leslie A., 1900–75
Whorf, Benjamin Lee, 1897–1941
Willis, Roy G., 1927–
Wilmsen, Edwin N., 1932–
Wilson, Edward O., 1929–
Wilson, Godfrey, 1908–1944
Wilson, Monica (Monica Hunter), 1908–82
Wissler, Clark, 1870–1947
Worsley, Peter, 1924–

Appendix 2
Glossary

ablineal relative A blood relative (e.g., a cousin) who is neither in ego's line of descent nor the brother or sister of one who is (cf. **co-lineal relative, collateral relative**).

action-centred approaches Approaches which emphasize social action over social structure, such as transactionalism.

affine, affinal relative A relative by marriage.

age-area hypothesis Wissler's notion that older culture traits tend to be those on the periphery of a culture area, rather than in the centre. His hypothesis is based on the idea that things are invented in the centre and diffuse outwards.

age set A category of people united by common age, often those initiated into adulthood at the same time.

agenda hopping D'Andrade's notion of researchers changing their interests when old paradigms yield fewer and fewer insights (cf. **Kuhnian**)

androcentric Male-centred.

animism A belief in a spiritual presence within things such as rocks and trees.

anthropogeography The nineteenth-century German university subject, roughly equivalent to human geography. It gave birth to diffusionism.

anthropology In its widest sense, the subject which includes social or cultural anthropology, anthropological linguistics, prehistoric archaeology, and biological or physical anthropology (cf. **four fields**). In a narrower sense, a short name for social anthropology.

Apollonian An aspect of drama or culture characterized by measure, restraint, and harmony (cf. **Dionysian**).

articulation of modes of production Interaction between different modes of production, for example as when colonial capitalist and lineage-based societies come into contact.

associative Saussure's term for what are now usually called paradigmatic relations in a language or symbolic system.

avunculate   The relationship between a child and his or her mother's brother. More specifically, the term usually refers to accepted informal behaviour between a boy and his mother's brother, contrasted to formality between the boy and his father.

avunculocal   Another word for viri-avunculocal (residing with the husband's mother's brother).

barbarism   In evolutionist theory, the stage of society which lies between savagery and civilization. It is characterized by the possession of things such as pottery, livestock, etc. (cf. **savagery**, **civilization**).

base   The material aspect of society, believed by Marxists to be determinant of the superstructure or ideological aspect of society (cf. **infrastructure**, **superstructure**).

basic needs   In Malinowskian theory, the seven biological needs (e.g., safety) which are served by seven corresponding cultural responses (e.g., protection).

Boasian   Referring to the ideas of Franz Boas, especially with reference to his cultural relativism.

bridewealth   Marriage gifts or payments made from the family of the groom to the family of the bride.

British structuralism   Originally a synonym for structural-functionalism (in the 1950s), but later used to refer to the work of British anthropologists who had taken up French structuralist ideas (from the 1960s). British structuralists (in the latter sense) tended to be interested in structural elements of one culture at a time (cf. **Dutch structuralism**, **French structuralism**).

centre   In opposition to periphery, the economically dominant place. Its centrality does not have to be geographical. For example, in world-systems theory a colonial power may be defined as the 'centre' and its colonies the 'periphery'.

civil society   In the eighteenth century, generally a synonym for government or the state. (More recently the term has been used to refer to anti-state groupings or occasionally to 'society' in contrast to 'the state'.)

civilization   In evolutionist theory, the highest level of society, characterized by urbanization, social hierarchy, and complex social structure (cf. **savagery**, **barbarism**).

cognitive anthropology   The branch of anthropology or perspective within anthropology which emphasizes the relation between cultural categories and structures or processes of thought.

cognitive relativism   The form of relativism which holds that all statements about the world are culturally contingent (cf. **moral relativism**).

cognitive science   A somewhat broader term for cognitive anthropology, or any field which emphasizes the relation between cultural categories and structures or processes of thought.

'cold' societies   Lévi-Strauss' term for societies he believed to be essentially static. 'Cold' societies have a concern with myth rather than history (cf. **'hot' societies**).

co-lineal relative   Ego's brother or sister or the brother or sister of someone who is in ego's line of descent (e.g., an uncle or nephew) (cf. **ablineal relative, collateral relative**).

collateral relative   A blood relative who is not in ego's line of descent (e.g., a cousin). Sometimes brothers and sisters are included and sometimes not (cf. **lineal relative, direct relative**).

collective conscience, collective consciousness   Durkheim's term for the collective understandings which people within a given society share (French, *conscience collective*).

collective representation   Any of the collective understandings which people in a given society share (cf. **collective conscience**).

communitas   Turner's term for an unstructured realm of 'social structure', where often the normal ranking of individuals is reversed or the symbols of rank inverted. This sense of 'community', he said, characterizes rites of passage.

community   A group of people who share common values. The term has come to be regarded as safer than 'society', whose existence has been challenged by some postmodernist thinkers (as well as some politicians).

comparative philology   An older term for the study of historical or structural relations between languages.

comparative sociology   A term occasionally used by Radcliffe-Brown to mean 'social anthropology'.

competence   In linguistics, the ability or knowledge required by a native speaker to tell intuitively whether a construction is grammatical or not (cf. **performance**).

complex structures   According to Lévi-Strauss, those kinship systems based on rules about whom one may not marry (e.g., that marriage between close relatives is forbidden) (cf. **elementary structures**).

component   In componential analysis, a synonym for 'significatum'.

componential analysis   A method or theoretical perspective which examines the relation between cultural categories as parts of a system of such categories, for example the system of colour terms in a given language.

conjectural history Originally an eighteenth-century term for the methods of historical reconstruction favoured by thinkers such as Adam Smith and much later by evolutionists and diffusionists.

connotatum An element in componential analysis which implies connotation rather than signification (e.g., 'uncle-like behaviour' as opposed to a more formal defining feature of the category 'uncle') (cf. **significatum**).

consanguine, consanguineal relative A relative by blood.

conscience collective Durkheim's term for the collective understandings which people within a given society share (in English, 'collective conscience' or more commonly 'collective consciousness').

consonant triangle Jakobson's term for the structural relations between p, t, and k as representing a system defined according to relative loudness and pitch (cf. **vowel triangle**).

controlled comparison Any form of comparison which involves limiting the range of variables, such as by confining comparisons to those within a region.

couvade A custom whereby a man feels or pretends to be pregnant when his wife is about to give birth, often to draw malevolent forces away from his wife and child.

cross-cousins The children of a brother and those of a sister. In many societies, cross-cousins are marriageable whereas parallel cousins are not (cf. **parallel cousins**).

'Crow' terminology A type of kinship terminology in which the father's sister's daughter is called by the same term as the father's sister, or more generally one in which ego calls several members of his or her father's matrilineal kin group by the same term (cf. **'Omaha' terminology**).

Crow-Omaha systems Lévi-Strauss' term for systems lying in-between elementary and complex ones: systems with 'Crow' or 'Omaha' terminologies in which all those called by kin terms are forbidden as possible spouses.

culinary triangle A structural model proposed by Lévi-Strauss in which roast, smoked, and boiled foods are seen as analogous to raw, cooked, and rotted foods.

cultural anthropology The branch of anthropology or the academic discipline which is concerned with the study of cultural diversity. The term is typically used in the North American traditions, whereas in other traditions 'ethnology' or 'social anthropology' are the more common terms, often with slightly different subject matter (cf. **ethnology, social anthropology, four fields**).

cultural core, culture core In Steward's cultural ecology, the aspects of culture most susceptible to ecological influence (e.g., subsistence, patterns of migration) (cf. **total culture**).

cultural determinism   The notion that culture, rather than biology, regulates the ways in which humans perceive the world.

cultural ecology   The study of relations between culture and the natural world, especially in the theoretical perspective of Julian Steward.

cultural materialism   The theoretical perspective of Marvin Harris, who argues that there is a direct causal relation between material forces and aspects of culture (cf. **vulgar materialism**).

cultural relativism   Any of several theoretical perspectives in anthropology, including descriptive relativism, epistemological relativism, and normative relativism.

cultural responses   In Malinowskian theory, the seven basic aspects of culture (e.g., protection) each of which serves a biological need (in this case, safety).

cultural studies   The discipline concerned with the study of mass culture, popular culture, etc. Although it touches on anthropological interests, it has its origins in and its most direct links with literary criticism and sociology.

culture   In anthropology, usually taken as the totality of ideas, skills, and objects shared by a community or society. In other contexts, it is sometimes useful to distinguish the 'high culture' of the elite or the (often transient) 'popular culture' of the majority.

'culture and personality'   The perspective of Ruth Benedict and her followers which emphasizes the 'personality' of whole cultures rather than individuals.

culture area   A cluster of related cultures, normally those occupying a geographical region.

culture circle   A cluster of related culture traits, or the geographical area where these are found. The idea is fundamental to German-Austrian diffusionists, who saw these circles as spreading progressively over earlier culture circles (German, *Kulturkreis*).

culture trait   Any individual item of culture, either material or non-material.

culturo-genesis   The origin of culture, or more usually, of symbolic culture.

Darwinian   Referring to the ideas of Charles Darwin, for example in his opposition to Lamarckian ideas (cf. **Darwinism**).

Darwinism   Any of several related perspectives derived from the evolutionist theory of Charles Darwin, and especially the idea of evolution through natural selection.

deconstruction   Derrida's term for a method of literary analysis which seeks to expose the underlying assumptions of a text.

deductivism, deductivist   Any approach which proceeds from general assumptions to specific conclusions (cf. **inductivism**).

degeneration theory, degenerativist theory   The anti-evolutionist notion that organisms or societies decline in physical or moral quality.

delayed direct exchange   Lévi-Strauss' term for a type of marital exchange between kin groups where women move in one direction in one generation, and in the opposite direction in the next. It is a logical consequence of men marrying fathers' sisters' daughters (cf. **direct exchange, generalized exchange**).

denotatum   In componential analysis, a member of a given category.

descriptive relativism   The form of relativism which holds that culture regulates the ways in which humans perceive the world, and therefore that cultural variability will produce different social and psychological understandings among different peoples (cf. **epistemological relativism, normative relativism**).

designatum   In componential analysis, the term for a given category.

diachronic perspective   A perspective through time (e.g., evolutionism), rather than one in the same time frame (cf. **synchronic perspective**).

différance   Derrida's term implying roughly 'a delay in difference', in that the differences which define something in opposition to what it is not, cannot, in his view, be fully conceptualized. There is always, he argues, something beyond such differences.

diffusion   The movement of culture traits from one people to another.

diffusionism, diffusionist   A perspective which emphasizes diffusion (or sometimes migration) over evolution as the greater cause of cultural change in the world.

Dionysian   An aspect of drama or culture characterized by emotion, passion, and excess (cf. **Apollonian**).

direct exchange   Lévi-Strauss' term for a type of marital exchange between kin groups where exchanges of women may go in either direction. It is a logical consequence of men exchanging sisters with each other or marrying women of a category which includes both mothers' brothers' daughters and fathers' sisters' daughters (cf. **delayed direct exchange, generalized exchange**).

direct relative   A lineal relative or the brother or sister of a lineal relative (cf. **collateral relative**).

discourse   A complex concept involving the way people talk or write about something, the body of knowledge implied, or the use of that knowledge, such as in structures of power (e.g., in the work of

Foucault). The term can also have the meaning (as in linguistics) of units of speech longer than a sentence.

dispositions   In Bourdieu's terminology, tendencies or choices individuals have within the habitus (see also **habitus**).

distinctive features   Those features whose presence or absence defines a given phenomenon. For example, in phonology the feature of voicing defines the difference between a *p* (voiceless) and a *b* (voiced).

Durkheimian   Referring to the ideas of Emile Durkheim, especially his emphasis on social structure as a determinant of belief and ideology.

Dutch structuralism   Structuralism in The Netherlands, arguably as early as the 1920s, which emphasized regional structures such as that of the cultures of the Malay Archipelago taken as a whole (cf. **British structuralism, French structuralism**).

ecosystem   In ecology and ecological anthropology, the system which includes both social and natural environments.

ego   In discussions of kinship, the person from whose point of view a relationship is traced (meaning 'I' or 'self').

eidos   According to Bateson, the form or structure of culture or cultural phenomena (cf. **ethos**).

Elementargedanken   'Elementary thoughts', those beliefs and aspects of culture held by Bastian to be common to all humankind (cf. **psychic identity, Völkergedanken**).

elementary structures   According to Lévi-Strauss, those kinship systems based on categories between which marriage is prescribed (e.g., the category of the cross-cousin) (cf. **complex structures**).

embodiment   The notion that social or cultural categories are inseparable from the bodies of the individuals who possess them.

emic   Relating to a culture-specific system of thought based on indigenous definitions (cf. **etic**).

empiricism, empiricist   The doctrine which holds that knowledge is derived from experience rather than from prior reasoning (cf. **rationalism**).

enculturation   The process by which people, especially children, acquire culture (cf. **socialization**).

Enlightenment   The mainly eighteenth-century movement which stressed the importance of reason for the critical understanding of nature and society.

epistemological relativism   The form of relativism which holds that human nature and the human mind are culturally variable, and therefore that all general theories of culture are fallacious (cf. **descriptive relativism, normative relativism**).

epistemology   In philosophy, the theory of knowledge.

esprit general   Montesquieu's term (meaning 'general spirit') for the fundamental essence of a given culture.

esprit humain   Lévi-Strauss' term (meaning 'human spirit') for the psychic unity or collective unconsciousness of humanity as a whole. In his usage it implies a structure of thought universal among humanity.

ethnography   Literally, 'writing about peoples', the term also implies the practice of anthropological fieldwork.

ethnology   The study of ethnic groups, broadly a synonym for social or cultural anthropology. The term was in general use in Britain prior to the 1870s, but since then has been more common on the Continent and to some extent in North America (cf. **cultural anthropology**, **social anthropology**).

ethnoscience   Most literally, the scientific notions of indigenous peoples. More commonly the term implies methods such as componential analysis, designed to elucidate such knowledge.

ethos   According to Bateson, the distinctive character or spirit of an event or a culture (cf. **eidos**).

etic   Relating to categories held to be universal or based on an outside observer's objective understanding (cf. **emic**).

evolution   A change or development, such as from simple to complex. Usually this change is regarded as gradual (cf. **revolutionist**).

evolutionism, evolutionist   Any perspective which stresses change for the better or advancement from simple to complex. In contrast to diffusionism, a perspective which emphasizes evolution over diffusion or migration as the greater cause of cultural change in the world. In contrast to a revolutionist perspective, one which argues for gradual over revolutionary change.

extended case study   A case study presented in detail within an ethnographic article or book, in order to illustrate a more general point. The idea came into anthropology from legal studies and is characteristic of the Manchester School.

feminism, feminist   The movement which developed to counteract male-dominant representations and male dominance generally.

feral child   A child existing in a 'natural' state, unsocialized by humans but sometimes believed to have been reared by wild animals.

fetishism   The belief in fetishes, or objects believed to have supernatural power.

fetishization   The act of treating something as a fetish or as being like a fetish. It is used especially in the latter, metaphorical sense (e.g., Marxist references to the 'fetishization of commodities').

forces of production   In Marxist theory, things such as raw materials and technology which form the material as opposed to the social aspect of the economic base; or the interaction of these elements of the means of production with labour (cf. **base, mode of production, relations of production**).

Foucauldian, Foucaultian   Referring to the ideas of Michel Foucault (cf. **discourse**).

four fields   The classic division of American and Canadian anthropology: cultural anthropology, anthropological linguistics, prehistoric archaeology, and biological or physical anthropology. In other countries these 'four fields' tend to be treated as separate disciplines rather than as branches of the same subject.

French structuralism   In its widest sense, the ideas of Claude Lévi-Strauss and his admirers. In a narrower sense, the perspective within anthropology which emphasizes structures of the human mind rather than structures in the minds of members of particular cultures or people from particular culture areas (cf. **British structuralism, Dutch structuralism**).

function   A term variously used to denote the purpose of a custom or social institution in the abstract, or its relation to other customs or social institutions within a social system.

functionalism, functionalist   Any perspective which emphasizes the functions of customs or social institutions. In anthropology it refers especially to the perspectives of either B. Malinowski (regarded as a 'purer' functionalist) or A. R. Radcliffe-Brown (a structural-functionalist).

Geertzian   Referring to the ideas of Clifford Geertz (cf. **interpretivism**).

Geist   Literally, the 'ghost' or 'spirit' of a society.

genealogical grid   The set of statuses believed to lie at the foundation of all kinship systems, no matter how relatives are classified in any given culture or society.

general spirit   Montesquieu's term (*esprit general*) for the fundamental essence of a given culture.

generalized exchange   Lévi-Strauss' term for a type of marital exchange between kin groups where 'exchanges' of women are in one direction only, for example where a son may marry into the same kin group as his father but a daughter may not. It is a logical consequence of men marrying mothers' brothers' daughters (cf. **delayed direct exchange, direct exchange**).

genotype   The genetic makeup of an organism (cf. **phenotype**).

global comparison, global-sample comparison   Comparison on a world-wide basis in the search for universal cross-cultural generalizations or predictions.

globalization   The process of increasing contact between societies, especially in the economic sphere, across the globe (cf. **localization, re-localization**)

'God's truth'   In linguistics and cognitive anthropology, the view that a good analysis of a set of emic categories will represent the true psychological reality of informants (cf. **'hocus-pocus'**).

Great Chain of Being   The view of the world as consisting of a hierarchy of entities from God to humanity to animals to plants, etc. It was prevalent in the sixteenth, seventeenth, and eighteenth centuries and, in contrast to the theory of evolution, based on a notion of the fixity of species.

grid   Mary Douglas' term for the 'dimension' of constraint through individual isolation (cf. **group, grid/group analysis**).

grid/group analysis   The analysis of 'grid' and 'group' constraints in the style of Mary Douglas.

group   Mary Douglas' term for the 'dimension' of constraint on individuals as members of groups (cf. **grid, grid/group analysis**).

gumlao, gumsa   Among the Kachin of Burma, the two social formations, *gumlao* being egalitarian and *gumsa* being hierarchical.

habitus   In Bourdieu's terminology, the culturally defined system of knowledge and social action made up of 'dispositions' or choices available to individuals (see also **dispositions**).

heliocentrism, heliocentric   Literally 'with the sun at the centre', the extreme diffusionist perspective of the early twentieth century which held that the sun-worshipping ancient Egyptians were the source of greatest invention in human culture.

historicist   Any approach which emphasizes historical or diachronic aspects of culture or society.

'hocus pocus'   In linguistics and cognitive anthropology, the view that a good analysis of a set of emic categories will be one which correctly accounts for the data but which will not necessarily represent the (elusive) 'true' psychological reality of informants (cf. **'God's truth'**).

'hot' societies   Lévi-Strauss' term for societies he believed to be essentially dynamic. 'Hot' societies have a concern with history rather than myth (cf. **'cold' societies**).

hypergamous   Involving marriage where the man is of higher status than his wife (cf. **hypogamous**).

hypogamous   Involving marriage where a woman is of higher status than her husband (cf. **hypergamous**).

ideal types   Weber's notion of the basic forms of social phenomena, simplified from observed cases. For example, his studies of Protestantism assume an ideal type which is not necessarily an accurate representation of *all* Protestant societies.

ideographic   Referring to the specific rather than the general (e.g., the description of exact instances rather than generalizations on social processes) (cf. **nomothetic**).

ideology   Literally, the study of ideas. It generally carries the meaning of a system of values, such as those Marxists and some postmodernists argue give power to one group over another.

illustrative comparison   Comparison of specific ethnographic cases, for example to highlight some feature of culture or social structure which may be unusual.

inductive computation   Malinowski's term for the process of discovery of the 'invisible facts' which govern the interconnection of facets of social organization.

inductivism, inductivist   Any approach which proceeds from specific examples to general conclusions (cf. **deductivism**).

infrastructure   Another word for the 'base' or material aspect of society (cf. **base, superstructure**).

interactive perspective   Any perspective in anthropology which emphasizes action over structure.

interpretation   Intuitive understanding, or more precisely the understanding of culture as being like a language, to be 'translated'.

interpretive   An approach or method based on interpretation.

interpretivism, interpretivist   A perspective which emphasizes the interpretation of culture over the quest for formal structures. Geertz's anthropology is the most commonly cited example.

intersubjective   Referring to methods which privilege equally the ethnographer and his or her informants.

intertextual, intertextuality   Referring to relations between texts, where each represents a commentary on another.

irony   A verbal construction, often humorous, in which words are used to mean the opposite of what they normally mean.

'Iroquois' terminology   A type of kinship terminology in which cross-cousins are distinguished from parallel cousins. Often parallel cousins are classed together with siblings.

Kuhnian   Referring to the ideas of Thomas Kuhn, especially his notion of science as a sequential series of paradigms.

kula   In the Trobriand Islands and surrounding areas, the formalized system of exchange of bracelets for armshells.

Kulturkreis   A cluster of related culture traits, or the geographical area where these are found. The idea is fundamental to German-Austrian diffusionists, who saw these circles as spreading progressively over earlier culture circles (English, 'culture circle').

Lamarckian   Referring to the ideas of Jean-Baptiste de Lamarck, especially that learned traits can be passed from parent to child.

langue   Saussure's term for language in the sense of linguistic structure or grammar; by analogy, this can be the grammar of culture as well as of language as such (cf. **parole**).

Lévi-Straussian   Referring to the ideas of Claude Lévi-Strauss (cf. **structuralism**).

lineal relative   A relative who is in ego's line of descent (e.g., a grandmother or granddaughter).

localization   The interplay between local forms of knowledge and external pressures (cf. **re-localization, globalization**).

Malinowskian   Referring to the ideas of Bronislaw Malinowski, either as a fieldwork methodologist or a functionalist theorist.

Manchester School   The school of thought centred around Max Gluckman at Manchester in the 1950s, 1960s, and 1970s.

manitoo   In Ojibwa belief, the guardian spirit of an individual (cf. **totem**).

Marxism, Marxist   Referring to the ideas of Karl Marx. In anthropology, the term implies a theoretical interest in the connections between material forces and relations of power but not necessarily adherence to Marx's political ideology.

matrilineal descent, matrilineality   Descent through women, from mother to child, etc. (cf. **patrilineal descent**).

means of production   In Marxist theory, the organized arrangement of raw materials, tools, and know-how; the technological system of a society, especially in relation to subsistence (cf. **mode of production**).

metanarrative   Lyotard's term for grand theory.

metaphor   An analogy, or relation of similarity across different levels of analysis (e.g., a red traffic light means 'stop').

metonymy   A relation between objects in the same level of analysis (e.g., a red traffic light in relation to a green traffic light).

mode of production   In Marxist theory, the combination of either the means of production or the forces of production (mode of subsistence plus the social capability to exploit the environment), coupled with the relations of production (the ways in which production is organized) (cf. **means of production, relations of production**).

modern   In contrast to postmodern, emphasizing a holistic, coherent view of the world.

moiety   Literally 'half' a society, defined by membership in one or the other of two unilineal descent groups.

monogenesis   One origin for all human 'races' (cf. **polygenesis**).

monogenist   A person who believes in monogenesis (also the adjectival form of 'monogenesis').

monotheism   Belief in only one deity (cf. **polytheism**).

moral relativism   The form of relativism which holds that aesthetic and ethical judgements must be assessed in terms of specific cultural values (cf. **cognitive relativism**).

morpheme   The smallest meaningful unit of language (e.g., the English word *cars* consists of two morphemes: 'car' and 'plural').

morphological   In linguistics, referring to the level of the morpheme.

multilinear evolutionism   The theory of social evolution which emphasizes cross-cultural diversity and the influence of the environment in the process.

mytheme   In Lévi-Strauss' terminology, a unit within a mythological corpus which may be combined with similar units to make up a given myth.

Mythologiques   Literally, 'mytho-logics', Lévi-Strauss' four volumes on mythology.

naiscent society   Rousseau's notion of an idyllic, egalitarian society before the emergence of 'artificial' inequalities.

natural law   The theory of law or the essence of law in that theory, as embedded in human nature. It was characteristic of Enlightenment legal theory, but opposed by later conceptions of law as a set of rules.

natural selection   The Darwinian notion (also called sexual selection) that individuals with superior characteristics will tend to breed more often than other individuals, thus giving rise to better-adapted individuals in later generations.

naturism   Not to be confused with nudism, F. Max Müller's notion of early religion as nature-worship.

naven   Ceremonies of the Iatmul of Papua New Guinea involving transvestism and other ritual reversals of ordinary behaviour.

neo-Darwinism   In its most usual meaning today, the perspective in human biology which combines Darwinian theory with modern genetics in seeking biological explanations of human social behaviour.

neo-evolutionism   A broad concept embracing late twentieth-century evolutionist ideas in anthropology, including especially those of Julian Steward.

network analysis   A methodological tool which emerged as part of the Manchester School. It seeks an understanding of social relations through chains or networks of individual associations.

new archaeology   In the 1960s, a perspective in archaeology which emphasizes ethnographic analogy.

new ethnography   In the 1960s, a perspective essentially synonymous with the cognitive anthropology of the time. In the 1980s, a rather different perspective essentially synonymous with the approach or approaches typified by Clifford and Marcus' edited volume, *Writing Culture*.

noble savage   A seventeenth- and eighteenth-century notion of the goodness of natural humanity or primitive social humanity embodied in 'savages'. Typically, these were identified with the populations of Native North America.

nomothetic   Referring to the general rather than the specific, e.g., the search for regularities or general laws rather than the description of specific instances (cf. **ideographic**).

normative relativism   The form of relativism which holds that because cultures judge each other according to their own internal standards, there are no universal standards to judge between cultures. There are two positions within normative relativism: cognitive relativism and moral relativism (cf. **descriptive relativism, epistemological relativism**).

normative rules   Idealized descriptions of correct social behaviour, as distinct from actual social behaviour.

occidentalism   A relatively recent term for the stereotyping of the West by oriental or other non-Western peoples (cf. **orientalism**).

Oedipus complex   In psychiatry, the complex of emotions of desire for the parent of the opposite sex (especially a boy for his mother).

Oedipus myth   The Greek myth in which, by a strange sequence of events, Oedipus kills his father and marries his mother.

'Omaha' terminology   A type of kinship terminology in which the mother's brother's son is called by the same term as the mother's brother, or more generally one in which ego calls several members of his or her mother's patrilineal kin group by the same term (cf. **'Crow' terminology**).

Orang Outang   In the eighteenth century, a term roughly equivalent to the modern generic concept of the 'ape', but often believed to be human or nearly human. Not to be confused with the orang-utan of Southeast Asia as known to science today.

organic analogy   The notion that society is 'like an organism' in being composed of evolving or interrelated parts or systems.

orientalism   In anthropology, the stereotyping of the East by Western peoples, especially as described by Edward Said (cf. **occidentalism**).

Paideuma   Greek for 'education', though in Frobenius' German usage it identifies the 'soul' of a culture (cf. **Volksgeist**).

paradigm   Thomas Kuhn's term for a set of suppositions common to practitioners of a given science at a given time. It constitutes a large theory or perspective (e.g., Newtonian physics, Einsteinian physics). In the social sciences, the term bears much the same meaning (e.g., evolutionism and functionalism are anthropological paradigms).

paradigmatic   In structuralist usage, the relation between elements which might occupy the same position in a syntagmatic chain (e.g., Mary and Sally, in the sentences 'John loves Mary' and 'John loves Sally'). In the anthropology of symbolism, paradigmatic relations are those of metaphor as opposed to metonymy.

parallel cousins   The children of two brothers or two sisters. In many societies parallel cousins are treated as brothers and sisters and sharply distinguished from cross-cousins (cf. **cross-cousins**).

parole   Saussure's term for speech in the sense of actual utterances; by analogy, it refers also to the social action as opposed to social structure (cf. **langue**).

participant observation   The fieldwork methodology in which the ethnographer learns through both observation and participation in the social life of the people under study.

patrilateral parallel-cousin marriage   Marriage of a man to his father's brother's daughter (or a woman to her father's brother's son).

patrilineal descent, patrilineality   Descent through men, from father to child, etc. (cf. **matrilineal descent**).

performance   In linguistics, the actual utterances which make up language (cf. **competence**).

periphery   An economically weak or dependent place or region, in contrast to the 'centre'. The concept is important in Marxist anthropological theory (cf. **centre**, **world system**).

phenotype   The physical makeup of an organism, as produced by both genetic and environmental factors (cf. **genotype**).

phone   A sound. In phonetics, the smallest unit of speech.

phoneme   The smallest meaningful unit of sound, more specifically one which exists within a language-specific system of sounds.

phonemics   The study of systematic relations between sounds (as phonemes).

phonetics   The study of speech sounds (phones) in their fundamental essence.

phonological   Relating to sounds as part of a system of phonemes.

phonology   The systematic relations between sounds (as phonemes), or the study of these (in the latter sense, synonymous with phonemics).

phratry   A large unilineal descent group, usually a cluster of smaller groups such as clans.

pinalua   In Hawaii, a relationship of intimacy or of common sexual possession.

polygenesis   Multiple and separate origins for the different human 'races' (cf. **monogenesis**).

polygenist   A person who believes in polygenesis (also the adjectival form of 'polygenesis').

polytheism Belief in more than one deity (cf. **monotheism**).

postmodern   A term originally employed in architecture and the arts to denote a reaction against 'modernism' (e.g., modern architecture) and a revival of classical traditions, often mixed indiscriminately (cf. **postmodern condition, postmodernism**).

postmodern condition   Jean-François Lyotard's term for the state of society characterized by, among other things, globalization and a complexity of social groupings.

postmodernism, postmodernist   Any perspective which emphasizes a breakdown of Enlightenment ideals. In anthropology and other social sciences, the term implies the rejection of the validity of purported objective categories or scientific methods (cf. **postmodern, postmodern condition**).

poststructuralism, poststructuralist   Any perspective based on a rejection of structuralist methodology or classic structuralist distinctions such as *langue/parole* or synchronic/diachronic.

potlatch   A ceremony performed by peoples of the North West Coast of North America involving feasting and the giving away (or sometimes the destruction of) their own movable property, thereby redistributing goods and gaining prestige for themselves.

practice theory   Any perspective which emphasizes practice (or individual action) over social structure.

Prague School   In linguistics, the school of thought whose analysis was based on the identification of distinctive features, especially in phonology. It originated in Central Europe and was transplanted to New York during the Second World War.

praxis   Especially in Marxist theory, practice or action related to the furtherance of social good.

pre-logical mentality   Lucien Lévy-Bruhl's term for the supposed thought processes of peoples who are culturally not equipped to distinguish cause from effect.

presentist   In the study of the history of anthropology, the position which sees the past through the concerns of the present. The term is usually used disparagingly.

processualism, processualist   Any perspective which emphasizes social process over social structure, or which sees social or symbolic structures in terms of their propensity for transformation.

psychic identity, psychic unity   The idea that all humankind shares the same mentality (cf. **logical mentality, pre-logical mentality**).

Radcliffe-Brownian   Referring to the ideas of A. R. Radcliffe-Brown (cf. **structural-functionalism**).

rationalism, rationalist   The doctrine which holds that knowledge can be derived from reason without the necessity of prior experience (cf. **empiricism**).

rationality debate   A debate among philosophers and anthropologists, roughly from the 1960s to the 1980s, over the degree to which 'primitive peoples' were culturally capable of rational thought.

reciprocal altruism   In sociobiological theory, the notion of performing acts for others with the expectation of a return gain.

reflexivism, reflexivist   A perspective which holds reflexivity as central to anthropological method and theory.

reflexivity   The reflection on the place of one's self (the ethnographer) in ethnographic practice.

regional comparison   A form of controlled comparison which confines comparisons to those within a region (e.g., Aboriginal Australia, Great Plains North America, etc.).

relations of production   The social relations around which production is organized; more technically, the appropriation of surplus labour on the basis of control over the forces of production and especially the means of production (cf. **mode of production**).

relativism, relativist   A view of the world which opposes the assumption of cultural universals or universal values. In anthropology, broadly a synonym for 'cultural relativism'. In other words, any of several theoretical perspectives which include descriptive relativism, epistemological relativism, and normative relativism.

re-localization   The assertion, rediscovery or invention of locally based knowledge, especially knowledge which can be used in agrarian economic and social development (cf. **localization, globalization**).

representations collectives   French for 'collective representations'.

reproduction   In Marxist theory, not merely reproducing children but reproducing existing aspects of culture or society through the generations.

restricted exchange   A synonym for 'direct exchange' (as opposed to 'delayed direct' or 'generalized'). Lévi-Strauss and his followers use the terms interchangeably.

revolutionist   The view that social evolutionary change is the result of revolutionary events such as a literal 'social contract' or the invention of symbolism.

rites of passage   Rituals to mark the transition from one stage of life to another (such as adolescence to adulthood).

role   What an individual does, or more technically the dynamic aspect of a social status (cf. **status**).

Sapir–Whorf hypothesis   The hypothesis that the structure of the language people speak has an unconscious determining effect on their worldview. It was formulated by Benjamin Lee Whorf on the basis of his own research and that of his mentor, Edward Sapir, on Native North American languages. Also known as the Whorfian hypothesis.

Saussurian   Referring to the ideas of Ferdinand de Saussure (e.g., his distinction between *langue* and *parole*).

savage   In earlier times and to some extent in Lévi-Strauss' usage, 'wild' or 'natural'. In the eighteenth century the term often had positive overtones (in opposition to 'polished' or 'civil' society, believed to exhibit less of human nature). In the nineteenth century, it was a term identifying the earliest and lowest level of society (cf. **savagery**).

savagery   In evolutionary theory the earliest and lowest level of society, characterized by egalitarianism and a low level of material culture (cf. **barbarism, civilization**).

semantics   In linguistics, the study of meaning; the highest level of linguistic analysis (above phonetics, phonology, and syntax).

semi-complex systems   A synonym for 'Crow-Omaha systems', so-called because in Lévi-Strauss' theory of kinship they contain attributes of both 'elementary structures' and 'complex structures' (cf. **Crow-Omaha systems**).

semiology, semiotics   The study of 'signs', which include signifiers and the objects signified (cf. **signifier, signified**).

shamanism   The practice of mediation between the ordinary world and the spirit world by a ritual specialist (a shaman). The term is from Tungus, a Siberian language, and refers especially to such practices as trance, out-of-body travel, etc., as practised by Siberian, Arctic, and Amerindian shamans.

sign In Saussurian linguistics, the combination of the signifier (a word) and what is signified by it. By extension, any similar pairing in the study of symbolism.

significatum An element of componential analysis which, along with other significata, defines a given category (cf. **connotatum**).

signified An object or concept which is represented by a signifier (cf. **sign**).

signifier The word or symbol which stands for something (the object 'signified'; cf. **sign**).

sociability An eighteenth-century concept implying both sociality and conviviality (cf. **sociality**).

social action In opposition to social structure, what people actually do, i.e., the roles they play as opposed to the social statuses they occupy.

social anthropology The branch of anthropology or the academic discipline which is concerned with the study of society in cross-cultural perspective. The term is typically used in British and certain other traditions, whereas in North America 'cultural anthropology' is the more common term (cf. **cultural anthropology, ethnology**).

social drama Turner's characterization of a ritual process, such as a pilgrimage or a rite of passage, with pre-crisis and post-crisis phases.

social fact Durkheim's term for the smallest unit of social structure: a custom, institution, or any aspect of society.

social institution An element of a social system (e.g., marriage is an aspect of the kinship system).

social organization The dynamic aspect of social structure, i.e., the activities people engage in as part of the social structure.

social processes A general term employed for cyclical changes in society or changes in society over time.

social structure The relations between elements of society, either with reference to specific individuals (Radcliffe-Brown's usage) or to the statuses they occupy (cf. **structural form**).

social system A term variously referring to specific systems within society (economics, politics, kinship, religion) or to the society as a whole in its systematic aspects.

social theory The branch of sociology which deals with grand theoretical problems, or any area of the social sciences concerned with similar phenomena.

social values The values people acquire by virtue of membership in a community or society.

sociality   The capacity for living in a society, a concept of importance in theoretical perspectives as diverse as seventeenth-century political philosophy and late twentieth-century sociobiology.

socialization   The process by which people, especially children, acquire a knowledge of how to live in society (cf. **enculturation**).

society   A social unit equivalent variously to a language group, a cultural isolate, or a nation state. Also the social relations which exist between members of such a unit.

sociobiology   The study of social relations in a biological framework. More specifically, a discipline or theoretical position which treats human culture and society as adjuncts of humankind's animal nature.

sound shift   A systematic change in a language, such as where one set of sounds is transformed into another set (e.g., voiced stops b, d, g become the equivalent voiceless stops p, t, k).

state of nature   The notion of humanity without society, an idea prevalent in the eighteenth-century European social theory.

status   The position an individual occupies within a social structure (cf. **role**).

Stewardian   Referring to the ideas of Julian H. Steward (cf. **cultural ecology**).

stratigraphy   In archaeology, the relation of layers of earth in a site. From these the relative age of artefacts, the remains of dwellings, etc. can be inferred.

structural form   Radcliffe-Brown's term for generalities based on observations of the social structure. As his notion of 'social structure' was more concrete than that of others (referring to individuals), his term 'structural form' thus carried the more generic meaning which others ascribed to the term 'social structure'.

structural-functionalism, structural-functionalist   Referring to the ideas of A. R. Radcliffe-Brown, who emphasized functional relations between social institutions (cf. **functionalism**).

structural opposition   In structuralist theory, the relation between two elements of a structure according to the presence or absence of some distinctive feature.

structuralism, structuralist   Any perspective which emphasizes structural relations as a key to understanding. For structuralists, things acquire meaning through their place in a structure or system. In anthropology, it is the perspective identified most closely with Claude Lévi-Strauss.

subaltern studies   A perspective in history and literary criticism, and prominent in South Asia, which emphasizes the position of the subordinate rather than the dominant group. It has been of influence in feminist anthropology.

superstructure   The ideological aspect of society, which in Marxist theory is determined by the base or infrastructure (cf. **base**).

surface reading   For Althusser, a reading (of Marx) which focuses on the actual words rather than the deeper meaning of the text (cf. **symptomatic reading**).

symbolic culture   The domain of culture concerned with symbols and symbolism, as opposed to material objects, social relations, etc.

symptomatic reading   For Althusser, a reading (of Marx) which focuses on the deeper meaning of the text rather than the actual words (cf. **surface reading**).

synchronic perspective   A perspective in the same time frame (e.g., functionalism), rather than one through time (cf. **diachronic perspective**).

synecdoche   A figure of speech in which a part represents a whole, or vice versa.

syntactic   In linguistics, either the level concerned with the structure of the sentence or more broadly the domain which lies between the phonological and semantic levels. By extension, any analogous aspect of the structure of culture.

syntagmatic   In structuralist usage, the relation between sequential elements such as words in a sentence. In the anthropology of symbolism, syntagmatic relations are those of metonymy as opposed to metaphor (cf. **associative**, **paradigmatic**).

theism   Belief in one or more deities (cf. **monotheism, polytheism**).

theory   In science or social science, any discourse, perspective or statement which leads to some conclusion about the world. Anthropological theory is centrally concerned with making sense of ethnography and with generalizations about culture or society.

theory of the gift   Mauss' notion that gifts are given because of social obligations and not simply voluntarily. These social obligations entail relations of reciprocity which are fundamental to society, though perhaps in some parts of the world (e.g., Polynesia, Melanesia, the North West Coast of North America) more than in others.

thick description   Geertz's notion of good ethnography as consisting of a multiplicity of detailed and varied interpretations (both the ethnographer's and those of the people under study).

three-age theory   In archaeology, the idea of human prehistory as consisting of three ages, namely the Stone Age, the Bronze Age, and the Iron Age.

total culture In Steward's cultural ecology, the general aspects of culture, especially those least susceptible to ecological influence (e.g., language, religious belief) (cf. **cultural core**).

totem In Ojibwa belief, the spirit of a patrilineal clan, represented by an animal (cf. **manitoo**). By extension, a similar spirit among any people (cf. **totemism**).

totemism Any belief system which entails the symbolic representation of the social (e.g., clan membership) by the natural (e.g., animal species and their characteristics). As phenomena described as 'totemism' are so varied across the world, some anthropologists have questioned the utility of calling them all by this one term (cf. **totem**).

transactionalism, transactionalist A perspective which emphasizes transactions between individuals as the basis for social analysis.

trope A figure of speech, such as metaphor, metonymy, synecdoche, or irony.

unilinear evolutionism The theory of social evolution which holds that all humankind passes through the same stages of evolution irrespective of environment or specific historical influences.

universal evolutionism The theory of social evolution which emphasizes broad, general stages rather than specific unilinear sequences of evolution.

uxorilocal Residing with the wife's group (cf. **virilocal**). Uxorilocal residence repeated through the generations creates localized matrilineal kin groups centred on women.

Verstehen German for 'understanding' or 'interpretation', the basis of Max Weber's sociology.

viri-avunculocal Residing with the husband's mother's brother's group (also called **avunculocal**; cf. **uxorilocal, virilocal**). Viri-avunculocal residence repeated through the generations creates localized matrilineal kin groups centred on men.

virilocal Residing with the husband's group (cf. **uxorilical, viri-avunculocal**). Virilocal residence repeated through the generations creates localized patrilineal kin groups centred on men.

vital sequences Malinowski's notion of the biological foundations of all cultures.

Völkergedanken 'Peoples' thoughts', those beliefs and aspects of culture held by Bastian to be specific to given cultures and not common to all humankind (cf. **Elementargedanken**).

Völkerkunde The study of peoples, a German synonym for 'ethnology' but distinguished sharply from *Volkskunde*.

Volksgeist   The spirit or soul of a people or culture.

Volkskunde   In Germany and some other countries, the study of folklore and local customs, including handicrafts, of one's own country (cf. **Völkerkunde**).

vowel system   The set of vowels found in a particular language and the structural relations which define them.

vowel triangle   Jakobson's term for the structural relations between *u*, *i*, and *a* as representing a system defined according to relative loudness and pitch (cf. **consonant triangle**).

vulgar materialism   Jonathan Friedman's disparaging term for what Marvin Harris calls 'cultural materialism'. It is 'vulgar' in the sense that it does not distinguish base from superstructure (cf. **cultural materialism**).

Weberian   Referring to the ideas of Max Weber, especially his emphasis on action over social structure (cf. **Durkheimian**).

Wechselwirkung   Simmel's notion of 'reciprocal effect', i.e., that the social exists when two or more people engage in interaction with each other, and when the behaviour of one is seen as a response to the behaviour of the other.

Weltanschauung   German for 'worldview'.

Whorfian hypothesis   Another name for the Sapir–Whorf hypothesis.

world system   Wallerstein's idea of a system which links the economies of the smallest societies to the powerful capitalist economies of the West and the Far East.

worldview   A loan translation of German *Weltanschauung*, the term used especially by Boasian anthropologists for the broad perspective on the world maintained by a people through their culture.

References

Abu-Lughod, Lila. 1986. *Veiled Sentiments: Honour and Poetry in a Bedouin Society.* Berkeley: University of California Press.

1990. The romance of resistance: tracing transformations of power though Bedouin women. *American Ethnologist* 17: 41–55.

1991. Writing against culture. In Richard G. Fox (ed.), *Recapturing Anthropology: Working in the Present.* Santa Fe: School of American Research, pp. 137–62.

Adams, William Y. 1998. *The Philosophical Roots of Anthropology.* Stanford: CSLI Publications (CSLI Lecture Notes no. 86).

Ahmed, Akbar S. 1976. *Millennium and Charisma among Pathans: A Critical Essay in Social Anthropology.* London: Routledge & Kegan Paul.

Althusser, Louis. 1969 [1965]. *For Marx* (translated by Ben Brewster). Harmondsworth: Penguin Books.

Althusser, Louis and Etienne Balibar. 1970 [1968]. *Reading 'Capital'* (translated by Ben Brewster). London: New Left Books.

Anderson, Stephen R. 1985. *Phonology in the Twentieth Century: Theories of Rules and Theories of Representations.* Chicago: University of Chicago Press.

Andreski, Stanislav (ed.). 1971. *Herbert Spencer: Structure, Function and Evolution.* London: Thomas Nelson & Sons.

Ardener, Edwin. 1989 [1970–87]. *The Voice of Prophecy and Other Essays* (edited by Malcolm Chapman). Oxford: Basil Blackwell.

Asad, Talal (ed.). 1973. *Anthropology and the Colonial Encounter.* London: Ithaca Press.

Atran, Scott. 1990. *Cognitive Foundations of Natural History: Towards an Anthropology of Science.* Cambridge: Cambridge University Press.

Augé, Marc. 1982 [1979]. *The Anthropological Circle: Symbol, Function, History.* Cambridge: Cambridge University Press.

1995 [1992]. *Non-Places: Introduction to an Anthropology of Supermodernity* (translated by John Howe). London: Verso.

Bachofen, J. J. 1967 [1859–1916]. *Myth, Religion, and Mother Right: Selected Writings of J. J. Bachofen* (translated by Ralph Manheim). Princeton: Princeton University Press (Bollingen Series LXXXIV).

Badcock, C. R. 1975. *Lévi-Strauss: Structuralism and Sociological Theory.* London: Hutchinson & Co.

Barfield, Thomas (ed.). 1997. *The Dictionary of Anthropology.* Oxford: Blackwell Publishers.

Barnard, Alan. 1983. Contemporary hunter-gatherers: current theoretical issues in ecology and social organization. *Annual Review of Anthropology* 12: 193–214.

1992. Through Radcliffe-Brown's spectacles: reflections on the history of anthropology. *History of the Human Sciences* 5(4): 1–20.

1995. *Orang Outang* and the definition of *Man*: the legacy of Lord Monboddo. In Han F. Vermeulen and Arturo Alvarez Roldan (eds.), *Fieldwork and Footnotes: Studies in the History of European Anthropology* (E.A.S.A. Monographs Series). London: Routledge, pp. 95–112.

1996. Regional comparison in Khoisan ethnography: theory, method and practice. *Zeitschrift für Ethnologie* 121: 203–20.

1999. Modern hunter-gatherers and early symbolic culture. In Robin Dunbar, Chris Knight, and Camilla Power (eds.), *The Evolution of Culture: An Interdisciplinary View*. Edinburgh: Edinburgh University Press, pp. 50–68.

Barnard, Alan and Anthony Good. 1984. *Research Practices in the Study of Kinship*. London: Academic Press.

Barnard, Alan and Jonathan Spencer (eds.). 1996. *Encyclopedia of Social and Cultural Anthropology*. London: Routledge.

Barrett, Stanley R. 1996. *Anthropology: A Student's Guide to Theory and Method*. Toronto: University of Toronto Press.

Barth, Fredrik. 1959. *Political Leadership among Swat Pathans*. London: Athlone Press.

1966. *Models of Social Organization*. London: Royal Anthropological Institute (Occasional Papers no. 23).

1969. Introduction. In Fredrik Barth (ed.), *Ethnic Groups and Boundaries: The Social Organization of Culture Difference*. Bergen: Universitetsforlaget/London: George Allen & Unwin, pp. 9–38.

Bateson, Gregory. 1958 [1936]. *Naven: A Survey of the Problems Suggested by a Composite Picture of the Culture of a New Guinea Tribe Drawn from Three Points of View* (second edition). Stanford: Stanford University Press.

1973 [1972] [1935–71]. *Steps to an Ecology of Mind: Collected Essays in Anthropology, Psychiatry, Evolution and Epistemology*. St. Albans: Paladin.

Benedict, Ruth. 1934. *Patterns of Culture*. Boston: Houghton Mifflin.

1946. *The Chrysanthemum and the Sword*. Boston: Houghton Mifflin.

Berlin, Brent. 1992. *Ethnobiological Classification: Principles of Categorization of Plants and Animals in Traditional Societies*. Princeton: Princeton University Press.

Berry, Christopher J. 1997. *Social Theory of the Scottish Enlightenment*. Edinburgh: Edinburgh University Press.

Bloch, Maurice (ed.). 1975. *Marxist Analyses and Social Anthropology* (A.S.A. Studies 2). London: Malaby Press.

1983. *Marxism and Anthropology: The History of a Relationship*. Oxford: Oxford University Press.

1991. Language, anthropology and cognitive science. *Man* (n. s.) 26: 183–98.

Bloor, Celia and David Bloor. 1982. Twenty industrial scientists: a preliminary exercise. In Mary Douglas (ed.), *Essays in the Sociology of Perception*. London: Routledge & Kegan Paul, pp. 83–102.

Boas, Franz. 1938 [1911]. *The Mind of Primitive Man* (revised edition). New York: Macmillan.

1940. *Race, Language, and Culture*. New York: Macmillan.

Bock, Phillip K. 1980. *Continuities in Psychological Anthropology: A Historical Introduction*. San Francisco: W. H. Freeman & Co.

1988. *Rethinking Psychological Anthropology: Continuity and Change in the Study of Human Action*. San Francisco: W. H. Freeman & Co.

Bonte, Pierre and Michel Izard (eds.). 1991. *Dictionnaire de l'ethnologie et de l'anthropologie*. Paris: Presses Universitaires de France.

Boon, James A. 1973. *From Symbolism to Structuralism: Lévi-Strauss in a Literary Tradition*. Oxford: Basil Blackwell.

Borofsky, Robert. 1997. Cook, Lono, Obeyesekere, and Sahlins. *Current Anthropology* 38: 255–82.

Bourdieu, Pierre. 1977 [1972]. *Outline of a Theory of Practice* (translated by Richard Nice). Cambridge: Cambridge University Press.

1990 [1980]. *The Logic of Practice* (translated by Richard Nice). Cambridge: Polity Press.

Bowler, Peter J. 1989. *The Invention of Progress: The Victorians and the Past*. Oxford: Basil Blackwell.

1990. *Charles Darwin: The Man and His Influence*. Oxford: Basil Blackwell.

Bratlinger, Patrick. 1990. *Crusoe's Footprints: Cultural Studies in Britain and America*. New York: Routledge.

Brockman, John (ed.). 1977. *About Bateson: Essays on Gregory Bateson*. New York: E. P. Dutton.

Buffon, George Louis Leclerc, comte de. 1749–1804. *Histoire naturelle, générale et particulière* (44 vols.). Paris: De l'Imprimerie Royale.

Caplan, Pat. 1997. *African Voices, African Lives: Personal Narratives from a Swahili Village*. London: Routledge.

Carrier, James G. (ed.). 1995a. *Occidentalism: Images of the West*. Oxford: Oxford University Press.

1995b. Preface. In James G. Carrier (ed.), *Occidentalism: Images of the West*. Oxford: Oxford University Press, pp. vii–x.

Chalmers, A. F. 1982 [1976]. *What is This Thing Called Science? An Assessment of the Nature and Status of Science and Its Methods* (second edition). Milton Keynes: Open University Press.

Cheater, Angela (ed.). 1999. *The Anthropology of Power* (A.S.A. Monographs 36). London: Routledge.

Childe, V. Gordon. 1936. *Man Makes Himself*. London: Watts & Co.

1942. *What Happened in History*. Harmondsworth: Penguin.

Chomsky, Noam. 1965. *Aspects of the Theory of Syntax*. Cambridge, MA: M.I.T. Press.

Clifford, James. 1986. On ethnographic allegory. In James Clifford and George E. Marcus (eds.), *Writing Culture: The Poetics and Politics of Ethnography*. Berkeley: University of California Press, pp. 98–121.

1988. *The Predicament of Culture: Twentieth-Century Ethnography, Literature and Art*. Cambridge, MA: Harvard University Press.

Clifford, James and George E. Marcus (eds.). 1986. *Writing Culture: The Poetics and Politics of Ethnography.* Berkeley: University of California Press.

Cohen, Anthony P. 1985. *The Symbolic Construction of Community.* Chichester: Ellis Horwood/London: Tavistock Publications.

1994. *Self Consciousness: An Alternative Anthropology of Identity.* London: Routledge.

Collier, Jane F. and Michelle Z. Rosaldo. 1981. Politics and gender in simple societies. In Sherry B. Ortner and Harriet Whitehead (eds.), *Sexual Meanings: The Cultural Construction of Gender and Sexuality.* Cambridge: Cambridge University Press, pp. 275–329.

Comaroff, Jean. 1985. *Body of Power, Spirit of Resistance: The Culture and History of a South African People.* Chicago: University of Chicago Press.

Comte, August. 1869 [1839]. *Cours de philosophie positive,* vol. IV (third edition). Paris: J. B. de Baillіäre et Fils.

Corbey, Raymond and Bert Theunissen (eds.). 1995. *Ape, Man, Apeman: Changing Views since 1600.* Leiden: Department of Prehistory, Leiden University.

Crapanzano, Vincent. 1992. The postmodern crisis: discourse, parody, memory. In George E. Marcus (ed.), *Rereading Cultural Anthropology.* Durham, NC: Duke University Press, pp. 87–102.

Csordas, Thomas J. 1990. Embodiment as a paradigm for anthropology. *Ethos* 18: 5–47.

(ed.). 1994. *Embodiment and Experience: The Existential Ground of Culture and Self.* Cambridge: Cambridge University Press.

Cucchiari, Salvatore. 1981. The gender revolution and the transition from bisexual horde to patrilocal band: the origins of gender hierarchy. In Sherry B. Ortner and Harriet Whitehead (eds.), *Sexual Meanings: The Cultural Construction of Gender and Sexuality.* Cambridge: Cambridge University Press, pp. 31–79.

Culler, Jonathan. 1976. *Saussure.* Glasgow: Fontana/Collins (Fontana Modern Masters).

Daiches, David, Peter Jones, and Jean Jones (eds.). 1986. *A Hotbed of Genius: The Scottish Enlightenment, 1730–1790.* Edinburgh: Edinburgh University Press.

D'Andrade, Roy. 1995. *The Development of Cognitive Anthropology.* Cambridge: Cambridge University Press.

Darwin, Charles. 1859. *On the Origin of Species by Means of Natural Selection.* London: John Murray.

1871. *The Descent of Man, and Selection in Relation to Sex.* London: John Murray.

De George, Richard T. and Ferdinande M. de George (eds.). 1972. *The Structuralists: From Mauss to Lévi-Strauss.* Garden City, NY: Doubleday & Co.

De Heusch, Luc. 1982 [1972]. *The Drunken King, or the Origin of the State* (translated by Roy Willis). Bloomington: Indiana University Press.

1985. *Sacrifice in Africa: A Structuralist Approach.* Manchester: Manchester University Press.

Denzin, Norman K. 1997. *Interpretive Ethnography: Ethnographic Practices for the 21st Century.* Thousand Oaks, CA: Sage Publications.

Derrida, Jacques. 1976 [1967]. *Of Grammatology* (translated by Gayatri Chakravorty Spivak). Baltimore: Johns Hopkins University Press.

1978 [1967]. *Writing and Difference* (translated by Alan Bass). Chicago: University of Chicago Press.

Douglas, Mary. 1966. *Purity and Danger: An Analysis of Concepts of Pollution and Taboo*. London: Routledge & Kegan Paul.

1969. *Natural Symbols: Explorations in Cosmology*. London: Routledge & Kegan Paul.

1978. *Cultural Bias*. London: Royal Anthropological Institute (Occasional Papers no. 35).

1980. *Evans-Pritchard*. Glasgow: Fontana/Collins (Fontana Modern Masters).

1982. Introduction to grid/group analysis. In Mary Douglas (ed.), *Essays in the Sociology of Perception*. London: Routledge & Kegan Paul, pp. 1–8.

1996. *Thought Styles: Critical Essays on Good Taste*. London: Sage Publications.

Dumont, Louis. 1980 [1967]. *Homo Hierarchicus: The Caste System and Its Implications* (revised edition, translated by Mark Sainsbury, Louis Dumont, and Basia Gulati). Chicago: University of Chicago Press.

Durkheim, Emile. 1915 [1912]. *The Elementary Forms of the Religious Life*. London: George Allen & Unwin.

1963 [1898]. *Incest: The Nature and Origin of the Taboo* (translated by Edward Sagarin). New York: Stuart.

1966 [1897]. *Suicide: A Study in Sociology* (translated by John A. Spaulding and George Simpson). New York: The Free Press.

Durkheim, Emile and Marcel Mauss. 1963 [1903]. *Primitive Classification* (translated by Rodney Needham). London: Cohen & West.

Edholm, Felicity, Olivia Harris, and Kate Young. 1977. Conceptualizing women. *Critique of Anthropology* 3 (9/10): 101–30.

Eggan, Fred. 1950. *Social Organization of the Western Pueblos*. Chicago: University of Chicago Press.

Ellen, Roy F. 1993. *The Cultural Relations of Classification: An Analysis of Nuaulu Animal Categories from Central Seram*. Cambridge: Cambridge University Press.

Encyclopaedia Britannica; or a Dictionary of Arts and Sciences, Compiled upon a New Plan (3 vols.). 1771. Edinburgh: A. Bell and C. Macfarquhar.

Engels, Frederick [Friedrich]. 1972 [1884]. *The Origin of the Family, Private Property and the State, in the Light of the Researches of Lewis H. Morgan*. London: Lawrence & Wishart.

Evans-Pritchard, E. E. 1937. *Witchcraft, Oracles, and Magic among the Azande*. Oxford: Clarendon Press.

1940. *The Nuer: A Description of the Modes of Livelihood and Political Institutions of a Nilotic People*. Oxford: Clarendon Press.

1951a. *Kinship and Marriage among the Nuer*. Oxford: Clarendon Press.

1951b. *Social Anthropology: The Broadcast Lectures*. London: Cohen & West.

1956. *Nuer Religion*. Oxford: Clarendon Press.

1962 [1932–61]. *Essays in Social Anthropology*. London: Faber & Faber.

1965 [1928–63]. *The Position of Women in Primitive Societies and Other Essays in Social Anthropology*. London: Faber and Faber.

Fardon, Richard (ed.). 1990. *Localizing Strategies: Regional Traditions of Ethnographic Writing*. Edinburgh: Scottish Academic Press/Washington: Smithsonian Institution Press.

1998. *Mary Douglas: An Intellectual Biography.* London: Routledge.

Fernandez, James W. 1986. *Persuasions and Performances: The Play of Tropes in Culture.* Bloomington: Indiana University Press.

(ed.). 1991. *Beyond Metaphor: The Theory of Tropes in Anthropology.* Stanford: Stanford University Press.

Ferguson, Adam. 1966 [1767]. *An Essay on the History of Civil Society.* Edinburgh: Edinburgh University Press.

Finnegan, Ruth and Robin Horton (eds.). 1973. *Modes of Thought.* London: Faber.

Firth, Raymond. 1936. *We the Tikopia: A Sociological Study of Kinship in Primitive Polynesia.* London: George Allen & Unwin.

1961 [1951]. *Elements of Social Organization* (second edition). Boston: Beacon Press.

1956. Alfred Reginald Radcliffe-Brown, 1881–1955. *Proceedings of the British Academy* 62: 287–302.

(ed.). 1957. *Man and Culture: An Evaluation of the Work of Bronislaw Malinowski.* London: Routledge & Kegan Paul.

Fortes, Meyer. 1945. *The Dynamics of Clanship among the Tallensi.* London: Oxford University Press.

1949. *The Web of Kinship among the Tallensi.* London: Oxford University Press.

1969. *Kinship and the Social Order: The Legacy of Lewis Henry Morgan.* London: Routledge & Kegan Paul.

Fortes, Meyer and E. E. Evans-Pritchard (eds.). 1940. *African Political Systems.* London: Oxford University Press for the International African Institute.

Foucault, Michel. 1973 [1966]. *The Order of Things: An Archaeology of the Human Sciences.* New York: Vintage Books.

1974 [1969]. *The Archaeology of Knowledge and the Discourse on Language* (translated by A. M. Sheridan-Smith). London: Tavistock Publications.

1977 [1975]. *Discipline and Punish: The Birth of the Prison* (translated by Alan Sheridan). London: Allen Lane.

Fox, Richard G. 1991. Introduction: Working in the present. *Recapturing Anthropology: Working in the Present.* Santa Fe: School of American Research Press, pp. 1–16.

Fox, Robin. 1975. Primate kin and human kinship. In Robin Fox (ed.), *Biosocial Anthropology* (A. S. A. Studies 1). London: Malaby Press, pp. 9–35.

Frake, Charles O. 1980. *Language and Cultural Description: Essays by Charles O. Frake (Selected and Introduced by Anwar S. Dil).* Stanford: Stanford University Press.

Frank, Andre Gunder. 1967. *Capitalism and Underdevelopment in Latin America: Historical Studies of Chile and Brazil.* New York: Monthly Review Press.

Frazer, James George. 1910. *Totemism and Exogamy: A Treatise on Certain Early Forms of Superstition and Society* (4 vols.). London: Macmillan & Co.

1922. *The Golden Bough: A Study in Magic and Religion* (abridged edition). London: Macmillan & Co.

Freeman, Derek. 1983. *Margaret Mead and Samoa: The Making and Unmaking of an Anthropological Myth.* Cambridge, MA: Harvard University Press.

Freud, Sigmund. 1960 [1913]. *Totem and Taboo* (translated by James Strachey). London: Routledge & Kegan Paul.

Friedman, Jonathan. 1974. Marxism, structuralism and vulgar materialism. *Man* (n.s.) 9: 444–69.

1975. Tribes, states, and transformations. In Maurice Bloch (ed.), *Marxist Analyses and Social Anthropology* (A.S.A. Studies 2). London: Malaby Press, pp. 161–202.

1996 [1979]. *System, Structure, and Contradiction: The Evolution of 'Asiatic' Social Formations* (second edition). Walnut Creek, CA: AltaMira Press.

Frobenius, Leo. 1933. *Kulturgeschichte Afrikas: Prologomena zu einer historischen Gestaltlehre*. Frankfurt: Frobenius Institut.

Gamble, Clive. 1993. *Timewalkers: The Prehistory of Global Colonization*. Stroud: Alan Sutton.

Geertz, Clifford. 1960. *The Religion of Java*. New York: The Free Press.

1963. *Agricultural Involution: The Process of Ecological Change in Indonesia*. Berkeley: University of California Press.

1966. Religion as a cultural system. In Michael Banton (ed.), *Anthropological Approaches to the Study of Religion* (A.S.A. Monographs 3). London: Tavistock Publications. pp. 1–46.

1968. *Islam Observed. Religious Developments in Morocco and Indonesia*. New Haven: Yale University Press.

1973. *The Interpretation of Cultures: Selected Essays*. New York: Basic Books.

1983. *Local Knowledge: Further Essays in Interpretive Anthropology*. New York: Basic Books.

1984. Anti anti relativism. *American Anthropologist* 86: 263–78.

1988. *Works and Lives: The Anthropologist as Author*. Stanford: Stanford University Press.

Geertz, Hildred and Clifford Geertz. 1975. *Kinship in Bali*. Chicago: University of Chicago Press.

Gellner, Ernest. 1982 [1981]. Relativism and universals. In Martin Hollis and Steven Lukes (eds.), *Rationality and Relativism*. Oxford: Basil Blackwell, pp. 181–200.

1985. *Relativism and the Social Sciences*. London: Cambridge University Press.

1992. *Postmodernism, Reason and Religion*. London: Routledge.

Gerth, H. H. and C. Wright Mills (editors and translators). 1946. *From Max Weber: Essays in Sociology*. New York: Oxford University Press.

Gierke, Otto von. 1934. *Natural Law and the Theory of Society, 1500 to 1800* (translated by Ernest Barker) (2 vols.). Cambridge: Cambridge University Press.

Givens, David B., Patsy Evans, and Timothy Jablonski. 1997. 1997 survey of anthropology PhDs. *American Anthropological Association 1997–98 Guide*. Arlington, VA: American Anthropological Association, pp. 308–21.

Gluckman, Max. 1955. *Custom and Conflict in Africa*. Oxford: Basil Blackwell.

1965. *Politics, Law and Ritual in Tribal Society*. Oxford: Basil Blackwell.

Godelier, Maurice. 1975. Modes of production, kinship, and demographic structures. In Maurice Bloch (ed.), *Marxist Analyses and Social Anthropology* (A.S.A. Studies 2). London: Malaby Press, pp. 3–27.

1977 [1973]. *Perspectives in Marxist Anthropology*. Cambridge: Cambridge University Press.

1986 [1982]. *The Making of Great Men: Male Domination and Power among the New Guinea Baruya* (translated by Rupert Swyer). Cambridge: Cambridge University Press/Paris: Editions de la Maison des Sciences de l'Homme.

Goodenough, Ward. 1956. Componential analysis and the study of meaning. *Language* 32: 195–216.

Goody, Jack. 1995. *The Expansive Moment: Anthropology in Britain and Africa, 1918–1970*. Cambridge: Cambridge University Press.

1996. *The East in the West*. Cambridge: Cambridge University Press.

Graburn, Nelson (ed.). 1971. *Readings in Kinship and Social Structure*. New York: Harper & Row.

Graebner, Fritz. 1911. *Die Methode der Ethnologie*. Heidelberg: Carl Winter's Universitäts Buchhandlung.

Grotius, Hugo. 1949 [1625]. *The Law of War and Peace* (translated by Louise R. Loomis). Roslyn, NY: Walter J. Black.

Guha, Ranajit and Gayatri Chakravorty Spivak (eds.). 1988. *Selected Subaltern Studies*. New York: Oxford University Press.

Hallpike, C. R. 1979. *The Foundations of Primitive Thought*. Oxford: Clarendon Press.

Hammond-Tooke, W. D. 1997. *Imperfect Interpreters: South Africa's Anthropologists, 1920–1990*. Johannesburg: Witwatersrand University Press.

Haraway, Donna. 1988. Situated knowledges: The science question in feminism and the privilege of partial perspective. *Feminist Studies* 14: 575–99.

1991. *Symians, Cyborgs, and Women: The Reinvention of Nature*. New York: Routledge.

Harris, Marvin. 1968. *The Rise of Anthropological Theory*. New York: Thomas Y. Crowell Company.

1977. *Cannibals and Kings: The Origins of Cultures*. New York: Random House.

1979. *Cultural Materialism: The Struggle for a Science of Culture*. New York: Random House.

Harris, Olivia and Kate Young. 1981. Engendered structures: some problems in the analysis of reproduction. In Joel S. Kahn and Josep R. Llobera (eds.), *The Anthropology of Pre-Capitalist Societies*. London: Macmillan, pp. 109–47.

Hart, Keith. 1982. *The Development of Commercial Agriculture in West Africa*. Cambridge: Cambridge University Press.

Hastrup, Kirsten. 1995. *A Passage to Anthropology: Between Experience and Theory*. London: Routledge.

Headland, Thomas., Kenneth L. Pike, and Marvin Harris (eds.). 1990. *Emics and Etics: The Insider/Outsider Debate*. Newbury Park: Sage Publications.

Helman, Cecil G. 1994 [1984]. *Culture, Health and Illness* (third edition). Oxford: Butterworth-Heinemann.

Hénaff, Marcel. 1998 [1991]. *Claude Lévi-Strauss and the Making of Structural Anthropology* (translated by Mary Baker). Minneapolis: University of Minnesota Press.

Héritier, Françoise. 1981. *L'exercice de la parenté*. Paris: Gallimard.

Herskovits, Melville J. 1926. The cattle complex in East Africa. *American Anthropologist* 28: 230–72, 361–88, 494–528, 633–64.

1930. The culture areas of Africa. *Africa* 3: 59–77.

Herzfeld, Michael. 1984. The horns of the Mediterraneanist dilemma. *American Ethnologist* 11: 439–54.

1987. *Anthropology through the Looking-Glass: Critical Ethnography in the Margins of Europe*. Cambridge: Cambridge University Press.

Hiatt, L. R. 1968. Gidjingali marriage arrangements. In Richard B. Lee and Irven DeVore (eds.), *Man the Hunter*. Chicago: Aldine Publishing Company, pp. 165–75.

1996. *Arguments about Aborigines: Australia and the Evolution of Social Anthropology*. Cambridge: Cambridge University Press.

Hindess, Barry and Paul Hirst. 1975. *Pre-Capitalist Modes of Production*. London: Routledge & Kegan Paul.

1977. *Mode of Production and Social Formation: An Auto-Critique of Pre-Capitalist Modes of Production*. London: The Macmillan Press.

Hjelmslev, Louis. 1953 [1943]. *Prolegomena to a Theory of Language* (Indiana University Publications in Anthropology and Linguistics, Memoir 7). Baltimore, MD: Waverly Press.

Hobbes, Thomas. 1973 [1651]. *Leviathan*. London: J. M. Dent & Sons.

Hollis, Martin and Steven Lukes (eds.). 1982. *Rationality and Relativism*. Oxford: Basil Blackwell.

Holy, Ladislav. 1996. *The Little Czech and the Great Czech Nation: National Identity and the Post-Communist Social Transformation*. Cambridge: Cambridge University Press.

Holy, Ladislav and Milan Stuchlik. 1983. *Actions, Norms and Representations: Foundations of Anthropological Inquiry*. Cambridge: Cambridge University Press.

Ingold, Tim, 1986. *The Appropriation of Nature: Essays on Human Ecology and Social Relations*. Manchester: Manchester University Press.

(ed.). 1994. *Companion Encyclopedia of Anthropology: Humanity, Culture and Social Life*. London: Routledge.

(ed.). 1996. *Key Debates in Anthropology*. London: Routledge.

Jakobson, Roman. 1962. *Selected Writings*, vol. I. The Hague: Mouton.

1971. *Selected Writings*, vol. II. The Hague: Mouton.

James, Allison, Jenny Hockey, and Andrew Dawson (eds.). 1997. *After Writing Culture: Epistemology and Praxis in Contemporary Anthropology* (A.S.A. Monographs 34). London: Routledge.

Jenkins, Richard. 1992. *Pierre Bourdieu*. London: Routledge.

Josselin de Jong, J. P. B. de. 1977 [1935]. The Malay Archipelago as a field of ethnological study. In P. E. de Josselin de Jong (ed.), *Structural Anthropology in the Netherlands*. The Hague: Martinus Nijhoff, pp. 166–82.

Josselin de Jong, P. E. de (ed.). 1977. *Structural Anthropology in the Netherlands*. The Hague: Martinus Nijhoff.

Kaberry, Phyllis. 1957. Malinowski's contribution to field-work methods and the writing of ethnography. In Raymond Firth (ed.), *Man and Culture: An Evaluation of the Work of Bronislaw Malinowski*. London: Routledge & Kegan Paul, pp. 71–91.

Kahn, Joel S. 1980. *Minangkabau Social Formations: Indonesian Peasants and the World Economy*. Cambridge: Cambridge University Press.

1981. Marxist anthropology and segmentary societies: a review of the literature. In Joel S. Kahn and Josep R. Llobera (eds.), *The Anthropology of Pre-Capitalist Societies*. London: Macmillan, pp. 57–88.

Kahn, Joel S. and Josep R. Llobera. 1981. Towards a new Marxism or a new anthropology. In Joel S. Kahn and Josep R. Llobera (eds.), *The Anthropology of Pre-Capitalist Societies*. London: Macmillan, pp. 263–329.

Kames, Lord. 1774. *Sketches of the History of Man* (2 vols.). London: W. Strahan and T. Cadell.

Kapferer, Bruce (ed.). 1976. *Transaction and Meaning: Directions in the Anthropology of Exchange and Symbolic Behavior* (A.S.A. Essays 1). Philadelphia: Institute for the Study of Human Issues.

Katz, Pearl. 1981. Ritual in the operating room. *Ethnology* 20: 335–50.

Kenyatta, Jomo. 1938. *Facing Mount Kenya: The Tribal Life of the Gikuyu*. London: Secker & Warburg.

Kloos, Peter and Henri J. M. Claessen (eds.). 1991. *Contemporary Anthropology in the Netherlands: The Use of Anthropological Ideas*. Amsterdam: VU University Press.

Kluckhohn, Clyde. 1936. Some reflections on the methods and theories of the Kulturkreislehre. *American Anthropologist* 38: 157–96.

1944. *Navaho Witchcraft* (Papers of the Peabody Museum of American Archaeology and Ethnology, vol. 22). Cambridge, MA: Peabody Museum.

Kluckhohn, Clyde and Dorothea Leighton. 1974 [1946]. *The Navaho* (revised edition). Cambridge, MA: Harvard University Press.

Knauft, Bruce M. 1996. *Genealogies for the Present in Cultural Anthropology*. New York: Routledge.

Knight, Chris. 1991. *Blood Relations: Menstruation and the Origins of Culture*. New Haven: Yale University Press.

Knight, Chris, Camilla Power, and Ian Watts. 1995. The human symbolic revolution: a Darwinian account. *Cambridge Archaeological Journal* 5(1): 75–114.

Knox, Robert. 1850. *Races of Men: A Fragment*. Philadelphia: Lea and Blanchard.

Korn, Francis. 1973. *Elementary Structures Reconsidered: Lévi-Strauss on Kinship*. London: Tavistock Publications.

Kroeber, A. L. 1909. Classificatory systems of relationship. *Journal of the Royal Anthropological Institute* 39: 77–84.

1931. The culture-area and age-area concepts of Clark Wissler. In Stuart A. Rice (ed.), *Methods in Social Science: A Case Book*. Chicago: University of Chicago Press, pp. 248–65.

1939. Cultural and natural areas of Native North America. *University of California Publications in American Archaeology and Ethnology* 38: 1-240.

1963 [1948]. *Anthropology: Culture Patterns and Processes* (from the revised edition of Kroeber's complete *Anthropology*). New York: Harcourt, Brace & World.

Kroeber, A. L. and Clyde Kluckhohn. 1952. *Culture: A Critical Review of Concepts and Definitions* (Papers of the Peabody Museum of American Archaeology and Ethnology, vol. 47, no. 1). Cambridge, MA: Peabody Museum.

Kropotkin, Peter. 1987 [1902]. *Mutual Aid: A Factor of Evolution*. London: Freedom Press.

Kuhn, Thomas S. 1970 [1962]. *The Structure of Scientific Revolutions* (second edition). Chicago: University of Chicago Press.

Kuklick, Henrika. 1991. *The Savage Within: The History of British Anthropology, 1885–1945*. Cambridge: Cambridge University Press.

Kuper, Adam (ed.). 1977. *The Social Anthropology of Radcliffe-Brown*. London: Routledge & Kegan Paul.

1979a [1977]. Regional comparison in African anthropology. *African Affairs* 78: 103–13.

1979b. A structural approach to dreams. *Man* (n.s.) 14: 645–62.

1982. *Wives for Cattle: Bridewealth and Marriage in Southern Africa*. London: Routledge & Kegan Paul.

1988. *The Invention of Primitive Society: Transformations of an Illusion*. London: Routledge.

1992. Post-Modernism, Cambridge and the Great Kalahari Debate. *Social Anthropology* 1: 57–71.

1994. *The Chosen Primate: Human Nature and Cultural Diversity*. Cambridge, MA: Harvard University Press.

1996 [1973]. *Anthropologists and Anthropology: The Modern British School* (third edition). London: Routledge.

1999. *Culture: The Anthropologists' Account*. Cambridge, MA: Harvard University Press.

Kuper, Adam and Jessica Kuper (eds.). 1996 [1985]. *The Social Science Encyclopedia* (second edition). London: Routledge.

Lacan, Jacques. 1977 [1966]. *Ecrits: A Selection* (translated by Alan Sheridan). London: Tavistock Publications.

Lakoff, George and Mark Johnson. 1980. *Metaphors We Live By*. Chicago: University of Chicago Press.

Lamarck, J. B. 1914 [1809]. *Zoological Philosophy: An Exposition with Regard to the Natural Philosophy of Animals*. London: Macmillan.

Lane, Harlan. 1977. *The Wild Boy of Aveyron*. London: George Allen & Unwin.

Langham, Ian. 1981. *The Building of British Social Anthropology: W. H. R. Rivers and his Cambridge Disciples in the Development of Kinship Studies, 1898–1931*. Dordrecht: D. Reidel Publishing Company (Studies in the History of Modern Science 8).

Lapointe, Francois H. and Claire Lapointe. 1977. *Claude Lévi-Strauss and His Critics: An International Bibliography of Criticism (1950–1976)*. New York: Garland (Reference Library of the Humanities, vol. 72).

Layton, Robert. 1997. *An Introduction to Theory in Anthropology*. Cambridge: Cambridge University Press.

Leach, Edmund R. 1954. *Political Systems of Highland Burma: A Study of Kachin Social Structure*. London: The Athlone Press.

1961a. *Pul Eliya, a Village in Ceylon: A Study of Land Tenure and Kinship*. Cambridge: Cambridge University Press.

1961b [1945–61]. *Rethinking Anthropology*. London: The Athlone Press (L.S.E. Monographs on Social Anthropology 22).

(ed.). 1967. *The Structural Study of Myth and Totemism* (A.S.A. Monographs 5). London: Tavistock Publications.

1970. *Lévi-Strauss*. Glasgow: Fontana/Collins (Fontana Modern Masters).

1976a. *Social Anthropology: A Natural Science of Society?* (Radcliffe-Brown Lecture, 1976). Oxford: Oxford University Press.

1976b. *Culture and Communication: The Logic by which Symbols are Connected.* Cambridge: Cambridge University Press.

Leacock, Eleanor. 1978. Women's status in egalitarian society: implications for social evolution. *Current Anthropology* 19: 247–75.

Leaf, Murray J. 1979. *Man, Mind, and Science: A History of Anthropology*. New York: Columbia University Press.

Lechte, John. 1994. *Fifty Key Contemporary Thinkers: From Structuralism to Postmodernity*. London: Routledge.

Lee, Richard B. 1979. *The !Kung San: Men, Women, and Work in a Foraging Society*. Cambridge: Cambridge University Press.

1981 [1980]. Is there a foraging mode of production? *Canadian Journal of Anthropology* 2: 13–19.

Lee, Richard B. and Mathias Guenther. 1991. Oxen or onions? The search for trade (and truth) in the Kalahari. *Current Anthropology* 32: 592–601.

1993. Problems in Kalahari historical ethnography and the tolerance of error. *History in Africa* 20: 185–235.

Legros, Dominique. 1977. Chance, necessity, and mode of production: a Marxist critique of cultural evolutionism. *American Anthropologist* 79: 26–41.

Levine, Donald N. 1995. *Visions of the Sociological Tradition*. Chicago: University of Chicago Press.

Lévi-Strauss, Claude. 1963 [1958] [1945–58]. *Structural Anthropology* (translated by Clare Jacobson and Brook Grundfest Schoepf). New York: Basic Books.

1966a. The future of kinship studies. *Proceedings of the Royal Anthropological Institute for 1965*, pp. 13–22.

1966b [1962]. *The Savage Mind*. Chicago: University of Chicago Press.

1968. The concept of primitiveness. In Richard B. Lee and Irven DeVore (eds.), *Man the Hunter*. Chicago: Aldine Publishing Company, pp. 349–52.

1969a [1949]. *The Elementary Structures of Kinship* (revised edition, translated by James Harle Bell, John Richard von Sturmer, and Rodney Needham). Boston: Beacon Press.

1969b [1962]. *Totemism*. Harmondsworth: Penguin Books.

1976 [1955]. *Tristes Tropiques* (translated by John and Doreen Weightman). Harmondsworth: Penguin Books.

1978a. *Myth and Meaning*. London: Routledge & Kegan Paul.

1978b [1968]. *The Origin of Table Manners: Introduction to a Science of Mythology, 3* (translated by John and Doreen Weightman). London: Jonathan Cape.

1988 [1950]. *Introduction to the Work of Marcel Mauss*. London: Routledge.

1997 [1993]. *Look, Listen, Read* (translated by Brian C. J. Singer). New York: Basic Books.

Lévi-Strauss, Claude and Didier Eribon. 1991 [1988]. *Conversations with Claude Lévi-Strauss* (translated by Paula Wissing). Chicago: University of Chicago Press.

Lévy-Bruhl, Lucien. 1926 [1910]. *How Natives Think* (translated by Lilian A. Clare). London: George Allen & Unwin.

1975 [1949]. *The Notebooks on Primitive Mentality* (translated by Peter Rivière). Oxford: Basil Blackwell & Mott.

Lewis, Oscar. 1951. *Life in a Mexican Village: Tepoztlan Restudied.* Urbana: University of Illinois Press.

Leyton, Elliott. 1974. Opposition and integration in Ulster. *Man* (n.s.) 9: 185–98.

Lienhardt, Godfrey. 1961. *Divinity and Experience: The Religion of the Dinka.* Oxford: Clarendon Press.

Linnaeus, Carolus. 1956 [1758]. *Systema Naturae. Regnum Animale* (tenth edition, vol. I). London: British Museum (Natural History).

Locke, John. 1988 [1690]. *Two Treatises of Government.* Cambridge: Cambridge University Press.

Long, Norman. 1996. Globalization and localization: new challenges to rural research. In Henrietta L. Moore (ed.), *The Future of Anthropological Knowledge* (The Uses of Knowledge: Global and Local Relations: A.S.A. Decennial Conference Series). London: Routledge, pp. 37–59.

Lovejoy, Arthur O. 1936. *The Great Chain of Being: A Study of the History of an Idea.* Cambridge, MA: Harvard University Press.

Lowie, Robert H. 1937. *The History of Ethnological Theory.* New York: Holt, Rinehart and Winston.

1947 [1920]. *Primitive Society* (second edition). New York: Liveright Publishing Company.

Lubbock, Sir John. 1874 [1870]. *The Origin of Civilisation and the Primitive Condition of Man.* New York: D. Appleton and Company.

Lucy, John A. 1992. *Language Diversity and Thought: A Reformulation of the Linguistic Relativity Hypothesis.* Cambridge: Cambridge University Press.

Lyotard, Jean-François. 1984 [1979]. *The Postmodern Condition: A Report on Knowledge* (translated by Geoff Bennington and Brian Massumi). Manchester: Manchester University Press (Theory and History of Literature, vol. 10).

McGrew, W. C. 1991. Chimpanzee material culture: what are its origins and why? In R. A. Foley (ed.), *The Origins of Human Behaviour.* London: Unwin Hyman, pp. 13–24.

McLennan, John F. 1970 [1865]. *Primitive Marriage: An Inquiry into the Origin of the Form of Capture in Marriage Ceremonies.* Chicago: University of Chicago Press.

Maine, Henry Sumner. 1913 [1861]. *Ancient Law: Its Connection with the Early History of Society and Its Relation to Modern Ideas.* London: George Routledge & Sons.

Malefijt, Annemarie de Waal. 1976. *Images of Man: A History of Anthropological Thought.* New York: Alfred A. Knopf.

Malinowski, Bronislaw. 1922. *Argonauts of the Western Pacific: An Account of Native Enterprise and Adventure in the Archipelagoes of Melanesian New Guinea.* London: George Routledge & Sons.

1927a. *The Father in Primitive Psychology.* New York: W. W. Norton & Company.

1927b. *Sex and Repression in Savage Society.* London: Kegan Paul.

1934. Introduction. In H. Ian Hogbin, *Law and Order in Polynesia: A Study of Primitive Legal Institutions.* London: Christophers, pp. xvii–lxxii.

1935. *Coral Gardens and Their Magic: A Study of the Methods of Tilling the Soil and of Agricultural Rites in the Trobriand Islands* (2 vols.). London: George Allen and Unwin.

1944 [1939–42]. *A Scientific Theory of Culture and Other Essays*. Chapel Hill: University of North Carolina Press.

1948 [1916–41]. *Magic, Science and Religion and Other Essays* (selected by Robert Redfield). Glencoe, IL: The Free Press.

1967. *A Diary in the Strict Sense of the Term*. London: Routledge & Kegan Paul.

Marcus, George E. and James Clifford. 1985. The making of ethnographic texts: a preliminary report. *Current Anthropology* 26: 267–71.

Marcus, George E. and Michael M. J. Fischer. 1986. *Anthropology as Cultural Critique: An Experimental Monument in the Human Sciences*. Chicago: University of Chicago Press.

Marx, Karl. 1965 [1857–8]. *Pre-capitalist Economic Formations*. New York: International Publishers.

1974 [1867]. *Capital: A Critical Analysis of Capitalist Production*, vol. 1 (edited by Frederick Engels [Friedrich Engels] and translated by Samuel Moore and Edward Aveling). London: Lawrence & Wishart.

Mason, Paul. 1990. *Deconstructing America: Representations of the Other*. London and New York: Routledge.

Mauss, Marcel. 1990 [1923]. *The Gift: The Form and Reason for Exchange in Archaic Societies* (translated by W. D. Halls). London: Routledge.

Mead, Margaret. 1928. *Coming of Age in Samoa*. New York: William Morrow and Company.

1930. *Growing Up in New Guinea*. New York: William Morrow and Company.

Meillassoux, Claude. 1964. *Anthropologie économique des Gouro de Côte d'Ivoire*. Paris: Mouton.

1972. From reproduction to production. *Economy and Society* 1: 93–105.

1981 [1975]. *Maidens, Meal and Money: Capitalism and the Domestic Economy*. Cambridge: Cambridge University Press.

Merleau-Ponty, Maurice. 1962. *Phenomenology of Perception* (translated by James Edie). Evanston, IL: Northwestern University Press.

Milner, Andrew. 1994. *Contemporary Cultural Theory: An Introduction*. London: UCL Press.

Milton, Kay. 1979. Male bias in anthropology. *Man* (n.s.) 14: 40–54.

Monboddo, Lord. 1773–92. *Of the Origin and Progress of Language* (6 vols.). London: T. Cadell.

1779–99. *Antient Metaphysics* (6 vols.). London: T. Cadell.

Montesquieu, C. L. de Secondat, baron de La Brède et de. 1964 [1721]. *The Persian Letters* (translated by George R. Healy). Indianapolis: Bobbs-Merrill.

1989 [1748]. *The Spirit of the Laws* (translated by Anne M. Cohler, Basia Carolyn Miller, and Harold Samuel Stone). Cambridge: Cambridge University Press.

Moore, Henrietta L. 1988. *Feminism and Anthropology*. Cambridge: Polity Press.

1994 [1993–4]. *A Passion for Difference: Essays in Anthropology and Gender*. Cambridge: Polity Press.

Moore, Jerry D. 1997. *Visions of Culture: An Introduction to Anthropological Theories and Theorists*. Walnut Creek, CA: AltaMira Press.

Morgan, Lewis Henry. 1871. *Systems of Consanguinity and Affinity of the Human Family* (Smithsonian Contributions to Knowledge, vol. 17). Washington: Smithsonian Institution.

1877. *Ancient Society; or, Researches in the Lines of Human Progress from Savagery through Barbarism to Civilization*. New York: Henry Holt.

Müller, F. Max. 1977 [1892]. *Anthropological Religion*. New Delhi: Asian Educational Services.

Murdock, George Peter. 1949. *Social Structure*. New York: Macmillan.

Myerhoff, Barbara. 1978. *Number Our Days*. New York: Simon & Schuster.

Nadel, S. F. 1957. Malinowski on magic and religion. In Raymond Firth (ed.), *Man and Culture: An Evaluation of the Work of Bronislaw Malinowski*. London: Routledge & Kegan Paul, pp. 189–208.

Needham, Rodney. 1962. *Structure and Sentiment: A Test Case in Social Anthropology*. Chicago: University of Chicago Press.

1972. *Belief, Language, and Experience*. Oxford: Basil Blackwell.

1973. Prescription. *Oceania* 42: 166–81.

1979. *Symbolic Classification*. Santa Monica, CA: Goodyear Publishing Company.

1981. *Circumstantial Deliveries*. Berkeley: University of California Press.

Obeyesekere, Gananath. 1992. *The Apotheosis of Captain Cook: European Mythmaking in the Pacific*. Princeton: Princeton University Press.

Okely, Judith. 1996 [1975–96]. *Own or Other Culture*. London: Routledge.

Okely, Judith and Helen Callaway (eds.). 1992. *Anthropology and Autobiography* (A. S. A. Monographs 29). London: Routledge.

O'Laughlin, Bridget. 1975. Marxist approaches in anthropology. *Annual Review of Anthropology* 4: 341–70.

Olson, David R. and Nancy Torrance (eds.). 1996. *Modes of Thought: Explorations in Culture and Cognition*. Cambridge: Cambridge University Press.

Ong, Aihwa. 1996. Anthropology, China and modernities: The geopolitics of cultural knowledge. In Henrietta L. Moore (ed.), *The Future of Anthropological Knowledge* (The Uses of Knowledge: Global and Local Relations: A.S.A. Decennial Conference Series). London: Routledge, pp. 60–92.

Ortner, Sherry. 1974. Is female to male as nature is to culture? In Michelle Z. Rosaldo and Louise Lamphere (eds.), *Woman, Culture and Society*. Stanford: Stanford University Press, pp. 67–88.

1984. Theory in anthropology since the sixties. *Comparative Studies in Society and History* 26: 126–66.

1995. Resistance and the problem of ethnographic refusal. *Comparative Studies in Society and History* 37: 173–93.

Ottenberg, Simon and Phebe Ottenberg (eds.). 1960. *Cultures and Societies of Africa*. New York: Random House.

Pals, Daniel L. 1996. *Seven Theories of Religion*. Oxford: Oxford University Press.

Parsons, Talcott. 1949 [1937]. *The Structure of Social Action*. New York: The Free Press of Glencoe.

Pasquinelli, Carla. 1996. The concept of culture between modernity and postmodernity. In Václav Hubinger (ed.), *Grasping the Changing World: Anthro-*

pological Concepts in the Postmodern Era. London: Routledge, pp. 53–73.

Perry, William James. 1923. *The Children of the Sun: A Study in the Early History of Civilization*. London: Methuen and Company.

Pike, Kenneth L. 1967. *Language in Relation to a Unified Theory of the Structure of Human Behavior* (second edition). The Hague: Mouton.

Pompa, Leon (editor and translator). 1982. *Vico: Selected Writings*. Cambridge: Cambridge University Press.

Pouillon, Jean and Pierre Maranda (eds.). 1970. *Echanges et communications: mélanges offerts à Claude Lévi-Strauss à l'occasion de son 60ème anniversaire* (2 vols.). The Hague: Mouton (Studies in General Anthropology, 5).

Prichard, James Cowles. 1973 [1813]. *Researches into the Physical History of Man*. Chicago and London: University of Chicago Press.

Pufendorf, Samuel. 1991 [1673]. *On the Duty of Man and Citizen* (edited by James Tully and translated by Michael Silverthorne). Cambridge: Cambridge University Press.

Quinn, Naomi. 1991. The cultural basis of metaphor. In James W. Fernandez (ed.), *Beyond Metaphor: The Theory of Tropes in Anthropology*. Stanford: Stanford University Press, pp. 56–93.

Rabinow, Paul. 1977. *Reflections on Fieldwork in Morocco*. Berkeley: University of California Press.

    1997. *Essays on the Anthropology of Reason*. Princeton: Princeton University Press.

Radcliffe-Brown, A. R. 1922. *The Andaman Islanders*. Cambridge: Cambridge University Press.

    1931. *The Social Organization of Australian Tribes*. Sydney: Oceania Monographs (no. 1).

    1952 [1924–49]. *Structure and Function in Primitive Society: Essays and Addresses*. London: Cohen & West.

    1957. *A Natural Science of Society*. Glencoe, IL: The Free Press.

    1958. *Method in Social Anthropology: Selected Essays by A. R. Radcliffe-Brown* (edited by M. N. Srinivas). Chicago: University of Chicago Press.

Radcliffe-Brown. A. R. and Daryll Forde (eds.). 1950. *African Systems of Kinship and Marriage*. London: Oxford University Press for the International African Institute.

Ramos, Alcida R. 1992. Reflecting on the Yanomami: ethnographic images and the pursuit of the exotic. In George E. Marcus (ed.), *Rereading Cultural Anthropology*. Durham, NC: Duke University Press, pp. 48–68.

Ratzel, Friedrich. 1891. Die afrikanischen Bögen, ihre Verbeitung und Verwandtschaften. *Abhandlungen der Königlichen Sächsische Gesellschaft der Wissenschaften. Philologischhistorischen Classe* 13: 291–346.

    1896–8 [1885–8]. *The History of Mankind* (translated by A. J. Butler) (3 vols.). London: Macmillan.

Redfield, Robert. 1930. *Tepoztlan: A Mexican Village*. Chicago: University of Chicago Press.

Reed-Donahay, Deborah. 1995. The Kabyle and the French: occidentalism in Bourdieu's theory of practice. In James G. Carrier (ed.), *Occidentalism: Images of the West*. Oxford: Oxford University Press, pp. 61–84.

Richards, A. I. 1939. *Land, Labour and Diet in Northern Rhodesia: An Economic Study of the Bemba Tribe*. London: Oxford University Press.

Rivers, W. H. R. 1968 [1914]. *Kinship and Social Organization* (L.S.E. Monographs on Social Anthropology, No. 34.). London: The Athlone Press.

Romney, A. Kimball and Roy Goodwin D'Andrade. 1964. Cognitive aspects of English kin terms. *American Anthropologist* 66(3), Special Publication, part 2: 146–70.

Rosaldo, Michelle Z. 1974. Woman, culture and society: a theoretical overview. In Michelle Z. Rosaldo and Louise Lamphere (eds.), *Woman, Culture and Society*. Stanford: Stanford University Press, pp. 17–42.

Rousseau, Jean-Jacques. 1973 [1750–62]. *The Social Contract and Discourses* (translated by G. D. H. Cole). London: J. M. Dent & Sons.

Sacks, Karen. 1979. *Sisters and Wives: The Past and Future of Sexual Equality*. Westport, CT: Greenwood Press.

Sahlins, Marshall. 1974 [1972]. *Stone Age Economics*. London: Tavistock Publications.

1976. *Culture and Practical Reason*. Chicago: University of Chicago Press.

1977 [1976]. *The Use and Abuse of Biology: An Anthropological Critique of Sociobiology*. London: Tavistock Publications.

1981. *Historical Metaphors and Mythical Realities: Structure in the Early History of the Sandwich Islands Kingdom*. Ann Arbor: University of Michigan Press (Association for the Study of Anthropology in Oceania, Special Publication no. 1).

1985. *Islands of History*. Chicago: University of Chicago Press.

1995. *How 'Natives' Think: About Captain Cook, for Example*. Chicago: University of Chicago Press.

Said, Edward W. 1978. *Orientalism*. New York: Pantheon.

Sapir, Edward. 1949 [1915–38]. *Selected Writings in Language, Culture, and Personality* (edited by David G. Mandelbaum). Berkeley: University of California Press.

Sarana, Gopala. 1975. *The Methodology of Anthropological Comparisons: An Analysis of Comparative Methods in Social and Cultural Anthropology*. Tuscon: University of Arizona Press (Viking Fund Publications in Anthropology 53).

Sarup, Madan. 1988. *An Introductory Guide to Post-structuralism and Postmodernism*. New York: Harvester Wheatsheaf.

Saussure, Ferdinand de. 1974 [1916]. *Course in General Linguistics* (edited by Charles Bally and Albert Sechehaye, translated by Wade Baskin). Glasgow: Fontana/Collins.

Schapera, I. 1947. *Migrant Labour and Tribal Life: A Study of the Condition of the Bechuanaland Protectorate*. London: Oxford University Press.

Scheper-Hughes, Nancy and Margaret Lock. 1987. The mindful body: a prolegomenon to future work in medical anthropology. *Medical Anthropology Quarterly* 1: 6–41.

Schmidt, Wilhelm. 1939 [1937]. *The Culture Historical Method of Ethnology: The Scientific Approach to the Racial Question* (translated by S. A. Sieber). New York: Fortuny's.

Schneider, David M. 1980 [1968]. *American Kinship: A Cultural Account* (second

232   References

edition). Chicago: University of Chicago Press.

1984. *A Critique of the Study of Kinship*. Ann Arbor: University of Michigan Press.

Service, Elman R. 1962. *Primitive Social Organization: An Evolutionary Perspective*. New York: Random House.

1985. *A Century of Controversy: Ethnological Issues from 1860 to 1960*. Orlando: Academic Press.

Shankman, Paul. 1984. The thick and the thin: on the interpretive theoretical program of Clifford Geertz. *Current Anthropology* 25: 261–79.

Shott, Michael J. 1992. On recent trends in the anthropology of foragers: Kalahari revisionism and its archaeological implications. *Man* (n.s.) 27: 843–71.

Skorupski, John. 1976. *Symbol and Theory: A Philosophical Study of Theories of Religion in Social Anthropology*. Cambridge: Cambridge University Press.

Slotkin, J. S. (ed.). 1965. *Readings in Early Anthropology*. Chicago: Aldine Publishing Company.

Smart, Barry. 1985. *Michel Foucault*. London: Routledge.

1993. *Postmodernism*. London: Routledge.

Smith, Adam. 1970 [1761]. *A Dissertation on the Origin of Languages*. Tübingen: Tübinger Beiträge zur Linguistik.

1981 [1776]. *An Inquiry into the Nature and Causes of the Wealth of Nations*. Indianapolis: Liberty Press.

Solway, Jacqueline S. and Richard B. Lee. 1990. Foragers, genuine or spurious? Situating the Kalahari San in history. *Current Anthropology* 31: 109–46.

Spencer, Jonathan. 1989. Anthropology as a kind of writing. *Man* (n.s.) 24: 145–64.

Sperber, Dan. 1975 [1974]. *Rethinking Symbolism* (translated by Alice L. Morton). Cambridge: Cambridge University Press.

1982. Apparently irrational beliefs. In Martin Hollis and Steven Lukes (eds.), *Rationality and Relativism*. Oxford: Basil Blackwell, pp. 149–80.

1985 [1982]. *On Anthropological Knowledge: Three Essays*. Cambridge: Cambridge University Press/Paris: Editions de la Maison des Sciences de l'Homme.

Spiro, Melford E. 1992. Cultural relativism and the future of anthropology. In George E. Marcus (ed.), *Rereading Cultural Anthropology*. Durham, NC: Duke University Press, pp. 124–51.

Steiner, P. (ed.) 1982. *The Prague School: Selected Writings, 1929–1946* (translated by Olga P. Hasty). Austin: University of Texas Press.

Steward, Julian H. (ed.). 1946–50. *Handbook of the South American Indians* (Bureau of American Ethnology, Bulletin 143, vols. 1–6). Washington, DC: Smithsonian Institution.

1955. *Theory of Culture Change: The Methodology of Multilinear Evolution*. Urbana: University of Illinois Press.

Stipe, Claude E. 1985. Scientific creationism and evangelical Christianity. *American Anthropologist* 87: 148–50.

Stocking, George W., Jr. 1968 [1962–6]. *Race, Culture, and Evolution: Essays in the History of Anthropology*. New York: The Free Press.

1971. What's in a name? The origins of the Royal Anthropological Institute. *Man* (n.s.) 6: 369–90.

(ed.). 1974. *A Franz Boas Reader: The Shaping of American Anthropology, 1883–1911.* Chicago: University of Chicago Press.

(ed.). 1983. *Observers Observed: Essays on Ethnographic Fieldwork.* Madison: University of Wisconsin Press (History of Anthropology 1).

(ed.). 1986. *Malinowski, Rivers, Benedict and Others: Essays on Culture and Personality.* Madison: University of Wisconsin Press (History of Anthropology 4).

1987. *Victorian Anthropology.* New York: The Free Press.

1996a. *After Tylor: British Social Anthropology, 1888–1951.* London: The Athlone Press.

(ed.) 1996b. *Volksgeist as Method and Ethic: Essays on Boasian Ethnography and the German Anthropological Tradition.* Madison: University of Wisconsin Press (History of Anthropology 8).

Strathern, Andrew and Pamela J. Stewart. 1998. Embodiment and communications. Two frames for the analysis of ritual. *Social Anthropology* 6: 237–51.

Strathern, Marilyn. 1981. Culture in a netbag: the manufacture of a subdiscipline in anthropology. *Man* (n.s.) 16: 665–88.

1987a. An awkward relationship: the case of feminism and anthropology. *Signs* 12: 276–92.

1987b. Out of context: the persuasive fictions of anthropology. *Current Anthropology* 28: 251–81.

1991. *Partial Connections.* Savage, MD: Rowan & Littlefield Publishers.

1992. Parts and wholes: refiguring relationships in a post-plural world. In Adam Kuper (ed.), *Conceptualizing Society* (E.A.S.A. Monographs Series). London: Routledge, pp. 75–104.

Swingewood, Alan. 1984. *A Short History of Sociological Thought.* Basingstoke, Hants: Macmillan.

Taussig, Michael. 1993. *Mimesis and Alterity: A Particular History of the Senses.* London: Routledge.

Terray, Emmanuel. 1972 [1969]. *Marxism and 'Primitive' Society* (translated by M. Klopper). New York: Monthly Review Press.

Trigger, Bruce G. 1989. *A History of Archaeological Thought.* Cambridge: Cambridge University Press.

Turner, Victor W. 1957. *Schism and Continuity in an African Society: A Study of Ndembu Village Life.* Manchester: Manchester University Press for the Rhodes-Livingstone Institute.

1967. *The Forest of Symbols: Aspects of Ndembu Ritual.* Ithaca: Cornell University Press.

Turner, Victor and Edith Turner. 1978. *Image and Pilgrimage in Christian Culture: Anthropological Perspectives.* New York: Columbia University Press.

Tyler, Stephen A. (ed.). 1969. *Cognitive Anthropology.* New York: Holt, Rinehart and Winston.

1986. Post-modern ethnography: from document of the occult to occult document. In James Clifford and George E. Marcus (eds.), *Writing Culture: The Poetics and Politics of Ethnography.* Berkeley: University of California Press, pp. 122–40.

Tylor, Edward Burnett. 1861. *Anuahac, or Mexico and the Mexicans, Ancient and Modern*. London: Longman, Green, Longman, and Roberts.

1871. *Primitive Culture: Researches into the Development of Mythology, Philosophy, Religion, Language, Art, and Custom* (2 vols.). London: John Murray.

Urry, James. 1993. *Before Social Anthropology: Essays on the History of British Anthropology*. Chur, Switzerland: Harwood Academic Publishers

Van der Geest, Sjaak. 1990. Anthropologists and missionaries: brothers under the skin. *Man* (n.s.) 25: 588–601.

Van Gennep, Arnold. 1960 [1909]. *The Rites of Passage* (translated by Monika B. Vizedom and Gabrielle L. Caffee). London: Routledge & Kegan Paul.

Vermeulen, Han F. 1995. Origins and institutionalization of ethnography and ethnology in Europe and the USA, 1771–1845. In Han F. Vermeulen and Arturo Alvarez Roldan (eds.), *Fieldwork and Footnotes: Studies in the History of European Anthropology*. London and New York: Routledge, pp. 39–59.

Wallace, Anthony F. C. and John Atkins. 1960. The meaning of kinship terms. *American Anthropologist* 62: 58–80.

Wallerstein, Immanuel. 1974–89. *The Modern World-System*, (3 vols.). New York: Academic Press.

Weber, Max. 1930 [1922]. *The Protestant Ethic and the Spirit of Capitalism* (translated by Talcott Parsons). London: George Allen & Unwin.

Werbner, Richard P. 1984. The Manchester School in South-Central Africa. *Annual Review of Anthropology* 13: 157–85.

White, Leslie. 1949. *The Science of Culture: A Study of Man and Civilization*. New York: Grove Press.

1959. *The Evolution of Culture: The Development of Civilization to the Fall of Rome*. New York: McGraw-Hill.

Whorf, Benjamin Lee. 1956. *Language, Thought and Reality: Selected Writings of Benjamin Lee Whorf* (edited by John B. Carroll). Cambridge, MA: The MIT Press.

Williams, Robert Charles. 1983. Scientific creationism: An exegesis for a religious doctrine. *American Anthropologist* 85: 92–102.

Willis, Roy. 1974. *Man and Beast*. London: Hart-Davis, MacGibbon.

1981. *A State in the Making: Myth, History, and Social Transformation in Pre-Colonial Ufipa*. Bloomington: Indiana University Press.

Wilmsen, Edwin N. 1989. *Land Filled With Flies: A Political Economy of the Kalahari*. Chicago: University of Chicago Press.

Wilmsen, Edwin N. and James R. Denbow. 1990. Paradigmatic history of San-speaking peoples and current attempts at revision. *Current Anthropology* 31: 489–524.

Wilson, Bryan R. (ed.). 1970. *Rationality*. Oxford: Basil Blackwell.

Wilson, Edward O., 1975. *Sociobiology: The New Synthesis*. Cambridge, MA: Harvard University Press.

1980. *Sociobiology: The Abridged Edition*. Cambridge, MA: The Belknap Press of Harvard University Press.

Wissler, Clark. 1923. *Man and Culture*. New York: Thomas Y. Crowell Company.

1927. The culture-area concept in social anthropology. *The American Journal of Sociology* 32: 881–91.

Wolf, Eric R. 1982. *Europe and the People without History.* Berkeley: University of California Press.

Wolff, Kurt H. (editor and translator). 1950. *The Sociology of Georg Simmel.* New York: The Free Press.

(editor and translator). 1965. *Simmel: Essays on Sociology, Philosophy and Aesthetics.* New York: Harper & Row.

Worsley, Peter. 1956. The kinship system of the Tallensi: a revaluation. *Journal of the Royal Anthropological Institute* 86: 37–73.

Yanagisako, Sylvia and Jane Collier. 1987. Toward a unified analysis of gender and kinship. In Jane Collier and Sylvia Yanagisako (eds.), *Gender and Kinship: Essays toward a Unified Analysis.* Stanford: Stanford University Press, pp. 14–50.

Yolton, John W. (ed.). 1991. *The Blackwell Companion to the Enlightenment.* Oxford: Blackwell Publishers.

Zwernemann, Jürgen. 1983. *Culture History and African Anthropology: A Century of Research in Germany and Austria.* Uppsala: Acta Universitatis Upsaliensis (Uppsala Studies in Cultural Anthropology 6)/Stockholm: Almqvist & Wiksell International.

Index